The Other Western Europe

Studies in International and Comparative Politics
Peter H. Merkl, Series Editor

The Other Western Europe SECOND EDITION

A POLITICAL ANALYSIS OF THE SMALLER DEMOCRACIES

Earl H. Fry
and
Gregory A. Raymond

In collaboration with
David E. Bohn
and
James L. Waite

ABC-Clio Information Services
Santa Barbara, California
Oxford, England

Cover illustration by Alyson Nethery

Library of Congress Cataloging in Publication Data

Fry, Earl H.
The other Western Europe.
(Studies in international and comparative politics; 14)

    Bibliography: p.
    Includes index.
    1. Europe—Politics and government.   2. Comparative government.   I. Raymond, Gregory A.   II. Bohn, David.
III. Waite, James L.   IV. Title.   V. Series.
JN94.A2F79   1983   320.94   82-20707
ISBN 0-87436-345-4
ISBN 0-87436-346-2 (pbk.)

10 9 8 7 6 5 4 3 2 1

ABC-Clio Information Services
2040 Alameda Padre Serra, Box 4397
Santa Barbara, California 93103

Clio Press Ltd.
55 St. Thomas Street
Oxford, OX1 1JG, England

Manufactured in the United States of America

To Elaine, Chris, Lisa, Anna, and Kimberly, and
To Christine

Contents

Preface

The purpose of the second edition of *The Other Western Europe* is identical to that of the first—to introduce students to the political systems of Western European countries normally neglected in most texts on European politics. Many works examine the political theories and machinations of only Great Britain, France, and West Germany. This volume, however, describes and compares these three nations with the Iberian, Adriatic, Benelux, Alpine, and Scandinavian countries. Concentrating on these territories, this book provides the material necessary for students to examine the diverse political behavior patterns occurring outside of London, Paris, and Bonn.

The authors retained the original organization of the first edition, but have made several improvements in the book's contents. Each of the original chapters has been revised and updated to account for recent events. For example, this volume includes the results and consequences of the most recent elections held in Spain and the Netherlands. In addition, an entirely new chapter has been added that examines the political systems of Italy and Greece. Regardless of changes made, however, we have attempted to keep the book as concise and readable as possible.

In preparing the second edition of *The Other Western Europe* Earl Fry wrote chapters four and five, and Gregory Raymond composed chapters one and two. The authors collaborated in writing chapters three and seven, as well as in editing the two chapters contributed by David Bohn and James Waite.

Needless to say, numerous others have contributed to the production of this book. We are especially grateful to Bonnie Simrell for encouraging us to prepare a second edition, and to Cecelia Albert for assisting us in bringing it to completion. We also wish to thank those who have used the first edition in the classroom and have shared their experiences with us. Finally, we acknowledge our indebtedness to those students who inspired us to write this book in the first place.

1.

An Introduction to the Comparative Analysis of European Politics

In college classrooms throughout the United States, Western Europe has become somewhat synonymous with the *Big Three*. This term is convenient shorthand for Great Britain, France, and West Germany. Almost without exception, these three states comprise the totality of undergraduate courses on Western European politics.

However, there is another Western Europe, which possesses a population roughly equal to the combined total of Great Britain, France, and West Germany. It is composed of a group of countries whose political systems show certain similarities with, and many marked differences from, those found in the Big Three. The purpose of this book is to introduce you to this "other" Western Europe. By viewing these countries in comparative perspective, we shall be in a position to identify, describe, and ultimately generalize about their most prominent political features.

The Comparative Analysis of Politics versus the Study of Foreign Government

Within the discipline of political science, there is considerable disagreement over the meaning of the term *comparative analysis*. To underscore the position taken throughout this book, let us begin with the following assertion: comparison is a method, not a substantive branch of any academic field. In other words, one studies politics comparatively; one does not study an entity called comparative politics.

But why compare? In essence, researchers utilize the comparative method for two general reasons. First, they employ it for descriptive purposes. For example, comparison may be used both as a procedure to clarify the meaning of theoretical concepts, and as a form of nonmetric (i.e., ordinal) measurement. Second, researchers also employ the method for explanatory purposes.

1

By comparing either several cases (e.g., cities, nations) at one point in time, or one case with itself at specific intervals over time, it becomes easier to identify those patterned regularities which are the source of empirical generalizations. Thus, putting these two general purposes together, it may be said that we compare in order to find an answer to what Abraham Kaplan has called the basic scientific question: "What the devil is going on around here?"[1]

Unfortunately, much of the past research done under the name of comparison could not respond adequately to this question, for it adopted the title rather than the actual methodology of comparative inquiry. At worst, these so-called comparative studies were simply legalistic discussions of the unique institutional aspects of a given foreign government. At best, they were mere juxtapositions of several such idiographic discussions. For an analysis to be truly comparative, it must be built on the logical foundation outlined by the following five rules.

1. Two or more instances of a phenomenon may be compared if and only if there exists some variable, say y, common to each instance.
2. No second variable, say x, is the cause of y, if it is not found when y is found.
3. No second variable, x, is the cause of y if it is found when y is not.
4. No second variable, x, is definitely the cause of y if there exists a third variable, say z, that is present or absent in the same circumstances as x.
5. No variable is the cause of y if it is not antecedent to y.[2]

These rules were devised to help researchers avoid making erroneous inferences regarding the causal connections between variables. They require that researchers establish empirically that both the independent variable, x, and the dependent variable, y, were present in the cases being compared, and that the value of x changed prior to the change in the value of y. Furthermore, the rules require that researchers control for the possible effects of any third variable, z, that might produce a spurious correlation between the independent and dependent variables. Omission of any of these rules can easily invalidate one's conclusions. Consider, for instance, the case of the "fabled gentlemen who got experimentally drunk on bourbon and soda on Monday night, scotch and soda on Tuesday night, and brandy and soda on Wednesday night—and stayed sober on Thursday night by drinking nothing. With a vast inductive leap of scientific imagination, they treated their experience as an empirical demonstration that soda, the common element each evening, was the cause of the inebriated state they had experienced."[3] Obviously the gentlemen had not adhered to rule four. Having failed to control for the effect of a third variable, alcohol, they made an erroneous inference about the cause of their condition.

Methodological Problems in Comparative Analysis

Of course, recognizing the existence of these rules is one thing, designing a research strategy to meet their demands is quite another. To illustrate some of these methodological problems, let us focus briefly on what is perhaps the best-known instance of comparative political analysis.

The ancient Greek philosopher, Aristotle, was among the first individuals who used the comparative method to examine political affairs. In his *Politics*, he sought to determine why certain city-states experienced more stability than others. So that he might assess this matter empirically, he collected data on the constitutions of 158 city-states and constructed a typology based on two defining criteria: the ends for which the state existed (i.e., the common interest of all, or the selfish interest of the rulers), and the kind of authority to which its citizens were subject (i.e., rule by one, a few, or many). From these two criteria, he derived six types of states: monarchies, aristocracies, polities, tyrannies, oligarchies, and democracies. But, dissatisfied with the number of rulers as a basis of categorization, he later went on to differentiate states according to the distribution of wealth among their classes. Once the final version of his typology was completed, he fit each state into its most appropriate cell, keeping in mind those states which were stable and those which were not. As a result of his comparison of the proportion of stable states within each cell, Aristotle concluded that polities which had a strong middle class were the stablest types of city-states.

Such, more or less, was the research strategy followed by Aristotle. Methodologically speaking, his was not very different from many of the analyses undertaken by contemporary political scientists. Hence we can use his research to highlight some of the major problems encountered by those seeking to use the comparative method today.

The first problem in doing comparative research centers on the technique of observation. In its most general sense, comparison means going beyond a detailed study of one case. This is not meant to imply that case studies are useless in political research. Among the many important functions they perform are (1) generating new hypotheses; (2) explaining some entity in depth to find out why it deviates from a general pattern; and (3) critically testing an instance where it is assumed that a particular theory will accurately predict the causal relationships between two or more variables. Yet, despite their value, case studies cannot establish the empirical generalizations upon which scientific explanations rest.

Given this limitation, scholars have increasingly turned to comparative analysis as an alternate road to knowledge. Nevertheless, there are many ways to travel along this road, each with its own advantages and drawbacks. For example, Aristotle used what could be called an intersocietal survey. In this kind of comparative research design, each case is viewed as an element in some larger universe of cases. The researcher either samples from the known population of cases or uses the entire population. If biases are not introduced by the sampling technique, and if the data on all of the selected cases are reliable and comparable, then an intersocietal survey can provide strong grounds for making empirical generalizations. However, there is a trade-off between the number of cases (n) included within this design and the number of variables (v) examined per case. Due to cost, time, and other such constraints, a large number of cases usually precludes collecting data on very many variables. Aristotle was able to compare 158 cases, but he only examined four variables. Hence the intersocietal survey assumes that all of the variables which characterize any case are not so interdependent that they cannot be studied independently of one another.

Another popular comparative design is based on a study of concomitant variation. Whereas in an intersocietal survey the size of n exceeds the size of v, in a concomitant variation design the ratio of n to v is often reversed. Take, for example, the "most-similar" system version of the concomitant variation design. When one engages in this type of comparison, two or more cases are selected which are as similar as possible. The objective is to hold constant, and thus control, as many variables as is conceivable (e.g., cultural heritage, geographic locale, level of economic development), so that if significant differences appear among these otherwise similar cases, the researcher can infer that variables held in common were irrelevant in accounting for these differences, while those "uncontrolled" variables which affected the cases in a manner corresponding to the observed differences were most likely the causal agents. Alternatively, under the "most-different" system version, a researcher selects two or more cases which are dissimilar in many ways, but share at least two features. If similar relationships between these common features are found, then one could infer that those variables not held in common were irrelevant as causes of that relationship. Thus, had Aristotle decided to study political stability by means of concomitant variation, he could have compared Athens with another democratic state in a most-similar system design, or Athens with Sparta in a most-different system design. In summary, concomitant designs have the disadvantage of observing a smaller number of cases than intersocietal surveys. Nonetheless, they have the advantage of potentially controlling for more variables than intersocietal surveys can.

After deciding which cases to observe, the researcher is faced with the task of classification. Before any two cases can be compared, they first must have been shown to share at least one variable. Returning again to our example, once Aristotle classified the city-states in accordance with his typology, he could rank order each of them, by category, in terms of the degree of stability they possessed. All classificatory schemes should be parsimonious, and contain categories which are mutually exclusive and jointly exhaustive. However, as Aristotle's dissatisfaction with the initial version of his own typology demonstrates, these requirements are difficult to meet whenever the criteria behind a

TABLE 1.1

A Statistical Profile of the "Other" Western Europe

Nation	Area (1,000 sq. km)	Agricultural Area (1,000 sq. km)	Population (thousands)	Density (per sq. km)	Gross Domestic Product (billion U.S. $)
Austria	83.1	37.8	7,513	90	48.1
Belgium	30.1	15.3	9,818	322	77.5
Denmark	43.1	29.4	5,073	118	42.2
Finland	337.0	27.7	4,729	14	30.0
Greece	132.0	88.5	9,167	69	25.7
Iceland	103.0	22.8	220	2	1.8
Italy	301.2	175.3	56,156	186	194.5
Luxembourg	2.6	1.3	356	137	2.6
Netherlands	40.8	20.8	13,770	338	105.3
Norway	324.2	9.0	4,027	12	36.0
Portugal	92.1	42.0	9,694	105	15.8
Spain	504.8	280.6	36,240	72	116.4
Sweden	450.0	37.4	8,219	18	78.0
Switzerland	41.3	20.1	6,346	154	60.3
France	549.1	323.2	52,927	96	379.1
Germany	248.6	132.7	61,531	248	510.1
Great Britain	244.0	185.1	55,959	229	242.3
United States	9,363.4	4,350.0	215,142	23	1,880.9

Sources: OECD Observer (March 1978), pp. 18–21; The Europa Year Book (London: Europa Publications Ltd., 1982).

TABLE 1.2

The "Other" Western Europe in an
Increasingly Interdependent World

Nation	Imports as % of GDP*	Exports as % of GDP
Austria	28.4	20.9
Belgium†	51.9	48.2
Denmark	32.2	23.7
Finland	26.3	22.5
Greece	27.3	11.5
Iceland	32.2	27.7
Italy	25.4	21.6
Luxembourg†	51.9	48.2
Netherlands	44.6	43.3
Norway	35.5	25.3
Portugal	26.8	11.5
Spain	16.7	8.3
Sweden	25.8	24.8
Switzerland	26.2	26.4
France	18.6	16.1
Germany	19.7	22.9
Great Britain	25.5	21.1
United States	7.2	6.8

* Imports and exports in terms of goods only
† Belgium-Luxembourg Economic Union

Source: OECD Observer (March 1978), pp. 22–23.

given typology are produced by the observer's intuitive assumptions about the phenomena under investigation.

In conclusion, comparison is but one part of a larger process used by social scientists to describe and explain the phenomena they study. Logically, comparison follows observation and classification. Before researchers can make meaningful comparisons, they must first solve the variety of methodological problems they encounter in these two prior steps.

A Look Ahead

Having briefly discussed some of the methodological issues involved in doing comparative research, we may now sketch how the comparative method will be used to analyze the "other" Western Europe. The approach we have selected applies the most-similar system design to the countries which make up the Iberian, Adriatic, Benelux, Alpine, and Scandinavian regions of Western Europe. Each country shares with its regional neighbors a wide variety of historical, cultural, and social attributes, therefore making it possible to hold constant, and thus control, the effects of third variables.

Tables 1.1 and 1.2 provide an introductory overview of the countries in these regions. As can be seen, they differ in many ways from the Big Three. Except in a few cases, these nations are smaller in area than France, Germany, or Great Britain. Aside from Italy, they have fewer inhabitants, although several have very high population densities. Beyond the obvious geographic and demographic differences between these nations and the United States, these statistics also show that foreign trade plays a predominant role in their economies, but a minor role in that of the United States. In short, these states are active participants on the international scene but, for a host of reasons, are too often neglected in the study of Western Europe.

The material which follows has been organized according to a common analytical framework. Listed below are the five categories which will be applied to compare the members of each region:

1. The historical setting
2. Political culture and socialization
3. Internal cleavages, political competition, and citizen participation
4. Governmental institutions and the policy-making process
5. Policy problems and prospects

To begin, we shall apply this framework to Iberia, a region composed of two countries which have recently become democracies after decades of authoritarian rule. Once we have compared Spain and Portugal, we shall consider two countries that share many similarities with the Iberian nations: Italy and Greece. Following our description of these relatively unstable southern European countries, we shall turn our attention to three regions which have had fairly stable democracies for some time: the Benelux, Alpine, and Scandinavian regions. We shall conclude by examining the part that all of the nations within these five regions play in Europe's intergovernmental organizations.

Notes

1. Abraham Kaplan, *The Conduct of Inquiry* (San Francisco: Chandler, 1964), p. 85.

2. Morris Zelditch, Jr., "Intelligible Comparison," in *Comparative Methods in Sociology*, edited by I. Vallier (Berkeley and Los Angeles: University of California Press, 1971), p. 167. Also see Patrick J. McGowan, "Meaningful Comparisons and the Study of Foreign Policy," in *International Events and the Comparative Analysis of Foreign Policy*, edited by Charles W. Kegley, Jr. et al. (Columbia: University of South Carolina Press, 1975), p. 66.

3. Julian L. Simon, *Basic Research Methods in Social Science* (New York: Random House, 1969), p. 70.

Selected Bibliography

Almond, Gabriel A., and Powell, G. Bingham, Jr. *Comparative Politics: System, Process, and Policy.* Boston: Little, Brown, 1978.

Bill, J. A., and Hardgrave, R. L., Jr. *Comparative Politics: The Quest for Theory.* Columbus, Ohio: Charles E. Merrill, 1973.

Chilocote, Ronald. *Theories of Comparative Politics.* Boulder, Colo.: Westview, 1981.

Czudnowski, Moshe M. *Comparing Political Behavior.* Beverly Hills, Calif.: Sage Publications, 1976.

Eckstein, Harry. "A Perspective on Comparative Politics, Past and Present." In *Comparative Politics,* edited by Harry Eckstein and David Apter, New York: Free Press, 1963.

Greenstein, Fred I., and Polsby, Nelson W., eds. *Strategies of Inquiry.* Vol. VII of *Handbook of Political Science.* Reading, Mass.: Addison-Wesley, 1975.

Haas, Michael. "Comparative Analysis," *Western Political Quarterly* 15 (June 1962): 294–303.

Holt, Robert T., and Turner, John E., eds. *The Methodology of Comparative Research.* New York: Free Press, 1970.

Kalleberg, Arthur. "The Logic of Comparison: A Methodological Note on the Comparative Study of Political Systems," *World Politics* 19 (October 1966): 69–83.

Kaplan, Abraham. *The Conduct of Inquiry.* San Francisco: Chandler, 1964.

Lasswell, Harold D. "The Future of the Comparative Method," *Comparative Politics* 1 (October 1968): 3–18.

Lijphart, Arend. "Comparative Politics and the Comparative Method," *American Political Science Review* 65 (September 1971): 682–693.

Mayer, Lawrence L. *Comparative Political Inquiry.* Homewood, Ill.: Dorsey, 1972.

Merkl, Peter H. *Modern Comparative Politics.* New York: Holt, Rinehart, and Winston, 1970.

Merritt, Richard L., and Rokkan, Stein, eds. *Comparing Nations: The Use of Quantitative Data in Cross-National Research.* New Haven: Yale University Press, 1966.

Przeworski, Adam, and Teune, Henry. *The Logic of Comparative Social Inquiry.* New York: Wiley-Interscience, 1970.

Pye, Lucian, ed. *Political Science and Area Studies: Rivals or Partners?* Bloomington: Indiana University Press, 1975.

Raymond, Gregory A. "Comparative Analysis and Nomological Explanation." In *International Events and the Comparative Analysis of Foreign Policy,* edited by Charles W. Kegley, Jr. et al. Columbia: University of South Carolina Press, 1975.

Sartori, Giovanni. "Concept Misformation in Comparative Politics," *American Political Science Review* 64 (December 1970): 1033–1053.

Scarrow, H.A. *Comparative Political Analysis*. New York: Harper and Row, 1969.

Simon, Julian L. *Basic Research Methods in Social Science*. New York: Random House, 1969.

Zelditch, Morris, Jr. "Intelligible Comparison." In *Comparative Methods in Sociology*, edited by I. Vallier. Berkeley and Los Angeles: University of California Press, 1971.

2.

Iberian Politics:
Beyond Corporatism?

The Historical Setting

An Overview

The Iberian Peninsula lies at the southwestern tip of Europe and is separated from the rest of the continent by the rugged Pyrenees Mountains. Much of the peninsula consists of a high plateau which is broken at regular intervals by mountain ranges and deep river valleys. For the most part, the population is distributed on the coastal lowlands that encircle the plateau. Except in the north and northwest, where the precipitation exceeds forty inches annually, agriculture is based upon winter wheat, olives, grapes, beans, and other crops which are naturally adapted to the prevailing climatic conditions of winter rainfall and summer drought. While major efforts at irrigation have added fruits and vegetables to the list of foodstuffs grown on the peninsula, the potential for increasing agricultural output remains limited by the poor quality of the soil. But though the topsoil generally lacks enough organic matter to support extensive agricultural development, the subsoil has yielded sizable deposits of copper in the Sierra Morena range, lead in the Sierra Nevada, and both coal and iron in the Cantabrian Mountains.

Many settlers have been attracted to the peninsula by these mineral resources. Archaeologists are uncertain about the origins of the first inhabitants. Perhaps the earliest were the Basques, who lived in the foothills of the Western Pyrenees. Since their language bears no resemblance to any other European tongue, etymologists consider them to be among the oldest native populations on the continent.

Regardless of who might rank as the oldest, it is clear that a wide variety of ethnic groups eventually migrated to the peninsula. Artifacts suggest that the

11

Iberians arrived from the eastern Mediterranean some time during the third millennium B.C. They were followed in subsequent centuries by the Celts, Phoenicians, Greeks, and later the Carthaginians. This ethnic diversity combined with the peninsula's topography to create several distinct cultural regions. Moreover, it was not until after the Roman victory over Carthage in the Second Punic War that those people residing within these regions were ever placed under the rule of one power.

The Romans brought political unity to the Iberian Peninsula for the first time. Nevertheless, the land they called Hispania was not easily subjugated. Because of its ethnic and cultural divisions, much of the conquest actually entailed defeating numerous independent tribes, one by one. The fanatical resistance put up by towns such as Numantia, as well as Rome's inability to crush the heroic Lusitanian chief, Viriathus, are still celebrated in the historical lore of Spain and Portugal, respectively. But, by 19 B.C., the conquest was completed and Hispania became an integral part of Rome's imperial system, providing the empire with grains, precious metals, and legionnaires.

In addition to political unity, the Romans also brought Hispania legal, linguistic, and, by the fourth century A.D., religious unity. Still, the impact of romanization was felt primarily in the urban south and east, where most immigrants settled after the conquest. From these areas came some of the most notable names in Roman civilization, including Seneca, Lucan, Trajan, Hadrian, and Marcus Aurelius. Yet, despite the vitality of the Hispano-Roman cities, the indigenous cultures of the interior did not vanish. New administrative units, for example, generally conformed to earlier tribal boundaries, and the large landed estates Rome introduced to the peninsula frequently were superimposed over existing agrarian structures.

When Roman military power began to erode, Hispania was invaded by the Suevi and the Vandals. Unable to respond himself, the Emperor Honorius persuaded the highly romanized Visigoths to occupy the peninsula in his name. Once the invaders were defeated, the Visigoths established a monarchy and governed Hispania under an imperial commission from Rome. Although Hispano-Romans continued as municipal administrators for this new warrior elite, urban life deteriorated and the church gradually emerged as a mediator between these two groups.

The Visigothic monarchy lasted three centuries but it never developed into a stable, integrated political structure. According to tradition, each new king was selected from the royal family and then ratified by the aristocracy. This transition process frequently was marked by family feuds and political intrigue. At times, the rivals of a designated heir would invite foreign powers to intervene on their behalf. Thus, when civil war erupted in 710 over the issue of succession, it was not surprising that the opponents of King Roderic called upon the Moors in North Africa for aid. The results of the call, however, were surprising. Within a year, Tarik ibn Zizad led an army across the Straits of Gibraltar. He was followed by a larger army and soon Muslim forces were in control of all the old Roman cities in the populous south and east.

The Moorish conquest divides ancient Hispania from medieval Spain and Portugal. As Visigothic defenses fell, many Christians converted to Islam and continued to direct their large estates. Others retained their religious beliefs but used Arabic in their daily economic transactions. All of these individuals, together with Syrians, Berbers, and Jews who originally came to the peninsula as Roman slaves, formed a society whose art and commercial goods became renowned throughout Europe. Yet the old problems of succession and factionalism continued to plague the peninsula. At the end of the tenth century a dictatorship was established by al-Mansur. Since this takeover broke the principle of legitimate descent from Mohammed, the dictatorship survived only six years longer than its founder. Afterwards the caliphate broke down into a welter of *taifa* (local faction) kingdoms. Political division weakened the Muslim grip on the peninsula; isolated, quarreling *taifas* could not defend themselves, let alone help defend each other.

Almost from the beginning of the Moorish occupation, Christians launched counterattacks from their remote mountain sanctuaries in the northwest.[1] Legend has it that the first Christian victory was won by the Visigothic noble Pelayo when, in 722, he ambushed an Arab patrol in the Cantabrian Mountains. His successors slowly extended control beyond Asturias to territories near the peninsula's heart, where they established their capital in the city of León. To gain additional support, *fueros* (special privileges) were given to local rulers along the Muslim frontier allowing them rights of taxation and semiautonomous government. Castile, one such frontier region, became an independent kingdom in 1004. Although it later rejoined León, this society of warriors (personified by a heroic knight called *El Cid*) had so eclipsed the latter in military strength that the new nation became known simply as Castile.

Another powerful combination emerged in the southeast. Fearing the possibility of Muslim advances, Frankish kings supported the creation of several buffer states along the Pyrenees. The kingdom of Aragón and the counties of Catalonia were part of this barrier. In 1137, they were united by a royal marriage and, a century later, the former Muslim kingdom of Valencia also became part of this Aragonese federation.

Both Aragón and Castile experienced growth and political instability. During the fourteenth century, for instance, the Aragonese federation vied with Genoa and Venice for commercial dominance in the Mediterranean. Similarly, throughout the next century Castile's merchant marine rivaled members of the Hanseatic League for control over Atlantic trade. But whereas war, the plague, and class conflict gradually weakened Aragón, Castile ultimately became the foremost state on the peninsula. The royal marriage of Ferdinand of Aragón to Isabella of Castile in 1469 united these two crowns and therein laid the foundation for the modern Spanish State.

Elsewhere on the peninsula another state had already been born. What is modern Portugal today originally was a dependency of León. During the eleventh century, Alfonso IV of Castile and León gave hereditary rule over Portugal to the Burgundian aristocrat Henri. Upon Alfonso's death, Henri gained substantial autonomy by selectively backing certain Leonese factions over others whenever they quarreled over the issue of succession. His son, Alfonso Henriques, defeated the Muslims at Ourique in 1139 and then declared himself king of Portugal.[2] This newly proclaimed House of Burgundy ruled until 1383. Under its leadership Portugal's borders were extended to their present limits, the navy enjoyed slow but steady expansion, and foreign merchant fleets regularly stopped en route between Italy and England. Although Portugal lacked the economic strength of its maritime rivals, the protection and incentives given to shipbuilding companies by the crown provided the basis for later growth.

In summary, both modern Spain and Portugal share a common heritage of political factionalism, ethnic heterogeneity, and center-periphery tensions. The two states were born during an undertaking that remains without parallel in human history. Once the eight-century reconquest was over, the leaders of Spain and Portugal turned their attention to another historic enterprise—transoceanic expansion.

The Rise and Decline of Spain

The year 1492 stands as a watershed in the flow of Spanish history. On one hand, the triumphal January entry of Ferdinand and Isabella into Granada marked the end of the reconquest, and on the other, Columbus's October discoveries represented the beginning of Spanish imperialism. Subsequently, under Charles I and Philip II, this new state developed a military capable of saving Christendom from the Turks in the Old World while simultaneously transporting the Gospel to the New World. Spain's position at the summit of global power was manifest politically by rule over the greatest empire yet known in the Western world, and culturally by the florescence of her literary and artistic genius throughout the sixteenth and seventeenth centuries.

However, this position was immutable to neither internal turmoil nor external threats. Inflation, agricultural problems, and a decline in manufacturing began to weaken Spain from within, while a series of foreign policy setbacks following the defeat of the Grand Armada ultimately eroded Spain's prestige abroad. Much of the wealth Spain took from the Americas was wasted in Europe to defeat Protestant armies and retain possessions in Italy and the Low Countries. In the years which followed, Spain became involved in the Thirty

Years' War on the side of the Catholic League and thus squandered even more resources at the very time when her American colonies began to exert pressure for economic independence.

Spain's plummet from the summit of global power was consummated in the eighteenth century. The War of Spanish Succession established a Bourbon dynasty in Madrid and Spanish foreign policy consequently became a virtual adjunct to that of France. Although under Charles III, Spain briefly enjoyed a semblance of her former international influence, incessant hostilities with England hindered effective control over her colonies during a period when ideas sparked by the French Revolution were taking root all over Spanish America. In 1808, Napoleon occupied Spain and placed his brother Joseph on the Spanish throne. As reports of these events spread throughout a colonial system already torn by economic grievance, Spanish Americans began substituting local rule for the administrators of the Intruder King. Between 1810 and 1824 Spain lost all of her American continental possessions. Still, the Spanish retained the hope that under the protocol of Troppeau other European monarchies would help them regain their erstwhile colonies.

The French Revolution had another impact on Spain. At the end of the eighteenth century, its political ideals spread among the people on the Iberian Peninsula and directly influenced the Spanish liberals who wrote the 1812 Cadiz constitution. However, within two years this remarkable document was abolished by King Ferdinand VII. When he died, war erupted between supporters of his daughter, Isabella, and supporters of his brother, Carlos de Borbón. In essence, the war pitted two groups of Spaniards against each other. The first, known as "red" Spain, was urban based, anticlerical, and in favor of centralization. The second, "black" Spain, was rural based, Catholic, and in favor of regional decentralization. Although the supporters of Isabella were victorious, the basic issues dividing these two Spains were not resolved. Moreover, since the new queen proved an ineffective ruler, Spain's political future remained in the hands of those generals who had saved her throne from the Carlists.

In 1868, Queen Isabella II was dethroned by a military coup. For the next six years the country experimented with different governments, but none received popular acceptance. As a result, the Bourbon monarchy was restored in 1874 under King Alfonso XII. To defuse the unrest which had scarred the nation for over four decades, a tacit agreement known as the *turno político* was reached between the Liberal and Conservative parties, allowing them to alternate in office. Nevertheless, toward the end of the century this informal pact began to break down as both those for and against the monarchy turned increasingly to violence. From 1902 to 1923 the country averaged one government every eighteen months. Consequently the military began to see the government as inefficient, corrupt, and a threat to national unity.

At the same time that military officers were complaining about a lack of civil order, the army found itself to be an object of popular criticism. Humiliated by the loss of the last vestiges of Spain's overseas empire in the Spanish-American War, and frustrated by its failure to carve out a new colony in Morocco, the army attempted to protect its swollen officer corps from outsiders by forming unions called *Juntas de Defensa*. When the army was routed by the Moors at Anual in 1921, public pressure forced the government to establish a commission of inquiry despite the fact that the juntas opposed any such investigation. Two years later, on the eve of the commission's final report, the army staged a coup and formed a new government under General Miguel Primo de Rivera.

The first few years of the new government were fairly successful; a major victory was won over the Moors at Alhucemas Bay, and a vast public works program was undertaken at home. However, when the depression hit Spain in 1929, Primo lost favor with his backers and soon resigned. The king briefly attempted to rule through another military dictator, but the monarchy too had lost support, thus prompting Alfonso XIII to leave Spain.

That summer a republic was proclaimed at a constitutional convention in San Sebastián. Spain had been a republic once before. Just prior to the Bourbon restoration of 1874, four different presidents unsuccessfully tried to organize a stable government. Now with the king in exile, the nation turned to a representative system again. But though the Second Republic began in an atmosphere of euphoria, it eventually suffered through more instabilities than the First Republic. During its first five years, there were eighteen different governments, which held power for an average of three and a half months each. Anarchists, communists, and revolutionary socialists on the far left of the political spectrum confronted monarchists, the Catholic church, and fascists on the far right. Each side feared the other's intentions; and neither side showed much willingness to compromise. In the Second Republic's last elections, a coalition of political parties from the left faced a coalition of parties from the right. When the official tabulations were published one important fact stood out: the country lacked a political center. Approximately 4.7 million votes had been cast for the left, 3.9 million for the right, but only 449,000 for the center. Owing to the republic's electoral system, the leftist plurality in the popular vote resulted in an absolute majority of seats in the parliament. Once this was known, many extremists began to draw parallels between Spain and the Russian Revolution. As the number of land seizures, strikes, and attacks on Catholic churches increased, elements on the far right demanded that the government take action to ensure public order. On July 17, 1936, less than a week after two political assassinations had rocked the country, the military staged a revolt in Morocco. Within twenty-four hours, successful uprisings occurred in various locations on the mainland, but prospects for a rapid coup evaporated when Barcelona and Madrid remained in the hands of loyal military and police officers. The insurgent officers, led by Francisco Franco, received troops, weapons, and air support from Mussolini and Hitler. Conversely, the republican government was aided to a lesser extent by the Soviet Union and thousands of volunteers from the Western democracies. What had begun as an attempted coup had thus developed into a bloody civil war with international ramifications.

After three years of war Franco defeated the republicans. In 1947, he turned Spain back into a monarchy but did not name a king. Don Juan de Borbón, son of the last reigning monarch, opposed the regime, so Franco ruled as regent while he groomed Don Juan's son, Juan Carlos, for the throne. On November 21, 1975, General Franco died. When Juan Carlos assumed power he proclaimed that a new era had begun in the history of Spain and then proceeded to initiate a variety of measures to transform Franco's authoritarian regime into a democracy.

The Rise and Decline of Portugal

Spain's western neighbor has also undergone a recent transformation from authoritarian rule to democracy. Like Spain, Portugal experienced hundreds of years of monarchy, followed in succession by a brief fling at republican government and then a right-wing dictatorship. Furthermore, Portugal once possessed a vast colonial empire that ultimately had detrimental effects on the domestic economy. Thus, in the period following the reconquest, the two states which grew out of ancient Hispania showed certain historical similarities. Of course, this is not to say that they were identical. It simply means that differences which arise from a comparison of similar cases can be accounted for by referring to a small range of independent variables, since such factors as culture, level of development, and so on have been held constant, and thus controlled. Having briefly outlined some of the major trends in Spanish history, let us now begin our "most-similar" system comparison by looking at the origins of the Portuguese colonial experience.

While Columbus had journeyed westward in search of Asia, Prince Henry the Navigator believed that Portugal could reach the same place by sailing in the opposite direction. When, in 1434, Gil Eanes sailed beyond Cape Bojador, he provided tangible evidence to support Henry's ideas. In succeeding years, Portuguese mariners rounded Africa and traveled to India, China, and Japan. Goods imported from Asia were less expensive for Europeans when they were taken by sea around Africa than when they were carted overland along the older trade routes. Thus, within a short time, the Portuguese were able to use this logistical advantage to build a vast empire.

To prevent conflict between the growing Spanish and Portuguese empires, the Treaty of Tordesillas divided the globe into two areas. Spain received the Philippines and the Americas; Portugal obtained Brazil and trade rights to Asia. However, neither country went on to build a modern economy. As revenues from silk, tea, and spices accumulated, the Portuguese began to purchase foreign manufactured goods rather than develop domestic industries. To make matters worse the price of Asian commodities on the European market fell in proportion to their newly increased availability. In order to raise profits, Portugal expanded the volume of its spice trade. Needless to say, this required that more money be allocated to shipbuilding, which in turn placed greater financial strain on the economy. Lacking enough resources to resolve these problems, Portugal gradually lost its premier position in Asia to competitors.

Portugal's position also came under attack elsewhere. During 1578, King Sebastião and much of the Portuguese nobility were killed by the Moors while trying to defend their holdings in Morocco. The country thus found itself virtually without either leaders or money in its treasury. Since the mother of Philip II of Spain was descendant from Portuguese royalty, the crowns of Portugal and Castile were united as parts of the Habsburg empire. Though the Portuguese initially benefited from access to Spanish America, they soon were pressed to pay increased taxes for defense at a time when Spain could not protect Portugal's remaining colonies. In 1640, Portugal broke away from Spain and eventually formed an alliance with England to preserve its independence.

Because nearly all commercial holdings in the Orient were lost during the years of Spanish rule, Brazil assumed a greater role in Lisbon's economic calculations once Portuguese independence was reestablished. Originally prized because of coffee exports, Brazil subsequently became an important source of gold and diamonds, too. By the early 1700s, Brazil's mineral wealth more than doubled the income which the Portuguese crown possessed following its break from Spain. But though this economic upswing revitalized some state institutions, overall Portugal's governmental machinery remained in desperate need of an overhaul. As trade revenues began to fall in mid-century, several ministers were appointed to streamline the bureaucracy. The most authoritarian of these, the Marques de Pombal, enacted a series of educational, military, and financial reforms which increased administrative efficiency at the same time that they weakened aristocratic political controls. Thus, when cotton exports from Brazil stimulated a new period of economic growth at the end of the century, middle-class merchants prospered for the first time in Portuguese history, while the wealth and power of the nobility declined.

Portugal, like Spain, lost its position in the western hemisphere after the Napoleonic wars. However, unlike Spain, Portugal did not engage in a protracted military struggle in an effort to keep its American colony. When French troops marched on Lisbon in 1807, the Portuguese court set sail for Brazil and left a council of regency behind to govern in its absence. Four years later, the French were driven out of the country by a British expeditionary force and several contingents of Portuguese troops which had been placed under the direction of Lord Beresford, a general in the British army. Since the royal family chose not to return from Brazil at this time, Beresford, acting as commander-in-chief of the Portuguese military, continued to dominate the affairs of state long after the fighting had ended. Between August 1820 and February 1821, revolts erupted in both Portugal and Brazil which prompted King João VI to return to Lisbon and name his liberal son, Dom Pedro, regent of Brazil. Meanwhile D. Pedro took steps to protect his new position by supporting the Brazilian independence movement. With Great Britain backing his move, the Portuguese had no choice but to grant Brazil its independence.

João VI proved much more tolerant of constitutional limitations on the monarchy than his Spanish counterpart, Ferdinand VII. Whereas the Spanish king abolished the Cadiz constitution, João VI accepted the liberal Portuguese constitution of 1822, which had also been inspired by the political ideals of the French Revolution. Nonetheless, upon his death, Portugal contained political divisions which were quite similar to those in Spain. Liberals criticized the clergy and the nobility, while conservatives spoke out in behalf of these groups. In an ill-fated attempt to unify the country, D. Pedro returned from Brazil and took two steps. First, he replaced the constitution with the more moderate Charter of 1826. Second, he planned to rally the nation behind the charter through a royal marriage between his daughter, Maria da Glória, and her conservative uncle, Dom Miguel. Yet, when the first opportunity arose, D. Miguel moved to revoke the charter and soon came into conflict with D. Pedro.

Just as the Carlist wars did not resolve the basic issues dividing Spain, the so-called Miguelist war likewise did not settle the constitutionalist-absolutist split within Portugal. Although the liberals reinstituted the charter after their victory over D. Miguel in 1834, three major changes occurred during the next eight years: the "Septembrist Revolt" of 1836 ended with a return to the constitution of 1822; the "Marshalls' Revolt" of 1837 led to the writing of a constitution which contained elements of both the charter and the 1822 document; while the "Chartist Revolt" of 1842 resurrected the charter once more. Thus, in order to bring stability to the government, liberals and conservatives finally agreed to alternate power. *Rotativismo*, as their system was called, functioned more smoothly than the Spanish *turno político* due to the greater talents of Portugal's reigning monarchs and the smaller number of conflicting interest groups within Portuguese society.

Even so, *rotativismo* came under severe criticism from those who felt that it merely perpetuated the rule of an upper-class oligarchy. Ultimately a severe financial crisis, the rising politicization of the middle class, and the government's acquiescence to British colonial demands in Africa all combined to further erode support for the constitutional monarchy. In February 1908, the king and his heir were assassinated. During the next thirty-two months, six different cabinets were formed to bolster the faltering regime. But when a rebellion broke out in Lisbon on October 4, 1910, the monarchy fell and was replaced by a parliamentary republic.

Much like Spain, Portugal experienced tremendous instability when it came under a parliamentary form of government. Republicans who had previously been united in their opposition to the monarchy splintered into rival factions when the vote was taken to select the first president. Civic life rapidly degenerated to the point that strikes, riots, terrorist attacks, and attempted coups became common. During this period, the country averaged no less than three governments a year. The political havoc ended in 1926, when the military overthrew the government. In contrast to Spain, Portuguese society had not been polarized under the parliamentary republic. Coupled with the fact that no strong mass movement developed among either the supporters or critics of the parliamentary system, this allowed Portugal to avoid the kind of civil war which decimated Spain.

Though Portugal was spared the ravages of war, it did not escape crippling inflation. To put the country back on a sound financial footing, the military turned to Dr. António de Oliveira Salazar, an economics professor at the University of Coimbra. Over the next seven years Salazar laid the foundation for his authoritarian *Estado Novo* (New State), which he directed as prime minister until suffering a stroke in 1968. Salazar's successor, Dr. Marcello Caetano, was toppled from power in 1974 by a military coup. When the junta took control it announced that a new era had begun and promised to initiate a series of reforms which would bring democracy to Portugal.

Thus far we have sketched the major events which preceded the recent transition from authoritarian to democratic governments in both Spain and Portugal. For the remainder of the chapter we shall focus in greater detail on this transition process. It has not been our intention to give a complete chronological account of either country, rather we have sought to describe the historical context in which these two new regimes currently operate. Contextual variables are important in comparative analysis because no government exists in a vacuum. At any moment in time it is affected by how precedents have been interpreted and passed on from one generation to the next. Having identified some of the most prominent features in the historical backgrounds of Spain and Portugal, we shall now examine the attitudinal patterns which have emerged from their past.

Political Culture and Socialization

Every nation possesses a particular cultural orientation toward political structures and behavior. This "political culture" is shaped by the collective history of a nation and the individual experiences of its members. All political cultures are characterized by beliefs, feelings, and judgments which affect the kinds of demands placed on a regime, as well as how these demands are converted into policy outputs. Of course, no country has a single political culture. There often are differences between the outlooks of elites and those of the mass public. Furthermore, when ethnic, linguistic, or religious cleavages exist within a society, distinct subcultures may also develop. In the analysis which follows, we shall describe the values that supported authoritarian regimes in Spain and Portugal and then examine the extent to which they were shared throughout these countries.

The Iberian Ethos

Deeply embedded in the history of the Iberian Peninsula lies a cultural orientation toward political structures and behavior which is essentially corporatist in nature. The main characteristics of this orientation have their roots in ancient Roman law, Thomistic thought, and feudalism as it was practiced during the reconquest. Not only did this cultural orientation provide a philosophic basis for the Spanish and Portuguese states which emerged in the fifteenth century, but its features could still be found in the regimes of Franco, Salazar, and Caetano well over four hundred years later.

Perhaps the most fundamental assumption in corporatism is that categories of people, rather than individuals, form the basic units of society. The major goal of the state is to find a way to bring order to the interactions between these units. Hence the relationship between society and the state is organic; in other words, government is seen as the natural means for achieving social harmony.

According to corporatist theory, societies are stratified horizontally in terms of distinct classes and differentiated vertically in terms of specific functional entities. Each class and functional entity has its own status, privileges, and responsibilities which allegedly conform to natural law. The best way for a state to achieve social harmony is to govern through a ruler strong enough to oversee and direct the associations between these units. Thus, under corporatism individual rights are subordinated to group rights, but group activities are regulated through patrimonial authority exercised by the head of state.[3] Consequently, for much of their histories Spain and Portugal possessed political cultures which contributed to a situation where most citizens were either unaware of national politics, or they understood the impact that the government could have on them but did not see themselves as potential participants in shaping the outcome of the political process.

Aside from stressing hierarchy and accepting one's station in life, the political cultures of Spain and Portugal also placed great emphasis on patronage ties. The nuclear family and, at times, extended kinship relations represented the primary source of an individual's physical security and economic well-being within these highly compartmentalized societies. Whenever circumstances arose which were beyond an individual's immediate control, he could frequently obtain assistance from a patron who was outside of the family. These patron-client arrangements had three main characteristics. First, they were asymmetrical because the two parties were unequal in status, wealth, and influence. Second, they involved reciprocity insofar as each party would ultimately gain something from the other. Finally, they were personalistic since the exchange agreements were based on face-to-face contact. In summary, the most prominent similarities in the historical development of the Spanish and Portuguese political cultures can be found in the cluster of values associated with corporatism and clientelism. This is not to minimize the various cultural differences between or within these two countries, but only to highlight some of their underlying similarities before we contrast their differences.

Problems in Perpetuating the Iberian Ethos

Political socialization is the process whereby an individual learns the values of a political culture. A welter of agents continuously socialize the individual throughout his or her life. Given that Franco and Salazar came to power after periods of considerable turmoil, and given that at least the corporatist values discussed above were not totally accepted in either country, both leaders soon faced the problem of how to organize a consistent, cumulative socialization process that would transmit a political culture congruent with the political structures in their regimes.

The first ten years of Franco's rule were marked by efforts to shape political attitudes through the control of youth organizations, the educational system, and the mass media. Let us look first at the political socialization of the youth. In 1937, Franco abolished all political parties and in their place named his National Movement (*Movimiento*) the sole official party. Although the *Movimiento* never created a school for cadre training, it was affiliated with a variety of bodies that supposedly would give proper ideological direction to the citizenry. Included among these bodies were a youth organization (*Organización Juvenil Española*, OJE) and a student organization (*Sindicato Española Universitario*, SEU). In an effort to unify the OJE and SEU, plus implant a strong organic-corporatist spirit in future generations, the Youth Front (*Frente de Juventudes*) was also established. Despite Franco's interest in using these bodies as socialization agents, by the 1950s they had atrophied so much that the bulk of their membership existed only on paper.[4]

Historically, the church played a greater role in political socialization than youth groups because it dominated Spain's educational system from elementary through the university level. As a strong supporter of hierarchy, order, and deference, the church received substantial criticism from nineteenth century liberals who encouraged the state to build public schools as a secular alternative to religious training. When the Franco regime came to power it was dissatisfied with the educational system and therefore undertook a series of moves to stress religious and political education. Textbooks were censored, teachers were placed under observation, and state-supervised boarding schools (*Colegios Mayores Universitarios*) were even introduced. These efforts notwithstanding, within a decade deviations from the regime's educational orthodoxy began to occur. By the 1960s demands for reform led to a number of improvements, the most notable being the curricula revision mandated under the 1970 Educational Reform Law.

Turning finally to the role of mass media in political socialization, we should note that except for a short time during the Second Republic the Spanish news media have been under some kind of state control since the fifteenth century. Throughout the Franco years the type of controls employed ranged from investigating the political sympathies of journalists to banning specific books and films. According to the press law of 1966 and its subsequent amendments, publications had to respect certain guidelines, namely, morality, public order, and the principles of the National Movement. Thus, while the regime's activities in the areas of youth organization and education lost much of their initial zeal by the end of World War II, controls were maintained over the media until Franco's death. Presently Spain is undergoing a political and moral *destape* (uncovering). Magazines and newspapers from virtually every part of the political (and erotic) spectrum currently appear on news stands. Films which were once forbidden because of their political content now play side by side with more lusty movies featuring necrophilia and other previously taboo subjects.

In short, while the first ten years of the Franco regime may have been marked by several attempts at active indoctrination, ultimately the socialization process was highly fragmented and the regime came to rest more on political apathy than political allegiance. Yet, as Juan Linz has pointed out, depoliticization is one way to reduce tension and consolidate power in a society that has recently suffered through considerable political strife.[5]

A similar conclusion may also be reached regarding political socialization during the Salazar-Caetano years in Portugal. Salazar, like his Spanish counterpart, had little use for the factionalism that he believed was inherent in multiparty systems. As a result, he abolished all existing political parties and in their place installed a political organization called the National Union (*União Nacional*). Except when the civil war was being fought in Spain, very little was done to mobilize the Portuguese population. Even membership in the youth group (*Mocidale Portuguesa*), which was organized to train school children in civic matters, declined after the war.

In large measure Salazar's control was based on passive compliance rather than on mass mobilization. To dampen political consciousness, "unreliable" teachers were removed from the educational systems and extensive censorship was placed on the mass media. Some cautious steps were taken to liberalize immediately after World War II and a few more were taken following Salazar's death. But the regime still retained its authoritarian character and, to borrow an old saw, continued its attempts to redirect popular attention from politics to the three F's: Fatima, football, and fado.

In summary, the political values which supported authoritarian regimes in Spain and Portugal were grounded in scholastic premises about society and the state. Yet, as suggested at the beginning of this section, these values were not uniformly shared throughout either country. Consequently, both Franco and Salazar made deliberate efforts to discourage political activism, especially among those who did not accept the notions of hierarchy, privilege, and patronage. To get a better picture of these political subcultures and how they may have contributed to the breakdown of authoritarianism, let us move away from our discussion of contextual variables to consider the impact of structural variables in Iberian politics.

Internal Cleavages, Political Competition, and Citizen Participation

Thus far we have covered the geographic, historical, and cultural contexts within which political behavior takes place. It is now time to focus on those structures which are actually engaged in the political process. For analytic purposes, we shall divide the political process into four main activities: interest articulation; interest aggregation; policy-making; and policy implementation. Our comparison of Spain and Portugal will continue with an analysis of the specialized structures involved in the first two of these activities.

Spain

The way in which demands are expressed by citizens, as well as the way in which they are formed into policy proposals, are influenced by the lines of cleavage that exist within a political system. Spain possesses as much diversity as any country in Europe. Visitors lured to Spain by travel agent promises that *España es diferente* are often astonished by its numerous subcultural divisions. As Ray Alan has observed, Spaniards come in a variety of sizes and shapes:

> Some are Castilians, strong on etiquette, elocution and subjunctives; some are Andalusians who swallow consonants like cockneys and sing like Moors. Others are Catalans who look like southern Frenchmen and speak a language similar to Langue-docien; Gallegos who look like Irishmen, speak Portuguese and drink like fish; Basques who look like lumberjacks and speak like nobody else on earth; and Aragonese who are bright-eyed and earnest and harbour grave doubts about the proud Castilians, wild Navarrans and surrealistic Catalans who surround them.[6]

In short, Spain is more than a land of whitewashed villages, gypsy guitars, and flamenco dancers. Indeed, there is some truth to the following reformulation of the old tourist slogan: *España es diferente, incluso de ella misma* ("Spain is different, even from itself").

Needless to say, there are many sources of heterogeneity in Spain. A nonexhaustive list would include differences in religious practice, cultural norms, language, political tradition, social stratification, and economic development. The most notable cleavages which have developed out of these differences are (1) church versus state; (2) center versus periphery; and (3) owner versus laborer. The first of these cleavages centers on the role of the Catholic church in national life. Beginning with the expulsion of the Jesuits in 1759, the Spanish church, perhaps the most conservative and intransigent in the Roman Catholic world, began to lose its grip on the nation's educational system. Criticism of the old ties between throne and altar continued throughout the next century and a half. Though Spaniards were said to be more papist than the pope, violent anticlericalism often accompanied political rebellions: priests were killed and churches were burned to protest religious influence in government affairs. The second cleavage was spawned by a lack of integration between the central government in Madrid and the inhabitants of various outlying regions. The dynastic marriage of Ferdinand and Isabella had combined territories with different social structures and political institutions. When attempts to centralize the Spanish state expanded dramatically after the War of Spanish Succession, they generated tremendous conflict in those regions which had long enjoyed some degree of autonomy under a full range of *fueros*. Finally, the third cleavage pertains to a complex set of class conflicts which have emerged in the urban north between industrial workers and managers, and in the rural south between agricultural workers and absentee landholders.

Whenever people who are grouped along one line of cleavage (e.g., region) are not also grouped together according to another kind of cleavage (e.g., class), we speak of crosscutting or overlapping cleavages. Many theorists contend that the greater the amount of crosscutting, the greater the stability of the political system, since people will not be divided into contending, mutually exclusive camps. An examination of cleavages in Spain reveals that there is a kernel of truth in a concept of the country as a series of water-tight compartments. For example, the most highly industrialized areas of Spain are "surrounded by rural areas with a stable and conservative peasantry while dominantly middle class cities in the South are often surrounded by a proletarian and potentially radical rural area."[7] What makes this situation explosive is that in certain cases cleavages do not crosscut between these hermetically sealed groups.

The two cases which attracted the most attention are Catalonia and the Basque provinces. Both areas possess a unique ethnolinguistic heritage but were repressed under the Franco regime. Moreover, both areas feel they have contributed disproportionately to Spain's economy in comparison to other parts of the country, but have not received their fair share of services from

TABLE 2.1

Demographic and Economic Characteristics of Selected Spanish Regions

	% of National Population	% of GNP	% of National Direct and Indirect Taxes	% of Expenditures
Regions with Tradition of Local Nationalism				
Catalonia	14.9	17.6	31.0	13.0
Basque provinces *	5.7	7.2	13.0	5.0
Region with Tradition of Administrative and Fiscal Autonomy				
Navarre	1.3	1.6	1.0	1.0
Regions Susceptible to Autonomy Appeals				
Galicia	7.8	5.7	5.0	9.0
Levant	8.6	8.5	9.0	9.0
Balearic Islands	1.5	1.7	2.3	2.2

*Vizcaya, Guipúzcoa, and Alava

Source: Adapted from Juan J. Linz, "Early State-Building and Late Peripheral Nationalism Against the State: The Case of Spain," in *Building States and Nations: Analyses by Region*, edited by S. N. Eisenstadt and Stein Rokkan (Beverly Hills, Calif.: Sage Publications, 1973), pp. 35, 87.

Madrid. Table 2.1 compares Catalonia and the Basque provinces with four additional regions which either once had some measure of autonomy or are susceptible to appeals for autonomy today.

As stated earlier, the pattern of cleavages within a political system has an impact on the structures which articulate and aggregate demands. Consider the case of the Basque country. Until the period of the Carlist wars, the Basques maintained considerable autonomy from Madrid due to *hidalgos de sangre* (nobility by virtue of blood pure from Moorish contamination) and the *fueros* they obtained during the reconquest. When the Basques began to lose their local rights, the *Partido Nacionalista Vaso* (Basque Nationalist Party, PNV) was organized to push for separatism, and Basques even set up their own trade union movement (the *Solidaridad de Obreros Vascos*). Yet, partially as a result of crosscutting, national parties continued to do relatively well in Basque provinces all the way up to the 1936 elections. In the waning days of the Second Republic, autonomy was given to the Basques, but because they opposed the Nationalists in the Civil War, they not only lost all of their special privileges when Franco came to power, but they were also repressed by his paramilitary *Guardia Civil* (Civil Guard). As conflict with the central government worsened, other cleavage lines were reinforced and a new, more militant organization called the *Euzkadi ta Azkatasuna* (Basque Homeland and Freedom, ETA) emerged to renew the demand for a separate Basque state. During the years which followed, the ETA and the *Guardia* became locked into a spiraling, escalatory pattern of terrorist violence that continues today.

Cleavages based on linguistic, ethnic, religious, and other such distinctions have played an important role in the history of Spanish party systems. But so long as Franco's *Movimiento* remained the single legal party in Spain, political opposition based on the kinds of cleavages illustrated by the Basque case expressed themselves outside of a competitive multiparty context. Simply stated, opposition during the Franco years took three forms: legal, alegal, and illegal. The legal opposition consisted of those dissident groups that had some stake in the regime but advocated different goals and policy objectives. The alegal opposition was basically composed of respected individuals who were tolerated by the regime despite their calls for change in its political institutions. Finally, the illegal opposition was made up of those who were viewed as enemies by the government.[8] Franco's death opened the door for all of these opposition groups to organize within a multiparty system. It had been over forty years since the last competitive elections in Spain. By the time a date was set, some 156 parties had registered and over 6,000 candidates were prepared to contest the 587 seats in the new parliament (Cortes).

Table 2.2 lists the major parties and electoral coalitions which were involved in the June 15, 1977, parliamentary race. One way to categorize these parties is to look at the positions they took on the role of democracy in post-Franco Spain. While some groups called for a continuation of the old regime,

TABLE 2.2

Major Spanish Political Parties

	Parties	Leaders
Electoral Coalitions on the Right		
Alianza Nacional 18 de Julio	Fuerza Nueva	Blas Piñar
	FE y JONS	Raimundo Fernández-Cuesta
	Comunión Tradicionalista	José M.ª de Oriol
	Confederación de Combatientes	José Antonio Girón
Alianza Popular	Partido Unido de AP	Manuel Fraga Iribarne
	Unión Nacional Española	Gonzalo Fernández de la Mora
	Acción Democrática Española	Federico Silva Muñoz
	Acció Regional de Catalunya	Laureano López Rodó
	Unió Catalana	Santiago Udina Martorell
	Partit Democràtic	José Antonio Linati
	Unió Lleidatana	Joaquín Viola Sauret
Electoral Coalitions in the Center		
Union del Centro Democratico	Partido Demócrata Cristiano	Fernando Alvarez de Miranda
	Partido Social-Demócrata	Francisco Fernández Ordóñez
	Unión Social-Demócrata Española	Eurico de la Peña
	Partido Social-Demócrata Independiente	Gonzalo Casado
	Federación Social-Demócrata	José Ramón Lasuén
	Partido Popular	Pio Cabanillas
	Federación de Partidos Demócratas	
	y Liberales	Joaquín Garrigues Walker
	Partido Demócrata Popular	Ignacio Comuñas
	Partido Progresista Liberal	Juan Garcia Madariaga
	Partido Liberal	Enrique Larroque
	Partido Social Liberal Andaluz	Manuel Clavero Arévalo
	Partido Gallego Independiente	José Luis Meilán Gil
	Acción Regional Extremeña	Enrique Sánchez de León
	Unión Canaria	Lorenzo Olarte Cullén
	Unión Demócrata de Murcia	Pedro Pérez Crespo

Coalition	Party	Leader
Equipo de la Democracia Cristiana	Federación de la Democracia Cristiana	Joaquín Ruiz-Ginénez
	Unió Democrática del País Valenciá	Vicente Ruiz Monrabal
	Partido Popular Galego	Fernando García Agudín
	Centre Catalá	Joaquín Molins Amat
	Unió Democrática de Catalunya	Antón Cañellas

Electoral Coalitions on the Left

Coalition	Party	Leader
Alianza Socialista Democrática	Partido Socialista Obrero Español (H)	Manuel Murillo Carrasco
	Partido Socialista Democrático Español	Antonio García López
Federación Laborista	Partido Reformista Independiente	José Manuel Somavilla
	Partido Laborista	Antonio Colomer
	Nueva Izquierda Nacional	José Redondo Gómez
PSOE	Partido Socialista Obrero Español	Felipe González
	Federación Catalana del PSOE	Josep M. Triginer
	Partit Socialista de Catalunya	Juan Raventós
Unidad Socialista	Partido Socialista Popular	Enrique Tierno Galvan
	Federación de Partidos Socialistas	Juan Garcés
Frente Democratico de Izquierdas	Partido Socialista Independiente	Lorento Bennasar
	Bloque Democrático y Social Independiente	Joaquín Vera Brijalba

Additional Major Parties Outside of Coalitions

	Party	Leader
	Partido Comunista Español	Santiago Carrillo

Source: Adapted from Carmelo Cabellos and Alfonso Montecelos, "¡A La Carrera ...!" La Actualidad Española (May 9–15, 1977): 18–19.

most political parties talked about extending democracy. Where they differed was over how much democracy would be extended. Opinions on the issue could be classified into three categories: those in favor of *apertura* desired slow change within Francoist institutions; supporters of *cambio* backed a gradual transition toward a more liberal regime; and, finally, advocates of *ruptura* wanted a total break with the past.

The major coalition on the right side of the Spanish political spectrum was the *Alianza Popular* (Popular Alliance, AP). Led by Manuel Fraga Iribarne, former Minister of Information under Franco, the AP spoke in vague terms about establishing democracy, but in a way that would not break with Franco's legacy. It received support during the campaign from some of Spain's largest banks and from various individuals located at the top of the church hierarchy.

The center of the political spectrum was occupied by a welter of parties committed to a gradual liberalization of the Spanish political system. The most notable coalition to be forged from this assortment of liberals, christian democrats, and social democrats was the *Union del Centro Democratico* (Democratic Center Union, UCD). Its standard-bearer, Adolfo Suárez Gonzáles had been appointed premier by King Juan Carlos to replace the more conservative head of the first post-Franco government, Carlos Arias Navarro. Suárez believed that a strong center was needed to avoid a confrontation between the old "red" and "black" Spains. Toward this end he stressed that the UCD would bring political change to Spain, but without any accompanying political trauma.

The left side of the Spanish political spectrum favored an abrupt break with the past but was split into two main groups, the socialists and the communists. Although much had been written about the possibility of the two groups forming a united front, there were several difficulties in creating such a coalition. Santiago Carrillo, the secretary-general of the *Partido Comunista Español* (Spanish Communist Party, PCE) worked diligently to heal the socialist-communist schism which had developed during the Civil War, yet many parties on the left remained suspicious of the communists. A good example could be seen in the relations between the PCE and the *Partido Socialista Obrero Español* (Socialist Worker's Party, PSOE). During the summer of 1974, the PCE organized a coalition known as the *Junta Democrática* (JD), which included some socialists and various liberal monarchists. While these noncommunist members of the coalition expressed their trust in the PCE's intentions, the PSOE organized a rival coalition called the *Programa Democrática* (PD) rather than join the JD. Even when the JD and PD later merged to form the *Coordinación Democrática*, Felipe Gonzáles, who held the post of first secretary of the PSOE, continued to insist that the socialist and communist alternatives were different. Communists were not believable as democrats, he noted, because their party structure was not democratic and they had never respected the rules of democracy when in power. If they were included in a coalition government, Gonzáles speculated that civil strife would increase and the military might stage a coup.

The second difficulty faced by the PCE in forming a broad coalition was the infighting among those who labeled themselves Spanish communists. For some time, the PCE had been challenged by the ultra left in the form of Trotskyite and Maoist splinter groups. However, once Santiago Carrillo criticized the Soviet Union for invading Czechoslovakia and later supported Eurocommunism, a split also occurred between his followers and a pro-Moscow faction. Speaking in almost religious terms, Carrillo likened his break with the Soviets to Martin Luther's rejection of Rome. When attacked during the campaign by the Kremlin, he frequently described himself as a victim of an inquisition or as a heretic who was being excommunicated.

Finally, the third difficulty in forming a broad leftist coalition pertained to the fact that in Spain national parties did not actually work in tandem with similar regional parties. Often Spain's regions had their own autonomous leftist parties. Thus, while the parties on the left were no longer illegal after Franco's death, these three major difficulties stood in the way of the type of coalition envisioned by Santiago Carrillo.

Having set the stage for the June 1977 parliamentary elections, we are now in a position to analyze their results. Table 2.3 gives the distribution of seats, by major party, in the Congress of Deputies and the Senate. Due to an election law which favored rural, conservative provinces, the popular vote actually was much closer than one would imagine when examining the percentages of seats won. The centrist UCD coalition of Premier Suárez received only 35 percent of the popular vote in the lower house, yet it obtained 47 percent of the seats. By way of comparison, Manuel Fraga's right-wing AP won 8 percent of the popular vote, but only obtained 4.6 percent of the seats. Because the UCD piled up most of its votes in rural areas and the PSOE won in most of the large cities, the UCD gained a stronger legislative position than might have been expected by their 980,425 vote victory over the PSOE.

As anticipated, the parties on the far right were unable to rally voters with the prospect of more Francoism. The AP's campaign of *apertura* did little better. On the other hand, the PCE polled only 9 percent of the popular vote but probably achieved Carrillo's long desired respectability. Hence this leaves the UCD and the self-proclaimed PSOE "democratic alternative" as the key actors in the next phase of Spain's transition to democracy.

Apart from the obvious questions which were raised about the political disaster suffered by the centrist parties not in the UCD, much of the speculation following the election concerned what type of party system was emerging in Spain. One view held that the UCD and PSOE would become a foundation for a two-party system. Another opinion was that the PSOE would eventually become a hegemonic party. A third point of view was that the election did not

TABLE 2.3

Results from the 1977 Spanish Parliamentary Elections

Congress of Deputies		
Party	Seats	%
Union del Centro Democratico (UCD)	165	47.1
Partido Socialista Obrero Español (PSOE)	118	33.7
Partido Comunista Español (PCE)	20	5.7
Alianza Popular (AP)	16	4.6
Others	31	8.9
	350	100.0

Senate		
Party	Seats	%
Union del Centro Democratico (UCD)	105	50.7
Partido Socialista Obrero Español (PSOE)	35	16.9
Partido Comunista Español (PCE)	12	5.8
Alianza Popular (AP)	2	1.0
Others	53	25.6
	207*	100.0

* King Juan Carlos also appointed 41 members to the Senate.

give an accurate picture of the future. According to this perspective, Spain was still in a state of flux because the UCD was an artificial, heterogeneous creation that might not remain as a strong power contender. Nor, it was argued, could the PSOE retain its popular appeal, for the PCE would soon adjust its strategy to reduce the socialists' influence.

Some idea about the future configuration of Spain's political party system was given during the spring of 1979. Following the approval of a new constitution in a national referendum on December 6, 1978, Premier Suárez dissolved the legislature and parliamentary elections were set for March. Although cold, rainy weather and a lackluster campaign cut voter turnout to roughly 12 percent below the 77 percent level registered two years earlier, the results for the major parties were quite similar. The UCD received 34 percent of the popular vote, the PSOE followed with 29 percent, while the PCE garnered only 10 percent and the coalition which AP joined received a mere 5 percent of the total. These figures translated into a slight decline in the number of parliamentary seats for the UCD, PSOE, and AP, but a modest increase in the number of seats held by the communists. In contrast to the major parties, regionalist parties did much better than in 1977. Catalonian nationalists retained their ten seats in the Cortes despite predictions that they would suffer an electoral defeat. Furthermore, Basque nationalists won twelve seats and other autonomists were elected from Andalusia and Aragon. Thus the 1979 parliamentary election formally ended Spain's transition from authoritarian rule to democracy. However, it showed that regardless of the UCD victory under a new constitution, uncertainties continued to exist about Spain's political future.

Portugal

In contrast with its eastern neighbor, Portugal is usually thought of as a country that possesses few cleavages. The two most prominent divisions are class- and territorial-based. Portugal's class inequalities have changed more slowly than those of almost any other country in Western Europe. At the top of the social pyramid lies a small elite of large landowners, industrialists, financiers, and so forth. Immediately below this upper echelon are small entrepreneurs, lower-level civil servants, skilled workers, and similar occupational groups. Estimates place the combination of these two groups at approximately one-quarter of the total population. These individuals have both wealth and prestige, and typically share many common political values.

Poverty among the remaining 75 percent of the people wears many faces. On the one hand, it is possible to distinguish between rural and urban workers and, on the other, between the pattern of agriculture in the north and that which exists in the south. The latter cleavage is particularly important from a political standpoint. Northern Portugal is a patchwork of *minifundios* (small family-owned plots of land), while the south contains numerous *latifundios* (large estates). This difference in landholding resulted when the territory in the south was given to Portuguese nobles after it was liberated from Moorish control. Often the nobility lived elsewhere and simply used this land as a hedge against inflation. Thus, over time, agricultural productivity in the south began to lag behind other portions of Europe since absentee landlords invested little capital to either improve their land or to purchase new equipment. Meanwhile, resentment against the wealthy grew among the many sharecroppers and landless peasants who tried to earn a living on the huge estates.

Whereas the southern poor were receptive to the expropriation calls made by leftists after Caetano's fall, the northern poor reacted in the opposite manner. Because almost everyone in the northern provinces owned their own fields, and because these farmers did not perceive themselves to be deprived relative to their neighbors, they did not see any benefit in collectivization. Thus, when attempts were made by the new regime to expropriate agricultural land, violent anti-government uprisings occurred throughout the north.

Another split with political overtones, aside from the historic class and territorial cleavages, recently surfaced in Portugal. One of the factors which precipitated the 1974 military coup was Caetano's effort to maintain Portugal's

TABLE 2.4

Significant Events in Portugal Following the 1974 Coup

Year	Month	Event
1974	May	MFA appoints General António Spínola provisional president. Adelino da Palma Carlos named prime minister by Spínola. First provisional government formed.
	July	Adelino da Palma Carlos and four moderate cabinet ministers resign when the Council of State rejects a series of policy proposals, including a referendum on the MFA constitution. Colonel Vasco dos Santos Gonçalves named prime minister. Second provisional government formed.
	September	Spínola supporters stage anti-Gonçalves demonstrations. Under heavy leftist pressure, Spínola resigns and is replaced by General Francisco da Costa Gomes.
	December	Third provisional government is formed; Gonçalves remains prime minister.
1975	March	Unsuccessful right-wing coup. Moderates in the MFA are purged; General Spínola goes into exile. Fourth provisional government formed; Gonçalves remains prime minister.
	April	Constituent Assembly elections result in a victory for the moderate political parties.
	June	MFA publishes its political action program, which would establish a system of people's assemblies to bypass the existing political parties.
	July	Moderate parties resign from the cabinet and demand the resignation of Gonçalves. MFA radicals place supreme power in Costa Gomes, Gonçalves, and General Otelo Saraiva de Carvalho, head of the army's Continental Operation Command.
	August	Moderates within the MFA issue the Document of the Nine, which called for greater political pluralism. Gonçalves forms fifth provisional government; all political parties excluded from the cabinet.
	September	Gonçalves dropped from the Council of the Revolution. Sixth provisional government formed.
	November	Unsuccessful left-wing coup. Communists and extreme leftists are purged.
1976	February	MFA leaders sign a pact with the political parties which limits the army to a minor constitutional role.
	April	Constituent Assembly completes the new constitution. Elections for the Assembly of the Republic result in a victory for the moderate parties.
	June	General António Ramalho Eanes elected president.
	July	Portugal's first democratic government since 1926 sworn in by President Eanes.

last possessions in Africa by fighting a protracted colonial war. When the *Movimento das Forças Armadas* (Armed Forces Movement, MFA) ousted Caetano, independence for Angola, Mozambique, and Portuguese Guinea did not seem far away. Consequently, Portugal was soon flooded with *retornados*, citizens who had once settled in the African colonies but had now returned to the safety of their mother country. As might be expected, this influx placed a

TABLE 2.5

Major Portuguese Political Parties

Parties Which Participated in Provisional Government Cabinets, 1974–1975
Movimento Democrático Português (MDP/CDE)
Partido Comunista Português (PCP)
Partido Popular Democrático (PPD)
Partido Socialista Português (PSP)

Additional Parties Which Ran in Either the 1975 or 1976 Elections	Ideological Position
Aliança Operária e Camponesa (AOC)	extreme left
Frente Eleitoral Comunista Marxista-Leninista (FEC-ML)	extreme left
Frente Socialista Popular (FSP)	moderate left
Liga Comunista Internacionalista (LCI)	extreme left
Movimento da Esquerda Socialista (MES)	moderate left
Movimento Reorganizativo do Partido do Proletariado (MRPP)	extreme left
Partido do Centro Democrático Social (CDS)	moderate right
Partido Comunista de Portugal (Marxista-Leninista) (PCP-ML)	extreme left
Partido da Democrácia Cristâô (PDC)	center right
Partido Popular Monárquico (PPM)	moderate right
Partido Revolucionária dos Trabalhadores (PRT)	extreme left
Partido Unidade Popular (PUP)	extreme left
União Democrática Popular (UDP)	extreme left

tremendous strain on an already sagging economy. Some individuals charged that the *retornados* were misusing their resettlement subsidies, others attributed a rise in the crime rate to their presence, and still others complained that they would ruin the job market. On the opposite side of the coin, the *retornados* felt betrayed by the MFA and, in turn, gave their support to conservative political causes.

The way in which these lines of cleavage affected Portuguese politics between the 1974 coup and the legislative and presidential elections of 1976 was extremely complex. During this period, six provisional governments were formed, two coups were attempted, and a new constitution was written. Table 2.4 outlines some of the significant events of this period. Since one of the first acts taken by the MFA was to abolish the *União Nacional*, let us examine the political parties which subsequently stepped forward to take its place.

Table 2.5 lists the four major parties which participated in cabinets that were formed by the provisional governments after Caetano's fall, as well as those parties which later ran candidates in either the 1975 or 1976 elections. The most important party on the right side of the political spectrum is the *Partido do Centro Democrático Social* (Social Democratic Center Party,

CDS). Although it did not participate in the cabinets of any provisional governments, the CDS was the only major party to significantly increase its popular vote between the 1975 and 1976 elections. Led by Diogo Pinto de Freitas do Amaral, the party contains many individuals who were administrators in the Caetano regime. Not surprisingly, the party has called for a suspension of agrarian reform and a denationalization of Portugal's industries.

The *Partido Popular Democrático* (Popular Democratic Party, PPD) occupies the center of the political spectrum. In the main, it is composed of liberals who, like Secretary-General Francisco Sá Carneiro, were previously members of Salazar's old National Assembly. Philosophically, the party claims to be an alternative to both capitalism and Marxism. It has favored state intervention in the economy and the nationalization of utilities but, much to the liking of farmers in the north, it also defended "socially useful" private property and initiative.

As in the case of Spain, the Portuguese left is dominated by socialists and communists. The *Partido Socialista Português* (Portuguese Socialist Party, PSP) is quite similar to other Western European socialist parties. Its platform calls for political pluralism, agrarian reform (though not expropriations), and a larger public sector in the Portuguese economy. In general, PSP backing lies mostly in urban areas, though it too has received some support from small landowners in the rural north. The party's leader, Mário Soares, is considered one of Portugal's most skilled and popular politicians.

If a united front between socialists, communists, and other parties on the left seemed problematic in Spain, it is even more difficult to imagine in Portugal. In the first place, Soares has stated that the PSP would cooperate with the *Partido Comunista Português* (Portuguese Communist Party, PCP) only if the latter would respect democracy. In the second place, Alvaro Cunhal, the PCP secretary-general, has claimed that he does not accept democratic elections or the concept of Eurocommunism. To put the matter in simple terms, the PCP is one of the most doctrinaire and inflexible communist parties in Western Europe. Similarly, it is one of the most disciplined and well-organized groups in Portugal, drawing support from the agricultural south and from working-class areas in Lisbon and Setuúbal.

Besides the PSP and PCP, there are numerous other leftist political parties in Portugal. Two which deserve special mention are the *Movimento Democrático Português* (Portuguese Democratic Movement, MDP), and the *União Democrático Popular* (Popular Democratic Union, UDP). What makes these parties interesting is their relationship to the PCP: the former has been called a front organization because of its joint platforms with the PCP on various issues; while the latter broke from the PCP in 1974 due to the revisionism which allegedly permeated the Communist Party.

On April 25, 1975, the first anniversary of the coup, Portuguese voters went to the polls in the first competitive, multiparty election that the country had

TABLE 2.6

Results from the 1975 and 1976 Portuguese Elections

Party	Constituent Assembly, 1975			Assembly of the Republic, 1976		
	Votes	Percentage	Delegates	Votes	Percentage	Seats
Partido Socialista Português (PSP)	2,145,392	37.9	115	1,887,180	35.0	107
Partido Popular Democrático (PPD)	1,494,575	26.4	80	1,296,432	24.0	73
Partido do Centro Democrático Social (CDS)	433,153	7.7	16	858,783	15.9	42
Partido Comunista Português (PCP)	709,639	12.5	30	785,620	14.6	40
União Democrática Popular (UDP)	44,546	0.8	1	91,383	1.7	1
Movimento Democrático Português (MDP)	233,362	4.1	5	Did not run	—	—
Others	605,040*	10.6	0	476,724*	8.8	0
TOTAL	5,665,707	100.0	247	5,396,122	100.0	263†

*Includes blank ballots
†Portuguese emigrants were allotted four seats

seen in half a century. At stake were 250 seats in the Constituent Assembly that would draft a new constitution to replace the one the MFA instituted after overthrowing Caetano. At best, the results of the election were discouraging to the radical elements in the MFA. As Table 2.6 shows, the returns gave a combined total of 64.3 percent of the vote and 197 seats to the moderate PSP and PPD. By way of contrast, the parties on the extreme left garnered a total of only 36 seats, with the Communist Party pulling down a mere 12.5 percent of the popular vote.

The parliamentary elections of 1976 confirmed, with one exception, the results of the year before. Once again, the moderate PSP and PPD led the field, picking up 59 percent of the vote and 180 seats. This time, however, the more conservative CDS doubled its vote to almost 16 percent, thus surpassing the PCP total of 14.6 percent. Nor did the distribution of electoral power change in the next two months. In June, António Ramalho Eanes, a moderate right-of-center general who was backed by the PSP, PPD, and CDS, took 61.5 percent of the vote on his way to winning the presidency. When he later swore in a fragile minority socialist government under Mário Soares, Portugal had completed a critical phase in its transition from authoritarian rule to democracy.

Governmental Institutions and the Policy-Making Process

We now turn our attention from those specialized structures which dominate the processes of interest articulation and interest aggregation to those structures which play key roles in the processes of policy-making and policy implementation. Let us begin by comparing Franco's Spain with post-Franco Spain.

Spain

In October 1936, Spain's youngest general, Francisco Franco y Bahamonde, was named chief of state and given the title *Caudillo de España* (Leader of Spain). For the next thirty-nine years, his personalistic rule remained the key to understanding the Spanish political system. Franco was a Galician, and at least in his case, many observers felt that Spanish tradition about a *gallego* rang true: "No one knows what goes on in his head. No one can be sure of what he will do next. And when he has done it, it is often hard to tell what has happened."[9] While on the surface Franco's political maneuvers might appear to have been engendered by impulse rather than design, upon closer scrutiny it is clear that an alternative interpretation is warranted, namely, domestic affairs were conducted with an eye toward balancing a set of diverse political interests so that none would ever grow too strong.

The closest thing Spain ever had to a constitution during the Franco years was the *Ley Orgánica del Estado* (Organic Law). Prior to its ratification by national referendum in 1966, Franco ruled under an assorted group of corporativist documents, the most important of which were (1) the 1942 Law of the Cortes; (2) the 1945 Charter of the Spanish People; (3) the Referendum Act of 1945; (4) the 1947 Law of Succession; (5) the 1947 Labor Charter; and (6) the 1958 Principles of the National Movement. In a nutshell, the Organic Law modified and consolidated these documents. Nevertheless, because he was the *Caudillo*, Franco still remained responsible "only to God and to history."

The Organic Law specified the functions of each governmental structure in the policy process. According to its provisions, absolute authority over all foreign and domestic policy resides in the chief of state. He is advised on important issues by several bodies, including the Council of State, National Economic Council, National Defense Junta, and the National Council of the Movement. However, these bodies are not the most salient decision-making structures. That distinction goes to the Council of Ministers, which in essence is a cabinet presided over by the president of government (i.e., prime minister) and composed of the heads of all government ministries. The number of cabinet members was not fixed. But regardless of how many there might be in a given year, all would have been appointed by the chief of state.

Until 1973, Franco was both chief of state and president of the government. Though he gave up the basically routine job of president of the government, he continued as chief of state for as long as he was physically able. It was this position that enabled him to legislate by decree, veto legislative proposals, and control the political makeup of the cabinet. Perhaps more than anything else, Franco's many cabinet changes showed his skills at balancing numerous unequal and seemingly incompatible power contenders. The military, the church, and the *Movimiento* were the three pillars which supported his regime from the very onset. Yet, over the years, the proportion of cabinet members affiliated with these pillars varied markedly. For instance, at the end of the Civil War military officers held considerable political influence, as evidenced by their filling over 40 percent of the cabinet positions. But, by the time Franco died, roughly half of these positions had been reshuffled to other groups. Usually these shake-ups would occur whenever Franco felt new additions would be useful. Thus, when he wanted to stimulate economic growth during the 1960s, the percentage of technocrats from the Catholic lay organization, *Opus Dei*, jumped significantly. In short, the cabinet became "the focus of coalitional politics, the place where the disparate forces supporting the regime came together to seek common ground before the Caudillo."[10]

The institution which had the strongest corporatist flavor in the Franco system was the Cortes (parliament). Members were not popularly elected, but rather were appointed directly by Franco or were selected to represent functional entities such as the military, the church, the *Movimiento*, professional groups, *sindicatos* (government-controlled unions), provinces, municipalities, and family units. The number of individuals in the Cortes varied from one session to the next, but on average it contained some 565 members who served three-year terms. A president of the Cortes typically would be appointed for each session by the chief of state to act as presiding officer. His job was to maintain discipline because, strictly speaking, the Cortes was only a consultative assembly; it could not bring down the government with a vote of no confidence, nor was it ever conceived as a forum for opposition viewpoints.

Given the limitations on the Cortes, it should not be surprising to find that the Spanish judicial system under Franco did not check executive power through judicial review. Judges could interpret the law but they could not question its validity. Today the Supreme Court, Spain's highest court of appeal, does have the jurisdiction to hear cases against government officials. Structurally it is divided into six chambers, one each for criminal, civil, administrative, and labor cases, plus two for lawsuits. The court is presided over by a chief justice who is appointed by the chief of state for a six-year term.

Below the Supreme Court are fifteen district high courts, fifty provincial high courts, and a number of specialized high courts. The district courts hear cases involving malfeasance and government liability, while the provincial high courts basically deal with criminal indictments that have come from courts of original jurisdiction. By way of contrast, the specialized high courts are involved in cases that pertain to salary disputes, breach of contract, job-related accidents, and so on.

At the lowest level of the judicial system are municipal courts and local peace courts. The former have jurisdiction over commercial, civil and criminal cases. The latter take up minor cases and function somewhat like a justice of the peace.

All of these governmental structures, from the Council of Ministers to those in the judicial system, comprised the infrastructure of Franco's regime. In order to guarantee that this infrastructure would not be overturned as soon as he passed from the political scene, Franco gave special powers to a body known as the Council of the Realm. Composed of seventeen conservative members, the council was given power under the Organic Law to return bills to the Cortes, dismiss government officials, and propose three names to the king for premier (head of government), from which the king had to choose one. Through these powers Franco hoped the council would ensure the continuation of his regime. However, Juan Carlos was able to have Adolfo Suárez included in the list of names that was given to him in 1976. Once Suárez was picked to be premier, he began putting together a cabinet to bring about the political reforms desired by the king.

On December 15, 1976, a national referendum was held on the new regime's Law of Fundamental Reform. Following its overwhelming approval, a bicameral legislature was created to replace Franco's Cortes. The new parliament contained a lower house (Chamber of Deputies) of 350 members elected for four years through proportional representation, and an upper house (Senate) of 248 members. Four senators would be elected by majority vote from each of fifty provinces, 7 by majority vote from Spain's islands and North African enclaves, and 41 would be appointed by the king. Like their counterparts in the lower house, the senators would serve four-year terms.

Under the reform law a bill needed an absolute majority to pass the Chamber of Deputies. Should a bill go on to the Senate, it was required to pass that body with the identical wording that made it through the lower house, otherwise it would go before a special commission composed of deputies and senators. Whenever any bill which dealt with a question of "national interest" went before the king, he had the option of either signing it or calling for a national referendum. If he selected the latter alternative, the results of the referendum would be binding on the Cortes.

In accordance with the reform law, primary responsibility for drafting a new constitution fell on the Cortes. A 7-member constitutional committee was established to formulate a document which could be examined by the Chamber of Deputies and the Senate, and a "mixed" committee of 5 deputies and 6 senators was elected to resolve the differences which arose in the revisions sought by these two chambers. On October 31, 1978, the Chamber of Deputies and the Senate accepted the new constitution. In the lower house, 325 members voted in favor, 6 against, and 14 abstained. In the upper house, 226 were in favor, 5 were opposed, and 8 abstained. Five weeks later, when the document was placed before the public in a national referendum, 87.8 percent of the voters gave it their approval.

Although the new constitution has thoroughly overhauled national institutions and has taken several steps to grant more rights to areas such as the Basque region, Spain still possesses a unitary form of government. Immediately below the national administrative level are fifty provinces, each headed by a civil governor. Under the reform law the civil governor was appointed by the chief of state for a six-year term and was responsible to the Ministry of the Interior. As a representative of the central government, the civil governor presided over the provincial council, a deliberative body composed of delegates from each municipality within his province.

Municipalities are the lowest administrative subdivisions within the Spanish system. They too have officials, known as mayors, who function as agents of the central government. Like the civil governors above them, the mayors have been responsible to the Ministry of the Interior and have presided over deliberative bodies called municipal councils. The major impact of the new constitution has been to extend the process of free and secret elections to the local level of government. On April 3, 1979, municipal elections were held for the first time in forty-eight years. Although nationwide the UCD won the largest number of municipal council seats and held a majority in most provincial councils, both the PSOE and PCE did well in many large cities.

Portugal

Whereas the Franco regime traced its constitutional roots to a series of charters, decrees, and statements of principle that were formulated over a number of years, the Salazar regime presented the Portuguese citizenry with a single document to inaugurate the *Estado Novo*. The Constitution of 1933 was proclaimed the world's first corporatist constitution. Under its provisions, the Portuguese would directly elect their president for a seven-year term.

As the head of state, the president of the republic possessed the authority to appoint government ministers, dissolve the legislature, and call for elections. According to the constitution, he would be advised by the Council of State, a consultative body composed of high-ranking officials and "public men of outstanding ability."

Under the corporatist framework engineered by Salazar, the president of the republic stood somewhat above the government. As it later turned out, the president of the Council of Ministers (a kind of prime minister) became the real source of power in the system. Both Salazar and Caetano held the position of prime minister. Needless to say, they both handpicked and controlled the president of the republic throughout their years in office.

The 1933 Constitution established the unicameral National Assembly as the regime's only legislative body. It was composed of 120 deputies who were directly elected to four-year terms. Although the constitution stipulated that the Assembly's major functions would include lawmaking, in practice the body performed much the same role as Franco's Cortes, namely, ratifying proposals issued by the executive branch.

Working alongside of the National Assembly was an advisory body called the Corporative Chamber (*Cámara Corporativa*). Its function was to evaluate all of the legislation that would come before the National Assembly. Without question, the chamber was unique. Whereas Spain had allocated a certain proportion of the seats in the Cortes to functional representatives, the entire membership of the chamber was to be selected from various professional associations and economic groups. In short, the chamber was perceived as the foundation for a much more extensive corporate edifice. During the next decade, laws were passed to create a host of additional corporatist organizations, including national syndicates for urban laborers and employers (*sindicatos nacionais*), compulsory employers' guilds (*grémios*), landowners' guilds (*grémios da lavoura*), Houses of the People (*Casas do Povo*) for rural workers and their employers, and Houses for the Fishermen (*Casas dos Pescadores*). All of these organizations were based on the thesis that functional patterns of representation would be more stable than interest patterns of representation. So long as labor and management, for example, were united within one organization based on their common branch of industry, neither labor nor management would join interest groups that would force them into mutually hostile camps.

After the initial decade of experimentation and rapid organizational development, the process of extending corporatism began to slow. In fact, it was not until 1956 that the corporations (*corporações*), the capstones of the entire edifice, were actually created. Moreover, by the time they were established, Portugal had grown into an administrative state characterized by a "multitude of semi-autonomous organizational units grouped together by sectors under the jurisdiction of central ministries."[11] Little information flowed between sectors, and communication was at best sporadic within sectors. In brief, the entire corporate complex had hardly any impact on the policy process. As Philippe Schmitter points out, until the 1960s, decision-making in Portugal was heavily personalist: Salazar surrounded himself with trusted acquaintances from the military, the church, commerce, industry, and so forth. But in the later years of his reign, and certainly after Caetano took over, these aging cronies were partially replaced by a younger group of technocrats.[12] Thus, instead of guaranteeing social justice and an avenue for effective political participation, the corporate agencies gradually evolved into instruments for controlling the lower classes.

The hollowness of these corporate structures became clear when they collapsed like a house of cards in 1974. Ultimately, Caetano proved ineffective in either reforming or shoring up the system he had inherited. His policies were so cautious and quickly reversed that people joked about how he would signal left and turn right. As one prominent banker complained: "There are too many people left in the cabinet who think that the ideal is to go through life without making mistakes, and therefore drive around at 20 miles per hour, honking their horns."[13]

After the military coup sent Caetano scurrying to Brazil, the Corporative Chamber was abolished and various provisions in the 1933 Constitution were replaced by the MFA program. However, the old office of president of the republic, the Council of State, the prime minister, and the cabinet were retained—albeit with new personnel. General António Sebastião Ribeiro de Spínola, the first provisional president, and the *Junta de Salvação Nacional* (Junta of National Salvation, JSN), a group of prestigious officers sympathetic to the MFA, had the task of implementing the program. Running parallel to these were several other structures, including an officers' General Assembly, the elite Continental Operations Command (COPCON), the MFA's Coordinating Committee, and a "military cabinet" known as the Council of the Twenty.

This proliferation of political organizations combined with a lack of clearly established lines of authority to create friction between *Spinolistas* and the more radical members of the MFA.

Following an abortive right-wing countercoup on March 11, 1975, MFA radicals moved to consolidate and strengthen their position by establishing the Council of the Revolution (*Conselho da Revolucão*, CR) to replace the JSN, Council of State, Coordinating Committee, and Council of the Twenty. Ironically, in less than a year the situation reversed itself. On November 25, elements from the far left tried to overthrow the government. In the aftermath of the second attempted coup, the CR began to rethink its position on the role of the military in politics. In February, the CR agreed to relinquish much of its previous legislative power. Under the provisions of the new constitution, which the Constituent Assembly completed that April, the CR became primarily a consultative body.

According to the new constitution, the next four years would be a transition period. The document went on to outline a governmental system for the transition that was quite similar to the French Fifth Republic. The president, who would be elected by direct popular vote, had the power to name a prime minister after consulting with the Council of the Revolution. The cabinet, in turn, was responsible to the Assembly of the Republic, a legislative organ whose membership would be determined by election under proportional representation. Although the president could veto bills passed by the assembly, the legislature could override the veto if the bill was passed once again by two-thirds vote of those present. Constitutional amendments were prohibited during the transition. However, at the end of the four years, a new legislature would be elected to revise the constitution, and therein end the transition period.

Some changes were made in the court system after the 1974 coup, but by and large, the judiciary and the subnational units of government have not been drastically altered. The major innovation introduced by the constitution was the Constitutional Commission. Chaired by a member of the CR, it consists of four judges and four appointees who together have the power to determine the constitutionality of any existing laws.

As in the case of Spain, the Portuguese court system has many layers, ranging from the Supreme Court of Justice in Lisbon to a group of appeals courts and finally to the municipal courts on the local level. Also included within the system are juvenile courts, justices of the peace, and numerous special courts for labor, administrative, and other such cases.

Finally, like Spain, Portugal is a unitary state where authority flows from the national government downward to the districts and municipalities. Under the Salazar-Caetano regime, districts were headed by a civil governor who was appointed by the Minister of Interior. He, in turn, was assisted by a council and a district committee. The municipalities contained a council which represented various corporate groups and a chamber led by a president who had been appointed by the civil governor. Following the 1974 coup, all of the corporate bodies at various levels of the Portuguese political system were dissolved and replaced by new, nonelective committees.

Policy Problems and Prospects

The two authoritarian regimes that had endured for decades on the Iberian Peninsula came to an end in the mid-1970s. The political futures of Spain and Portugal will, without a doubt, have a tremendous impact on both the United States and Western Europe. Let us conclude our comparison of these countries by looking at some of the problems which lie ahead during their transition to democracy.

One of the most basic problems faced by both regimes is legitimation. This issue has appeared in its most dramatic form in Spain, where Lt. Colonel Antonio Tejero Molina led an abortive coup against the government on February 23, 1981. Despite the failure of the rebels, the UCD coalition is not as stable as it was even a short while ago. Supporters of Leopoldo Calvo Sotelo have pushed for more conservative policies, while supporters of former Prime Minister Suárez have advocated centrist positions. Suárez himself resigned from the UCD and is attempting to forge a new centrist party to be known as the Democratic and Social Center. However, the weakness of the UCD was clearly shown when it won only 13 seats in the 1982 parliamentary elections, compared to 201 for the victorious PSOE and 106 for AP. Portugal, too, has experienced similar problems. Although General Eanes was re-elected to the presidency on December 7, 1980 with 56 percent of the vote, several governments have followed the Soares government. At present the center-right Democratic Alliance holds the largest number of seats in Parliament with only 47 percent of the 1980 vote.

Another basic problem faced by both regimes is economic. Since the end of the nineteenth century, Spain's economic structure has been aimed almost exclusively at the domestic market. Owing in some measure to a per capita income which was not high enough for industries to gain extensively from large-scale production, the economy gradually took shape without relying upon foreign sales. During the 1960s, however, the Spanish economy underwent a remarkable change. In essence, it had become interconnected with the economies of other European states due to foreign exchange generated by trade, investments, tourism, and emigrant remittances. Using a 1937 base figure of 100, industrial production as measured by the Moorsteen Powell Index stood at 339 in 1960, but climbed to 890 by 1969. At the end of the decade, the per capita gross domestic product had grown 138 percent, and the agricultural sector accounted for only 15 percent of that figure.[14] Thus Spain's largely agricultural economy had been transformed into a semi-industrial economy, and continued growth was interpreted by the Franco regime as a means of ensuring external prestige and internal stability. Not only did it make Spain more attractive to foreign investors, but it also engendered consumers, whose attention might well be diverted from the political realm. As Frederick Pike has written, "not until a person escapes from the compulsion of consumerism, not until he ceases to be manipulated . . . will he develop interest in gaining his political liberation and come to demand a voice in political decision making at the national level."[15]

Equally important, then, with the specific governmental reforms initiated by Juan Carlos are the political ramifications of Spain's current economic slump. Between 1971 and 1973 alone, wholesale and consumer prices rose 18 and 21 percent respectively—well over twice the increases experienced from 1969 to 1971. In addition, unemployment has been especially high in Andalusia and Galicia, the inflation rate has now risen to approximately 30 percent, labor costs have also gone up, and the average annual gross investment in Spain has been a negative figure since 1975. To put it quite simply, the perception by the mass public that it will no longer benefit from the fruits of continued economic growth could prove as volatile as the expectations unleashed by any decline in the prospects for further political reform.

In contrast to Spain, an economic miracle did not occur in Portugal during the 1960s. Portugal's economy was guided by Salazar's belief in balanced budgets and his distaste for external debt. Indeed, only as the cost of the guerrilla wars in Africa mounted did Salazar take steps to accelerate Portugal's economic development. Yet, despite the resulting upswing in productivity, the cost of living climbed faster than the increases in personal income. Furthermore, the economy remained shackled through the Caetano years by high amounts of defense spending, a shortage of skilled manpower, and an inefficient agricultural system.

Also, in contrast to Spain, Portugal did not undergo a cautious liberalization once the old regime was replaced. Enormous difficulties were created by an extensive, but hastily organized, program to nationalize private industrial and agricultural holdings. Wages rocketed upward at the same time that productivity fell. Moreover, the old manpower problem was further exacerbated when "workers' committees" began to replace managers in a variety of enterprises. Finally, to make matters worse, investment money dried up and the country's once sizable foreign exchange reserves were threatened by a growing balance of payments deficit.

It is often said, and not without some justification, that politics never allows an observer to finish his contemplation. This seems particularly true when one contemplates Iberian political affairs. In 1977, Spain, the first European colonial power to lose its colonies, and Portugal, the last to do so, both applied to become formal candidates for membership in the European Community. As a result of the events of 1974 and 1975, Europeans north of the Pyrenees have accepted the two Iberian states as democracies and are currently negotiating the terms of their entry into the Community. The pace of these negotiations will be influenced not only by the technical issues of coordinating agricultural and industrial economic policies, but also by how well both Spain and Portugal are able to strengthen their new democracies. In this regard, Spain faces more serious difficulty than Portugal insofar as it is pressured by at least two kinds of domestic violence. On the one hand, separatist groups, such as the ETA, the *Front d' Alliberament Catala* (FAC), and the *Organitzácio Lluita Armada* (OLlA) have hampered the new government in the Basque provinces and Catalonia. On the other hand, ideological groups like the right-wing *Guerrilleros de Cristo Rey* (Warriors of Christ the King) and their left-wing counterparts in the *Frente Revolucionario Antifascista Patriótica* (Revolutionary Antifascist Patriotic Front) have tested the new government's ability to deal with terrorism without ending the democratic reforms. This is not to say that Portugal has not had its share of terrorist groups. Right-wing groups such as the *Exército de Libertação Português* (Portuguese Liberation Army) and the *Movimento Democrático para a Libertação de Portugal* (Democratic Movement for the Liberation of Portugal) have launched some raids, and the far leftist *Liga de União e Açõ Revolucionária* (United League for Revolutionary Action) has engaged in others. But these groups do not represent the more fundamental problem of militant separatism that one finds in Spain's ethnonationalistic groups. Consequently, Spain today possesses a paradoxical quality that one does not find in Portugal: at the very time that the central government is moving to become integrated with the larger European Community, various regions are calling for the establishment of smaller, ethnically defined communities.

Notes

1. Two major parts of ancient Hispania had not been conquered: the mountainous regions of Asturias in the northwest and the Basque principality of Navarre in the Pyrenees. These areas existed outside the mainstream of both Roman and Visigothic life and thus did not offer the Muslims a prize worth the costs of a full-scale attack.

2. Scholars disagree on how Portugal was able to obtain its independence. Some historians have written that independence was an accident, but others contend that it was a result of long-standing socioeconomic differences between Portugal and the rest of the peninsula. Regardless of the underlying cause, León was unable to bring its erstwhile dependency back into the fold owing to a combination of domestic problems and renewed Muslim attacks.

3. Howard J. Wiarda, "Toward a Framework for the Study of Political Change in the Iberic-Latin Tradition: The Corporative Model," *World Politics* 25 (January 1973), 217–218.

4. Gino Germani, "Political Socialization of Youth in Fascist Regimes: Italy and Spain," in *Authoritarian Politics in Modern Society: The Dynamics of Established One-Party Systems*, edited by Samuel P. Huntington and Clement H. Moore (New York: Basic Books, 1970), p. 360.

5. Juan J. Linz, "An Authoritarian Regime: Spain," in *Mass Politics: Studies in Political Sociology*, edited by Erik Allardt and Stein Rokkan (New York: Free Press, 1970), pp. 261–262.

6. Ray Alan, "The New Spain," *The Economist* (April 2, 1977): 523.

7. Juan J. Linz and Amando de Miguel, "Within-Nation Differences and Comparisons: The Eight Spains," in *Comparing Nations: The Use of Quantitative Data in Cross-National Research*, edited by Richard L. Merritt and Stein Rokkan (New Haven: Yale University Press, 1966), p. 281.

8. Juan J. Linz, "Opposition In and Under an Authoritarian Regime: The Case of Spain," in *Regimes and Oppositions*, edited by Robert A. Dahl (New Haven: Yale University Press, 1973), pp. 191–231.

9. Alan Lloyd, *Franco* (London: Longman, 1969), p. 209.

10. Charles W. Anderson, *The Political Economy of Modern Spain: Policy-Making in an Authoritarian System* (Madison: University of Wisconsin Press, 1970), p. 73.

11. Lawrence S. Graham, "Portugal: The Decline and Collapse of an Authoritarian Order," *Sage Professional Papers in Comparative Politics*, V (Beverly Hills, Calif.: Sage Publications, 1975), p. 56.

12. Philippe C. Schmitter, "Corporatism and Public Policy in Authoritarian Portugal," *Sage Professional Papers in Political Sociology*, I (Beverly Hills, Calif.: Sage Publications, 1975), p. 28.

13. Robert Moss, "Between Africa and Europe," *The Economist* (February 26, 1972): 510.

14. The statistics cited in this section are based on data from the following sources: *Europa Year Book* (London: Europa Publications, 1977); *Informaciones Economicas* (various issues); B. R. Mitchell, *European Historical Statistics, 1950–1970* (New York: Columbia University Press, 1975); *OECD Observer* (various issues); and *United Nations Statistical Yearbook* (New York: Publishing Service of the United Nations, 1977).

15. Frederick B. Pike, "The New Corporatism in Franco's Spain and Some Latin American Perspectives," in *The New Corporatism: Social and Political Structures in the Iberian World*, edited by Frederick B. Pike and Thomas Stritch (Notre Dame: University of Notre Dame Press, 1974), p. 194.

Selected Bibliography

Anderson, Charles W. *The Political Economy of Modern Spain*. Madison: University of Wisconsin Press, 1970.

Baklanoff, Eric N. *The Economic Transformation of Spain and Portugal*. New York: Praeger, 1978.

Braga de Macedo, Jorge. *Portugal Since the Revolution: Economic and Political Perspectives*. Boulder, Colo.: Westview, 1981.

Bruce, Neil. *Portugal: The Last Empire*. New York: John Wiley, 1975.

Coverdale, John F. *The Political Transformation of Spain After Franco*. New York: Praeger, 1979.

Di Palma, Giuseppe. "Founding Coalitions in Southern Europe: Legitimacy and Hegemony," *Government and Opposition* 15 (Spring 1980): 162–189.

Germani, Gino. "Political Socialization of Youth in Fascist Regimes: Italy and Spain." In *Mass Politics: Studies in Political Sociology*, edited by Erik Allardt and Stein Rokkan. New York: Free Press, 1970.

Gonzalez Blasco, Pedro. "Modern Nationalism in Old Nations as a Consequence of Earlier State-Building: The Case of Basque Spain." In *Ethnicity and Nation-Building: Comparative, International, and Historical Perspectives*, edited by Wendell Bell and Walter F. Freeman. Beverly Hills, Calif.: Sage Publications, 1974.

Graham, Lawrence S. "Portugal: The Decline and Collapse of an Authoritarian Order." *Sage Professional Papers in Comparative Politics*, V. Beverly Hills, Calif.: Sage Publications, 1975.

Grason, George W. "Portugal and the Armed Forces Movement," *Orbis* 19 (Summer 1975): 335–378.

Harsgor, Michael. "Portugal in the Revolution." *The Washington Papers*. Beverly Hills, Calif.: Sage Publications, 1976.

Kay, Hugh. *Salazar and Modern Portugal*. London: Eyre and Spottiswoode, 1970.

Linz, Juan J. "An Authoritarian Regime: Spain." In *Mass Politics: Studies in Political Sociology*, edited by Erik Allardt and Stein Rokkan. New York: Free Press, 1970.

Linz, Juan J. "Early State-Building and Late Peripheral Nationalisms Against the State: The Case of Spain." In *Building States and Nations: Analyses by Region*, edited by S. N. Eisenstadt and Stein Rokkan. Beverly Hills, Calif.: Sage Publications, 1973.

Linz, Juan J. "From Falange to Movimiento-Organización: The Spanish Single Party and the Franco Regime, 1936–1968." In *Authoritarian Politics in Modern Society: The Dynamics of Established One-Party Systems*, edited by Samuel P. Huntington and Clement H. Moore. New York: Basic Books, 1970.

Linz, Juan J. "Opposition In and Under an Authoritarian Regime: The Case of Spain." In *Regimes and Opposition*, edited by Robert A. Dahl. New Haven: Yale University Press, 1973.

Linz, Juan J. "Spain and Portugal: Critical Choices." In *Western Europe: The Trials of Partnership*, edited by David S. Landes. Lexington, Mass.: D. C. Heath, 1977.

Linz, Juan J. "The Party System of Spain: Past and Future." In *Party Systems and Voter Alignments: Cross-National Perspectives*, edited by Seymour Martin Lipset and Stein Rokkan. New York: Free Press, 1967.

Linz, Juan J., and Miguel, Amando de. "Within-Nation Differences and Comparisons: The Eight Spains." In *Comparing Nations: The Use of Quantitative Data in Cross-National Research*, edited by Richard L. Merritt and Stein Rokkan. New Haven: Yale University Press, 1966.

Marques, António Henrique R. de Oliveira. *History of Portugal*. 2 vols. New York: Columbia University Press, 1972.

Martins, Herminio. "Portugal." In *Contemporary Europe: Class, Status, and Power*, edited by Margaret Scotford Archer and Salvador Giner. London: Weidenfeld and Nicolson, 1971.

Payne, Stanley G. *A History of Spain and Portugal*. 2 vols. Madison: University of Wisconsin Press, 1973.

Payne, Stanley. *Politics and the Military in Modern Spain*. Stanford: Stanford University Press, 1967.

Payne, Stanley. "Spain." In *The European Right: A Historical Profile*. Edited by Hans Rogger and Eugen Weber. Berkeley and Los Angeles: University of California Press, 1965.

Pike, Frederick B., and Stritch, Thomas, eds. *The New Corporatism: Social and Political Structures in the Iberian World*. Notre Dame: University of Notre Dame Press, 1974.

Salisbury, William T., and Theberge, James D., eds. *Spain in the 1970's: Economics, Social Structure, Foreign Policy*. New York: Praeger, 1976.

Schmitter, Philippe C. "Corporatism and Public Policy in Authoritarian Portugal." *Sage Professional Papers in Political Sociology*, I. Beverly Hills, Calif.: Sage Publications, 1975.

Wiarda, Howard J. "Toward a Framework for the Study of Political Change in the Iberic-Latin Tradition: The Corporative Model," *World Politics* 25 (January 1973): 206–235.

3.

The Adriatic Region: The Politics of Clientelism

The Historical Setting

An Overview

Italy and Greece have many characteristics in common with the Iberian nations. Like Spain and Portugal, both possess political cultures that stress the importance of kinship ties and local loyalties; both contain severe economic and geographic cleavages; and both have had their policy-making processes dominated by oligarchic institutions. Furthermore, like their western neighbors, they are both enmeshed in a clash between tradition and modernity that has accompanied their recent attempts to industrialize. In contrast to the Benelux, Alpine, and Scandinavian regions that we shall cover in subsequent chapters, the Adriatic region has had a history of chronic political instability.

Italy's imprint upon western civilization has been quite profound. The Roman Empire, at its height, included most of Europe, the Middle East, and the northern rim of Africa. Under the leadership of such stalwarts as Julius and Augustus Caesar, one could say with great justification that all roads led to Rome. Although the western Roman Empire fell apart more than 1,500 years ago, 300 million people today speak languages directly linked to Latin, the Roman tongue, and Roman law is still used extensively in Europe and Latin America.

Beginning with the Renaissance period of the early 1300s, Italy became the cultural leader of Europe, leaving to posterity the great works of such artists as Michelangelo, Leonardo da Vinci, and Raphael, and writers such as Petrarch and Boccaccio. Through the centuries, Italian soil has also spawned great explorers in the mold of Marco Polo and Christopher Columbus, distinguished scientists such as Galileo, and famous composers such as Puccini, Verdi, Paganini, and Vivaldi.

In marked contrast to the glories of ancient and Renaissance Italy, many scholars have depicted twentieth century Italian society as troubled and prone to political extremism on both the left and the right. For more than two decades, Italians tolerated the dictatorial rule of the fascist leader Benito Mussolini, and openly sided with Hitler during most of the Second World War. In the post–World War II period, political scientist Edward Banfield claims to have discovered an amoral subculture in Italy, and his colleagues Gabriel Almond and Sidney Verba have decried the Italian citizenry's lack of civic involvement and concern.[1] Entering the 1980s, the fourth largest party in Italy continued to espouse neo-fascist teachings and the Red Brigade on the left continued to dispense its own ultra-violent version of proletarian justice.

There can be little doubt that contemporary Italian society faces major challenges and much more must be done to convince the rank-and-file citizen that Italy's version of democracy can be both equitable and effective. A 1977 Gallup International Research Institute survey indicated that only 17 percent of Italians were highly satisfied with life, in comparison to 69 percent of Americans, 67 percent of Danes, 50 percent of the British, 41 percent of West Germans, and 26 percent of the French. Italy continues to suffer from major regional disparities and is plagued by secular-clerical cleavages. Moreover, postwar governments have been lucky to survive even for twelve months, and several political parties have experienced widespread corruption and cronyism.

On the other hand, there is still room for optimism concerning Italy's future; some of the gloom-and-doom portrayals of contemporary Italian society have been overstated or misleading. This nation of 58 million people, which is about the size of Arizona but has one-fourth the population of the entire United States, has experienced an economic miracle over the past few decades which rivals that of any European nation. The Italians have also embraced democracy for more than 35 years and have integrated themselves into the rest of Western Europe through membership in the European Community (EC) and the North Atlantic Treaty Organization (NATO). Thus, although the problems facing Italy are among the most serious in all of Western Europe, the Italians have shown great resiliency; most are steadfastly committed to making their republican system of government work.

One should remember that the inhabitants of the boot-shaped peninsula were among the last in Europe to achieve political unification. For several centuries, the peninsula was divided into city-states and principalities, which often feuded with one another. For example, Marco Polo represented the city-state of Venice in his thirteenth century trek to the Orient, and then returned to his native city to wage war against a neighboring city-state, Genoa.

Soon after Christopher Columbus, a native of Genoa, discovered America, the Italian peninsula underwent a wave of foreign invasions, most notably by France and Austria. Yet it was not until the era of Napoleon Bonaparte that a foreign power was able to consolidate control over most of the peninsula. Although Napoleonic rule lasted for less than twenty years, the French legal and administrative frameworks introduced during that era are still used extensively in contemporary Italy. Following Napoleon's defeat at Waterloo in 1815, the Austrians once again exerted great influence over Italian affairs, but support was growing among the local populace for independence from foreign domination and for some form of unification.

Under the leadership of Giuseppe Mazzini, groups of militants revolted in the 1820s and 1830s in efforts to establish an independent Italian republic. Their efforts were largely unsuccessful, however, and it was not until 1860 that the unification of most of the 700-mile-long peninsula was finally achieved. At that time, Giuseppe Garibaldi led the freedom army which paved the way for Victor Emmanuel II finally to declare the formation of the Kingdom of Italy in 1861. Even at that time, however, Venice and Rome refused initially to join the new kingdom. Venice finally cast its lot with the rest of the peninsula in 1866, but French troops remained in Rome to protect the interests of the pope. When France went to war with Prussia in 1870, the French troops were removed and the Italian army quickly marched in to take control of Italy's largest city.

To say the least, the *Risorgimento* (the nineteenth century movement for the liberation and unification of Italy) and the establishment of a constitutional monarchy were far from acceptable to a fair number of Italians. Unification was carried out largely by representatives of the northern state of Savoy-Piedmont, and the ruling family of that region was heavily influenced by French customs. The constitution, institutions, and many of the prevailing customs of Piedmont were to be extended to all of Italy after the kingdom was proclaimed. Inhabitants of the southern regions thus had little influence on the establishment of the new political order and many frankly regarded the kingdom as forced upon them against their will. As for the pope, he was livid over the loss of Rome and the Papal States and resented having his jurisdiction limited to the Vatican City area within Rome. To show its displeasure with the turn of events, the hierarchy of the Roman Catholic Church refused to recognize the legal existence of the new state and forbade Catholics from participating in political activities. This prohibition was to remain in effect until after World War I.

Italy eventually turned to a constitutional monarchy in 1870 and eligible voters were allowed to select a parliament. During the 1880s Italy pursued a policy of expansion by annexing Eritrea and Somalia in northeastern Africa. Following a war with Turkey in 1911 and 1912, Italy also occupied Libya and a group of islands in the Aegean Sea. Port facilities were also established in the Balkans and parts of Asia to foster Italian mercantilism.

Italy fought in World War I on the side of the Allies from 1915 on, but was disappointed in the territorial concessions which were offered to it by the victorious powers after the war. Soon after the end of hostilities, economic privation and rampant inflation took a heavy toll on Italian society and many people began to call for extremist solutions to these onerous problems. It was against the backdrop of economic despair that Benito Mussolini and his fascist movement gained favor with various sectors of Italian society, for he promised both jobs and order. Mussolini's fascist doctrine was extremely nationalistic and very much opposed to capitalist and democratic values. In October 1922, his fascist army marched on Rome and King Victor Emmanuel III named Mussolini Italy's premier. By 1927, Il Duce (the leader) ruled as a dictator. In order to patch up the strained relationship with the church, the Lateran Treaty was signed in 1929. As a result, for the first time since Italian troops took over Rome in 1870, the Holy See formally recognized the Kingdom of Italy. For its part, Italian authorities agreed to honor the sovereignty of the Holy See within the walls of the Vatican.

Mussolini eventually began to expand Italy's colonial empire and was condemned by the League of Nations for invading Ethiopia in 1935. A year later, Mussolini dispatched 70,000 men to help Franco win the civil war in Spain, and Il Duce entered into a Rome-Berlin axis pact with Hitler. In 1939, Italian troops overran Albania, and in 1940 Italy formally entered World War II on the side of Germany by invading southern France and then Greece. The war effort did not go well for Il Duce and when the Allies took control of Sicily in 1943, King Victor Emmanuel III ordered Mussolini's arrest and then surrendered the country. Mussolini was later rescued by German commandoes and was allowed to establish a puppet fascist state in northern Italy. In 1945, he was caught by Italian resistance fighters and was executed by a firing squad.

Because of its collaboration with Hitler's Germany, Italy was forced by the Allies to relinquish its colonial possessions and to cede some territory to France, Yugoslavia, and Greece. In a plebiscite held in June 1946, the Italian electorate voted to dump the monarchy altogether in favor of a republic. A new constitution legitimizing Italy's new parliamentary democracy went into effect on January 1, 1948. Italian leaders soon aligned the new republic closely with the West, first taking an active part in the Marshall Plan and later formalizing Italy's commitment to NATO in 1949, the European Coal and Steel Community (ECSC) in 1951, and the European Community in 1958. Although Italy has the strongest Communist Party in all of Western Europe, each and every postwar government has either been directed or heavily influenced by the moderate and pro-Western Christian Democratic Party. Barring severe domestic recessions or major upheavals within the Atlantic Alliance itself, there is little likelihood in the near future that Italians will want to abandon their republic system of government or their pro-Western foreign policy stance. Nonetheless, significant political changes may be in the offing and the direction in which these changes may go will be discussed in detail in the last section of this chapter.

GREECE

Greece (or more formally, the Hellenic Republic) lies at the southern edge of the Balkan Peninaula, and includes within its boundaries over 1,400 islands scattered throughout the Aegean and Ionian seas. It is common for students of Greek history to observe that while Greece is the home of Europe's oldest civilization, it is also one of Europe's youngest nation-states. The first Greek National Assembly met in December 1821 near the ancient theater of Epidaurus. A revolt against Ottoman rule had erupted in the northern Peloponnesus eight months earlier, and now that the rebels had achieved some military success, attention was given to the task of writing a constitution.

Although the origins of the modern Greek state lie in this war of independence, the roots of Greek national self-consciousness are embedded much deeper in the peninsula's history. The Greeks who took up arms in the spring of 1821 were the heirs of two traditions: a neo-classical tradition that drew its inspiration from the Hellenes of antiquity; and a Byzantine tradition that traced its ancestry to the Eastern Roman Empire. Each tradition contained a different image of what constituted Greece. Whereas the former emphasized the image of a nation (*ethnos*) that spoke Greek and shared a common descent from the ancient Hellenes, the latter stressed the broader image of a race (*genos*) composed of those who, regardless of language, lived under Ottoman rule, remained loyal to Orthodox Christianity, and internalized Greek culture. Thus the rebels of 1821 were torn between two visions of the future: one based on the image of a sovereign, independent national state; and the other based on the image of a multinational imperial state.[2] Despite efforts to combine both under the guise of the so-called Great Idea (*Megali Idhea*), ultimately the nationalism of Athens eclipsed the universalism of Constantinople.

Expulsion of the Turkish invaders had been a goal of the Greeks throughout the three and a half centuries of Ottoman rule. Greek social structure during this period resembled a pyramid-shaped grid.[3] At the apex stood the sultan, whose power was limited only by custom and Islamic law. Below him the pyramid was divided vertically by religion and horizontally by occupation. An individual's rights and duties were clearly defined by his position within this grid. For the majority of Greeks, who were neither Muslims nor employed by the state, Ottoman rule was harsh. But though most Greeks were united in the desire to cast off their foreign yoke, they quarreled over the revolution's secondary goals. Members of the upper class wanted Ottoman society without the Turks, various military leaders sought to carve out independent satrapies for themselves, while the peasant masses merely hoped to escape taxation and acquire land.[4] Given these differences, it is not surprising that the authors of the Epidaurus constitution have been described as "a motley collection of conflicting interests, varied political orientations, and rival personal ambitions."[5] Cognizant of their own vulnerabilities and fearful of the intentions of their peers, they agreed on little beyond the need to prevent authority from becoming concentrated in the hands of a strong executive. Although delegates to the second National Assembly held in `Astros a year later made some effort to centralize the provisional government, powerful local landowners known as the notables (*Kodjabashis*) continued to support regional control, based on the assumption that a diffusion of authority would best preserve the position they had acquired under Ottoman rule.

The problem of factionalism was exacerbated by the way the war of independence was fought. Rather than organizing a national army under a single command, the Greeks fought in small, autonomous guerrilla units, for which Greece's rugged terrain is well-suited. Moreover, many of the guerrilla leaders could draw upon skills they had acquired while living as *klephts* (brigands) in mountainous areas where Ottoman rule was weak. But a political liability accompanied these military advantages: The guerrilla bands distrusted outsiders and therefore resisted attempts to impose central control over their activities. In fact, the desire to protect local autonomy was so great that the Greeks frequently fought each other when they were not fighting the Turks. Over time, these internecine battles debilitated Greek military capability. Thus, in 1825 when the Pasha of Egypt landed an army of 11,000 disciplined troops on the Peloponnesus to help the Sultan, the Greeks were unable to stem their advance. By the time Athens fell two years later, the war appeared lost.

European public opinion strongly supported the Greek cause. Yet in spite of this support, the major European heads of state formulated their policies toward the Greek War of Independence in accordance with balance of power considerations rather than on the basis of romantic Philhellenism. Britain, France, and Russia all had commercial and strategic interests in the Eastern Mediterranean, and each was suspicious of the others' intentions toward the region. In order to prevent the unilateral actions of one great power from weakening the positions of the rest, the three states agreed to become joint mediators. Following the Sultan's rejection of their proposal to secure peace by granting Greece vassal status within the Ottoman Empire, an allied naval squadron sunk the Turco-Egyptian fleet in Navarino Bay. Six months later, in April 1828, Russia declared war on the Ottoman Empire over the presence of Turkish troops in the Danubian Principalities. As a result of these events, the great powers had become more than mediators. In February 1830, they formally recognized Greece's independence from the Ottoman Empire and pledged to guarantee the new state's sovereignty.

Yet the question still remained as to what form of government an independent Greece would possess. At the third National Assembly in 1827, the delegates had drawn up a new constitution and offered the presidency of the republic to John Capodistrias, a native of Corfu who once had worked in the Russian foreign service. Unfortunately, Capodistrias was assassinated in October 1831, and the republic soon degenerated into political anarchy. Consequently, Britain, France, and Russia agreed to establish a monarchy, and chose Prince Otho of Bavaria to be the first king.

Two themes emerge from an analysis of this period of Greek history: (1) the problem of political factionalism; and (2) the problem of dependence upon external powers. Compared to the Italian *Risorgimento* (liberation and unification) the Greek *enopiisis* (unification) was a long and costly process. Like the Italians, Greeks took pride in their cultural heritage, and they were influenced by the nationalist ideas of the Enlightenment and French Revolution. However, unlike the Italians, they had a single oppressor and no large, geographically concentrated population with which to begin their unification. As one historian has put it, the Greeks lacked a Piedmont. They had "no Piedmontese bureaucracy and diplomatic service, no well-equipped and well-supplied regular army."[6]

The twin themes of factionalism and dependence are not unique to the independence period; they also appear in most analyses of the political instability that has plagued Greece since independence. As can be seen in Table 3.1, Greece became what Samuel P. Huntington calls a "praetorian polity."[7] That is to say, it developed a political system that was divided into rival factions but had no effective political institutions capable of moderating group conflict. Until the late nineteenth century, the conflict was generally confined to personal struggles within the *tzakia*, a small number of oligarchic families. By the turn of the century, however, political participation broadened to include the middle class, and political conflict increasingly took the form of a clash between monarchists and republicans. Whereas previously the rival factions had accepted constitutional monarchy but had struggled for power within it, now the monarchy itself came under attack. In short, Greece began to experience regime instability, as well as governmental instability.

Given the absence of effective political institutions to moderate group conflict, the military often has intervened into politics, claiming that it is the only force capable of re-establishing order and stability. Since independence, the Greek military has staged numerous coups. Thus, when Colonel George Papadopulous led a successful coup on April 27, 1967, the event represented a continuation of the praetorian tradition that has characterized Greece since independence. Although the junta that ruled Greece until August 1974 did not last as long as the Franco and Salazar dictatorships that we examined in the previous chapter, the repression it engendered was very similar. Just as we gave special attention to the transition from dictatorship to democracy in the

TABLE 3.1

Political Instability in Greece since Independence

Year	Event

1833—An absolute monarchy is established under Otho, son of King Ludwig of Bavaria.

1843—A military revolt led by Colonel Kallergis forces Otho to accept constitutional limits on the monarchy.

1862—A military revolt occurs at Nauplion in February. The Nauplion revolt is followed by demonstrations throughout the country. In October, the Athens garrison revolts and Otho is deposed.

1863—William George, son of King Christian IX of Denmark, is selected by the protecting powers to ascend the throne as George I. A new constitution sets additional limits on royal power.

1909—A military revolt led by Colonel Zorbas forces a change in government.

1911—The constitution of 1864 is revised.

1913—King George I is assassinated. His son ascends to the throne as Constantine I.

1916—Eleutherios Venizelos establishes a provisional government at Salonika in opposition to King Constantine.

1917—Under British and French pressure, Constantine agrees to turn the throne over to his son Alexander.

1920—King Alexander dies and Constantine returns to claim the throne.

1922—A military coup led by Colonels Plastiras and Gonatas forces Constantine to abdicate. His son ascends to the throne as King George II. The constitution of 1911 is suspended.

1923—A military coup led by Generals Leonardopoulos and Gargalides fails to overthrow the government.

1924—Following a series of abortive coups, King George II is deposed and a republic is established.

1925—General Pangalos establishes a dictatorship after leading a military coup.

1926—The Pangalos dictatorship is overthrown by a coup organized by General Kondylis.

1927—A new constitution is established.

1933—General Plastiras leads an abortive coup.

1935—Led by General Papagos, the military overthrows the government, reinstates the 1911 constitution, and returns the throne to George II.

1936—Selected by King George II to form a government, General John Metaxas proclaims a state of emergency and establishes himself as a dictator.

1941—Following Metaxas' death, Germany conquers Greece and King George II goes into exile.

1944—Following the German withdrawal from Greece, Archbishop Damaskinos is appointed as regent.

1946—King George II returns from exile. After he dies, his brother Paul ascends to the throne. Civil war erupts between communist guerillas and the Greek government.

1949—The civil war ends.

1952—A new constitution is introduced.

1964—Upon the death of King Paul, his son ascends to the throne as Constantine II.

1967—Colonel Papadopulous leads a coup against the government and establishes a military regime.

1968—A new constitution is introduced.

1973—The 1968 constitution is modified. Colonel Papadopulous is overthrown by Generals Gizikis and Ioannidis.

1974—The military regime collapses during a conflict with Turkey over Cyprus. Civilian rule is restored and the monarchy is abolished by referendum.

1975—A new constitution is introduced.

Spanish and Portuguese cases, we shall also concentrate in this chapter on what the Greeks call the *metapolitefsi*, that is, the collapse of the military junta and the return to democracy.

Political Culture and Socialization

Italy

In certain respects, Italy may almost be considered as an island nation. It shares its only continental border in the north with France, Switzerland, Austria, and Yugoslavia, but is physically separated from most of these countries by the rugged Alps. To the east, west, and south, the peninsula is totally surrounded by water—the Adriatic, Ionian, Tyrrhenian, and Mediterranean seas.

Much of mainland Italy is also disjoined by mountainous terrain which for centuries helped to keep villages and cities isolated from one another. Consequently, groups in different valleys or mountain villages developed their own distinctive language patterns and lifestyles. As late as 1962, it was estimated that only 18 percent of the nation's population spoke standard Italian on a regular basis. This standard Tuscan form of Italian was the language mandated by the dominant ruling class of the northern region of Piedmont at the time of unification. By the mid-1970s, approximately one-quarter of the people were regularly speaking standard Italian and another one-third could use it when necessary.

The problem of not having a universally used national language is partially linked to the lack of educational training available to many Italians. In the late 1950s, 90 percent of the entire population of Italy had received no more than five years of schooling, and functional illiteracy was very high. Today, this situation has improved dramatically with almost 100 percent of elementary school age children attending classes and education from age six to fourteen being free and mandatory. The educational system in Italy is strictly controlled by the central government under the direction of the Ministry of Education. Illiteracy is now down to about 7 percent of the entire population and an increasing number of young people are beginning to use standard Italian instead of the dialects of their parents and grandparents. Approximately 90 percent of the elementary age children and 85 percent of high school students attend public institutions, with the remainder opting for parochial school training. Even in the parochial schools, however, the Ministry of Education mandates certain performance standards and curriculum offerings.

Rural school districts, especially in the south, still face special problems. Although education is free, the cost of transportation and supplies has been prohibitive for some villagers. In addition, budgetary problems have plagued the educational system and the rural areas are often the first to feel the financial pinch. Moreover, the Ministry of Education has had some difficulty in luring competent educators to these impoverished southern regions.

The Italian school system, family structure, and church institutions all tend to be quite authoritarian. Approximately 97 percent of all Italians are Roman Catholic, and almost one-half attend services on a fairly regular basis, twice as many as attend in neighboring France. The Roman Catholic Church has certainly had a major influence in socializing Italians, both religiously and politically. The Lateran Treaty of 1929 stipulates that there must be religious training in both public and parochial schools. Furthermore, the Catholic Church has not hesitated in the past in telling the faithful what attitudes should be adopted toward crucial political issues. As mentioned previously, the church instructed its membership to abstain from all political activity when the Kingdom of Italy was formed, and this edict was in effect until after World War I. In the post–World War II period, the church has been closely identified with the dominant Christian Democratic Party and has been a major foe of the Italian Communist Party. At the Italian Bishops' Conference held in May 1979, the clergy issued a communiqué stating that it was the duty of the believer to vote in accordance with his or her faith, which excluded choosing any party or candidate proposing solutions opposed in principle to the Christian conscience with regard to such matters as civil and religious liberties, the family, and respect for innocent lives. Although the Vatican has suffered some major defeats in recent years on divorce and abortion issues, and though the church leadership has become more circumspect in taking public stances on political issues, one should never underestimate the powerful influence which the church continues to exert in the political socialization of the Italian people.

In 1951, almost 43 percent of the Italian population was actively involved in agricultural work. In the 1970s, the number had dropped to 17 percent. As in almost all other industrialized countries, urbanization in Italy has helped bring about a loosening of familial ties. Nonetheless, authoritarian tendencies are still very strong, especially in the southern regions. Considerable political homogeneity still exists within family groups and a fairly high degree of continuity in party preferences is found from one family generation to the next. Family affiliation also remains a crucial factor in certain regions in terms of securing a job within the public bureaucracy or in the private sector.

The school, church, and home breed not only obedience in the Italian citizen, but cynicism and distrust as well. In school, the students learn about the disastrous actions of such past leaders as Mussolini, and about the major regional and class divisions that still plague Italian society. At church they are taught to be suspicious of the political system in general and certain political parties in particular. At home they learn that love and affection may always be found within the family unit, but that people not directly linked to the family should not be openly trusted.

The performance of the Italian public sector has, if anything, helped to fuel the fires of popular distrust and cynicism. In May 1981, the Forlani government resigned after it was revealed that almost one thousand leading national figures, among whom were cabinet members, politicians, and army and police officers, belonged to a secret Masonic Lodge known as P-2 which was implicated in a wide range of criminal activities. The activities carried out by some of the members of the lodge included tax evasion, financial and oil swindles, and right-wing terrorist operations.

The Italian people also recognize that many public service jobs are distributed solely on the basis of patronage and family ties and that many civil servants in the central government treat the general public in a shabby manner. Indeed, Censis, an eminent social research institute, recently estimated that an alarmingly high percentage of the civil servants in the national government apparently do not put in a full day's work. Censis divided worker absenteeism into three major categories. Traditional absenteeism occurs when civil servants take sick leave, which may range up to 150 days per year. Approximately 8 to 10 percent of the public employees seem to abuse the government's sick leave policy. Submerged absenteeism describes those civil servants who punch in on the time clock and then head for second jobs. In certain ministries, such as the postal service and pensions, up to 40 percent of the personnel might be moonlighting during regular working hours. About 20 percent of the public employees may also engage in entrepreneurial absenteeism, using office time for outside work or to sell goods during working hours. In certain extreme cases, offices have been transformed into Italian versions of oriental bazaars where employees peddle books, handbags, perfume, and a plethora of other items.[8]

Thus Italy's efforts to make a parliamentary democracy work leave much to be desired in terms of government efficiency and honesty, and it is not difficult to understand the cynicism toward political life shown by most Italians. On the other hand, the vast majority of the citizenry accept democracy and representative government as the type of system which Italy should have. Moreover, many Italians have enjoyed a marked improvement in their standard of living in the period from 1950 onward. Class divisions are still among the most flagrant in Western Europe, with a relatively small group of people enjoying vast riches and a large mass of people surviving at the subsistence level. Nonetheless, issues linked to class have been somewhat defused because of the general economic prosperity and the numerous job opportunities which have often been available in the northern regions. Furthermore, Italians have the right to seek work opportunities within the nations belonging to the European Community. It is estimated that nearly one-half of all the foreign labor used in the nine other member-states of the EC come from Italy. In times of recession, however, job opportunities dry up in northern Italy and the European Community countries, and dissatisfaction mounts against the government in power. In the future, lingering economic difficulties could certainly result in major clashes between the poor and the dominant economic class. Moreover, the people of the south remain deeply disturbed over the central government's inability to attract job-producing enterprises to their home regions.

The advancement in educational opportunities from the elementary to the university levels and the proliferation of state-controlled television and privately-owned radio stations have all played instrumental roles in developing a sense of national community in Italy. Young men reaching the age of 18 are also required to serve the nation in the armed forces, for an enlistment period ranging from 16 months in the army or air force to 28 months in the navy. Thus, in spite of their passivity and cynical perspectives, many Italians are well versed concerning political occurrences in Italy and abroad and the impact which these events may have on their nation in general and on their daily lives in particular. Although a relatively modest number in comparison to neighboring nations, approximately 90 newspapers are also published throughout the country on a daily basis with a combined circulation of 500,000. Many of these dailies are controlled by large corporations, political parties, or interest groups, but a good share provide a fairly accurate overview of important developments in Italy's political system.

A sense of national identity is certainly emerging in Italy and a far greater number of people than ever before now speak the same language, a crucial factor in forging Italian unity. The socialization process has also convinced the citizenry to accept in principle the institutions and policy-making processes outlined in the Republic of Italy's 1948 constitution, in spite of the authoritarian nature of school, church, and family training. However, they remain disappointed with the day-to-day operations of these political institutions and processes and would like to see the same substantive progress made in the political realm that has occurred in parts of the economic sector. If the moderate-conservative leadership circle that has dominated Italian politics since 1946 does not begin to clean up its act, the cynicism of the citizenry will intensify and many more people will opt for communist or neo-fascist solutions to the endemic political problems. In essence, the electorate has given a vote of confidence to Italy's first experiment with parliamentary democracy, but many elected officials and civil servants have thus far done little to warrant this public support.

Greece

Greek political culture contains many values that are similar to those found in southern Italy. The most important similarity between the two cultures lies in the importance attributed to the family. For a Greek, loyalty to family outweighs all other obligations. An individual's *philotimo*, or sense of honor and self-esteem, is affected by how he or she fulfills family duties. In contrast to the solidarity Greeks show toward family members, they display an intense distrust toward outsiders. Because those not belonging to the family are perceived as potential threats, it is considered acceptable to deceive and exploit them.

Several important consequences result from this value system. First, the family, rather than the individual, becomes the basic social unit. Thus, issues involving such diverse matters as amassing a dowry, obtaining a university education, determining water rights, and providing an inheritance are discussed by the entire family. When a decision is reached, there may be little concern over equal distribution within the family, since the entire family is thought to benefit from an advantage possessed by one member.[9] For instance, a large dowry may advance everyone's interest by helping a daughter attract a husband from a wealthy background. Similarly, family interests may receive special attention from the government if a good education provides one member with an opportunity to obtain public office.

A second noteworthy consequence of the Greek political culture is the difficulty of forming strong, secondary organizations. Nepotism and distrust of strangers have caused many Greeks to doubt whether the action of any group outside the family will be impartial.

The third major consequence of the Greek value system is clientelism. If nonfamily members cannot be expected to behave in a fair and impartial manner, then one must rely upon *rousfetti* (an exchange of favors) when interacting with those in the outside world. Such patron-client relationships involve reciprocal, face-to-face exchanges between individuals of unequal wealth, status, or power. Their origins in Greece can be traced to the period of Ottoman rule, when local notables often acted as intermediaries between the Turks and Greek villagers. After independence patron-client ties continued to provide an avenue for bypassing government bureaucracy. Typically, a wealthy local landowner was a patron to a group of poor villagers, as well as a client of a powerful regional politician. Thus a complex set of mutual obligations linked individuals from different levels of Greek society in a vast informal network, though, at times, clients attempted to formalize the relationship by having the patron become the *kumbaros* (godfather) to a newborn child.

In summary, the Greek political culture possesses a value system that is congruent with personalistic political structures. Greek political parties, for example, traditionally have been the personal creations of notables, and have more closely resembled patronage machines than mass, class-based organizations. But aside from being congruent with personalism, Greek political culture also contains many of the values associated with praetorianism. Social distrust, an expectation of scarcity, and a lack of moderation have fostered a political climate of intense inter-group conflict. Since the nation has lacked institutions that are commonly accepted as legitimate arbiters of such conflict, the Greek military has repeatedly intervened into politics.

Of course, a nation's political culture is not static. As conditions change, new norms arise and old ones gradually decay. The political culture we have just described arose out of Greek village life. Fifty years ago, the majority of Greeks lived in rural areas. Today, roughly 60 percent of the population lives in middle- to large-sized urban areas. Industrialization, urbanization, and the repatriation of Greeks from abroad have begun to change Greek political culture. While the nuclear family retains its importance, the role of the extended family has declined as more Greeks migrate from the countryside to the city. Likewise, the impact of the Orthodox Church of Greece has declined among Greek migrants. In short, the forces of social and economic modernization have weakened many of the traditional socializing agents in Greek society. Despite attempts by the recent military dictatorship to instill traditional values in Greek youth by passing laws on morality and purging the educational system, the forces of modernization continue to induce change within the Greek political culture.

Internal Cleavages, Political Competition, and Citizen Participation

Italy

Regional disparities based on class, distribution of wealth, and economic development are perhaps more profound in Italy than in any other country of Western Europe. Yet in spite of differences in dialects, Italy is linguistically homogeneous, with the notable exceptions of the South Tyrol, an area which borders Austria and in which more than one-half of the people speak German, and Valle d'Aosta, a small region nestled against France, which is dominated by French-speaking inhabitants. Northern Italy in general is quite prosperous and the "golden" triangle formed by Milan, Genoa, and Turin is as economically and industrially advanced as any region in Europe. Moreover, the Po Valley, which begins just south of the Alps and runs through part of central Italy, contains prime agricultural land and serves as the major breadbasket for the entire nation. This valley, which represents one-sixth of Italy's land mass, is home to 40 percent of the country's entire population. One's training and qualifications are generally the key factors in securing jobs in the northern region as merit usually takes precedence over party affiliation and family ties. On the other hand, class distinctions are quite noticeable and the Italian Communist Party (PCI) and other leftist movements have gained considerable support from the working class in the industrial belt. Moreover, northern Italians have had the habit of slighting and discriminating against the people of the southern regions who have come northward to seek jobs. The southerners naturally resent this treatment and ill will definitely exists between the two groups.

In sharp contrast to the relative prosperity of the north, the *Mezzogiorno*, which is all of Italy south of Rome (including the islands of Sicily and Sardinia), has regions that are as underdeveloped as many Third World countries. Quite frankly, in spite of well-publicized efforts to encourage the construction of so-called "cathedrals in the desert," large labor-intensive industrial plants, the Italian government has had only marginal success in upgrading the economic infrastructure of the south. Agriculture remains a major preoccupation of the population, but much of the land is arid and farming techniques are often outmoded. Family and friendship ties also continue to be vitally important in securing employment opportunities, although hundreds of thousands of people have had to abandon their towns and villages in order to seek jobs in northern Italy and northern Europe. Thus Italy's economic miracle, which was partially based on the ability of northern industrial cities to secure abundant and cheap labor from the south, has as yet had little impact on the *Mezzogiorno*, other than to drain the region of many of its young men and women, who have headed northward. From the point of view of many in the south, the northern regions of Italy have continuously dominated the nation's political and economic arenas from the days of unification until the present, and southerners have always been treated as second class citizens. As a consequence, some southern Italians continue to question what tangible benefits their regions have received from Italy's republican form of government and the nation's overall economic resurgence in the postwar period.

Another major cleavage in Italian society is linked to the differing priorities of the secular and clerical subcultures. As discussed earlier, the Roman Catholic Church plays a major role in the socialization of the Italian people with 97 percent of the entire population claiming to be Catholic. The Vatican, which serves as the world headquarters for the church, is situated entirely within the city of Rome but has been accorded the diplomatic status of an independent country by Italy and most other governments around the globe. Thus Italians are keenly aware of the spiritual and temporal guidance that comes not only from their neighborhood parish, but from the Holy See itself.

Since the end of World War II, the church has been closely identified with the Christian Democratic Party, which has dominated Italian politics for more than three decades. The church has also been strongly anticommunist, warning its membership to avoid Marxist movements like the plague. For example, prior to the 1979 general elections, a papal declaration reminded the faithful that a Catholic who voted for the Italian Communist Party or any other Marxist-oriented party would not be abiding by the principles of faith and morality.

The Catholic leadership has also spoken out strongly concerning certain moral matters, but seems to be losing ground to the secular camp on issues such as divorce and abortion. In May 1974, a referendum was held to decide whether or not to annul a liberalized divorce law which had been passed by the Italian parliament. In spite of the church's unequivocal stance against divorce, 60 percent of the electorate voted to keep the law, with only seven of Italy's twenty regions voting against it. In a referendum held in May 1981, over two-thirds of the voters also rejected broad changes in a liberalized abortion law which had been passed by parliament, with only one region this time voting for the repeal of the abortion law.

The secular subculture rejects the notion that the Catholic church should have a major role to play in making political, social, and economic policy in Italy. Indeed, some of the strongest anticlericalism in Italy today exists in the former Papal States, which were once directly governed by the church. Traditionally, the church has also been highly suspicious of most types of political systems that it has not been able to control directly. For example, centuries ago Italy was bitterly divided between the Guelphs and the Ghibellines, with the former group supporting the supreme spiritual and secular power of the pope, and the latter group the political preeminence of the leader of the Holy Roman Empire. The bitter hostility that the church hierarchy also showed toward the unification of the peninsula under the Kingdom of Italy and its criticism of some facets of the current republic have also not set well with many Italians. The communist and socialist movements generally claim that an Italian can be a good Catholic and an active member of their party at the same time, but the church has never recognized this point of view.

The church's influence over the daily lives of the Italian citizenry has certainly diminished in recent years and a greater number of Italians than ever before believe that the church leadership should confine itself generally to spiritual matters. This is especially true among the younger voters who have been brought up in a society offering a much improved standard of living, better educational opportunities, and higher expectations. These younger people have been raised in a much more secularized environment than their parents and now expect that there will be clear distinctions between the political and economic sectors of society on the one hand, and the church sector on the other. Even some elements within the church itself have become more circumspect about the Vatican's secular role in Italian domestic affairs, particularly since the selection of a non-Italian pope, John Paul II, has illustrated that the church is much more than simply an Italian institution.

Nevertheless, the subculture linked to the church remains very influential. The Christian Democrats continue to dominate the political and governmental sectors and the Lateran Treaty guarantees that the church will continue to enjoy some influence in the school systems. Catholic Action, a 3.5-million-member interest group which represents several Catholic-based organizations, also exerts a great deal of influence in political and economic circles. In addition, guidance from the local pulpit and from the Vatican will certainly have a significant impact on how Italians view certain sensitive moral and social issues. As an illustration of this influence, even though the voters rejected an opportunity to change the abortion law that allows a woman eighteen years or older to terminate a fetus within ninety days of pregnancy, they have also turned thumbs down to referendum issues which would remove most or all restraints on abortion. The movement in Italian society is most definitely in the secular direction, but the powerful Catholic subculture will insure that solutions to crucial social, moral, and political issues will generally be more conservative than those adopted in neighboring nations to the north.

Although the Italian voters are quite cynical about the workings of their political system, they nonetheless maintain one of the highest voter turnout records in the world. In the 1979 general elections for the Chamber of Deputies and the Senate, more than 90 percent of the eligible voters cast their ballots. Some commentators have speculated that people vote because of the good conduct certificates which are issued by the central government. Since the end of World War II, citizens who have failed to vote in a general election without a valid excuse have had this duly noted on their good conduct certificate, a document which is presented when seeking employment. Thus for pragmatic reasons, it makes good sense to vote. Nevertheless, voting is not compulsory and the Italian showing at the polling booth is much better than that in most of Western Europe and Canada and far superior to the anemic turnout for presidential elections in the United States. The Italian electorate is also provided an opportunity to vote in municipal and regional elections and on occasional referendum issues. The percentage of voter turnout is not as high as in general elections but is still very respectable.

Elections to the Chamber of Deputies and the Senate are held at the same time and must occur at least once within a five-year period. Citizens must be at least eighteen years old to vote for the Chamber of Deputies, and twenty-five years old to vote for the membership of the Senate. A rather complicated proportional representation voting system is used, which helps to encourage small parties and makes it extremely difficult for any one party to receive a majority of the seats. Indeed, a majority has been attained only once in the Republic of Italy and this was by the Christian Democrats in the "Christ-or-Communism" election of 1948. This election was held in April 1948, only two months after the infamous communist coup in Czechoslovakia. At that time, the Italian voters were extremely suspicious of anything that smacked of communism and offered an overwhelming mandate to the anti-communist Christian Democrats.

Italy is divided into thirty-two voting districts for elections to the 630-member Chamber of Deputies, with the number elected in each district determined by regional population. A citizen must cast his or her vote for only one party, but can select individual candidates from that party. Each party wins seats based on the total percentage of the vote it receives in the district. For example, if the Christian Democrats win 40 percent of the vote in a district which will send twenty representatives to the Chamber of Deputies in Rome, that party is entitled to eight seats. The eight candidates selected to represent the party will be those who received the most individual votes from the electorate. Elections to the 315-member Senate are fairly similar except there are only twenty voting districts instead of the thirty-two used for the Chamber of Deputies.

Citizens also participate in the political process through their involvement with any of the hundreds of interest groups which exist along the peninsula. Italy's political parties tend to be more clientelistic than their counterparts in neighboring Western European nations, catering quite openly to the demands of those interest groups which strongly support them. This has especially been the case with the parties involved in coalition governments. Each major party is closely aligned with a labor union, with the communist-socialist affiliated union being the largest in the country. Catholic Action and Confindustria, the major industrial association, are the interest groups which enjoy the easiest access to Christian Democratic representatives. Confindustria also maintains a close working relationship with personnel in the pivotal Ministry of Industry and Commerce.

As for political parties, the Christian Democrats continue to be Italy's leading political movement, winning somewhat less than 40 percent of the overall vote in recent elections. It has often been said that with 40 percent of the vote, the Christian Democrats control 80 percent of the nation's political and economic power. The Christian Democrats have always dominated government coalitions and have made sure that their own people are placed in pivotal positions within the bureaucracy, judiciary, and state-owned enterprises. Thus much of this party's power base is centered in institutions other than parliament.

The Christian Democrats pledge to preserve Catholic values and to protect the family structure, the business community, and small farmers. The party is very much anti-communist and very pro-Western, with leaders of the movement responsible for negotiating Italy's entry into NATO and the EC. In recent years, the party has been plagued by corruption and is widely blamed for the inefficiency of Italy's overall governmental system. Although many Italians still believe that it represents the only alternative to communist rule, the party must become more responsive to the needs of the people if it hopes to maintain its dominant political position. Some progress has been made in purging its ranks of unsavory elements and practices, but much more remains to be accomplished.

The Italian Communist Party (PCI) is the main challenger to the Christian Democrats and, although shut out of national cabinets since 1948, it has formed several regional and municipal governments. A good share of voters remain suspicious of the PCI, partly as a result of its undemocratic internal structure, its links to Moscow, and its occasional criticism of the Catholic Church. Nevertheless, the stigma of Stalinism has largely faded away and a majority of Italians have stated in surveys that they would not object to a national government which included PCI ministers.

The PCI has worked hard to build up a reputation as a movement which would work within the framework of Italy's parliamentary democracy and would always put Italy's interests first. Unlike its sister movement in France, the PCI has been harshly critical of the Soviet treatment of Jews and of its policies in Afghanistan and Poland, drawing strong rebukes from *Pravda* and other media sources in the Soviet Union. The PCI has also insisted that as long as Europe is divided into two major camps, Italy must remain a member of NATO. Moreover, the PCI has also supported Italy's continued participation in the European Community even though expressing regret over some of the capitalist priorities of that organization.

PCI leaders have consistently offered to cooperate with centrist movements in the formation of coalition governments, but their invitations have never been accepted formally. However, Enrico Berlinguer, the leader of the PCI, forged an unofficial historic compromise with the Christian Democrats and its allies during the 1977–1979 period. Although denied seats in the cabinet, the PCI was consulted on major issues and its votes in parliament were instrumental in passing a few significant bills and in keeping the government in power. The compromise was only marginally successful for Berlinguer and his compatriots, because the PCI in the 1979 elections lost twenty-seven seats in the Chamber of Deputies and seven seats in the Senate. Without a doubt, some of the more radical young voters and some of the workers in the major industrial cities abandoned the party because of its accommodationist policies toward the despised Christian Democrats. In the long run, however, Berlinguer's strategy to convince the voters that the PCI is a cooperative, mainstream party totally independent of Moscow may pay off, especially if the right-of-center governments continue to be ineffectual and corruption-prone.

Among left-of-center parties other than the PCI, the Italian Socialist Party (PSI) is the most important. The PSI receives about 10 percent of the national vote and has been a key coalition partner in several governments over the past twenty years. The party has suffered from a series of internal schisms and has not as yet challenged the ascendancy of either the Christian Democrats or the PCI, but is a potential swing partner that could enter into alliances with either major party. The Social Democratic Party (PSDI) split off from the PSI in 1947 and has frequently agreed to form coalitions with the Christian Democrats. The Socialist Proletarian Unity Party (PSIUP) also split off from the PSI in 1963 but in a decidedly leftward direction. Quite often, its policy stances are even to the left of the communists and it has refused to enter into coalitions with the Christian Democrats.

In the moderate-conservative camp, the Liberal Party (PLI) is pro-business but anticlerical. It musters less than 2 percent of the national vote but in a parliament with so many political movements, it has been a key partner for the Christian Democrats. An even more pivotal role is played by the Republican Party (PRI), a movement which advocates moderate economic planning and which is particularly attractive to intellectuals. The party receives about 3 percent of the national vote and, although anticlerical in orientation, has often been involved in coalitions with the Christian Democrats. Indeed, Giovanni Spadolini, a leader of the PRI, was selected as Italy's premier in 1981 even though his coalition government was dominated by ministers from the Christian Democratic Party.

The Italian Social Movement (MSI) occupies the far right position on the political spectrum. Members of this movement advocate certain neo-fascist positions and a return to order, discipline, and nationalist pride which they consider were hallmarks of the Mussolini era. The party is an unacceptable partner in any coalition and received only 6 percent of the vote in 1979 as compared to 9 percent in 1972. Nevertheless, the MSI continues to be the fourth largest party in Italy, a disturbing fact when one considers its anti-democratic reputation.

More than ten parties have been represented in the Chamber of Deputies over the past several years, making it extremely difficult to form stable coalitions. Italian governments continue to average only a year in office and recent elections have been held well within the five-year maximum lifespan of the parliament. Governments are generally weak and are wary of introducing controversial legislation for fear of losing coalition partners. Nonetheless, there is little chance that Italy will turn to a threshold law (such as exists in Germany, Sweden, and Denmark) which would require parties to receive a certain percentage of the national vote before being eligible for parliamentary seats. Some commentators believe that the Christian Democrats will eventually preempt the parties in the center and the right and the PCI will do the same on the left, leading to what is tantamount to a two-party system. How-

TABLE 3.2

Party Representation in Italy's Chamber of Deputies and Senate

| | Chamber of Deputies | | | | Senate | | | |
| | 1976 | | 1979 | | 1976 | | 1979 | |
Party	% Vote	Seats	% Vote	Seats	% Vote	Seats	% Vote	Seats
Christian Democratic (DC)	38.7	262	38.3	262	38.9	135	38.3	138
Communist (PCI)	34.4	228	30.4	201	33.8	116	31.5	109
Socialist (PSI)	9.6	57	9.8	62	10.2	29	10.4	32
Social Movement (MSI)	6.1	35	5.3	30	6.6	15	5.7	13
Social Democratic (PSDI)	3.4	15	3.8	20	3.1	6	4.2	9
Radical (PR)	1.1	4	3.4	18	0.8	0	1.3	2
Republican (PRI)	3.1	14	3.0	16	2.7	6	3.4	6
Liberal (PLI)	1.3	5	1.9	9	1.4	2	2.2	2
Proletarian Unity (PDUP)	1.5	6	1.4	6	—	—	—	—
South Tyrol People's (SUP)	0.5	3	0.6	4	0.5	2	0.5	3
Valle d'Aosta Autonomy	—	0	0.1	1	0.1	1	0.1	1
Trieste	—	0	0.2	1	—	—	—	—
Others	0.3	1	1.8	0	1.9	3	2.4	0

ever, there is little likelihood that a diminunition in the number of parliamentary parties will occur in the near future. The socialists, social democrats, and communists have too little in common to completely close ranks and form a permanent electoral alliance. The anticlerical sentiments of some of the center and right-of-center parties also make it extremely difficult for them to enter into a permanent electoral pact with the Christian Democrats. As a consequence, one should expect that a large number of parties will continue to be represented in the national parliament and that governments will be composed of at least three of these parties. Under such circumstances, significant changes in important policy matters may be made more easily through referenda than through the parliamentary route, which is a stinging indictment of a representative form of government.

Greece

The Greek and Italian political systems are divided by many of the same kinds of cleavages, though in some instances they are not as deep in Greece as they are in Italy. For example, there is no regional disparity in Greece comparable to the sharp difference between northern and southern Italy. This is not to say that Greek politics have been free from sectionalism. Since Greece was not administered as a single unit during the three and a half centuries of Ottoman rule, each region developed its own laws and customs. Thus, throughout the War of Independence various regional leaders attempted to preserve (and even expand) what local autonomy they possessed by resisting efforts to create a centralized government. But despite this history of sectionalism, Greece does not have anything comparable to the Italian *Mezzogiorno*.

Another deep division found in Italy but not in Greece is the cleavage that developed between church and lay cultures during the initial years of state-building. Under Turkish rule, Orthodox Christians were recognized as a separate *millet*, or nation, within the Ottoman Empire. The patriarch of Constantinople was both the head of the church and the leader of the millet. Aside from his religious responsibilities, he was also accountable for the civil administration of the millet. Hence the Orthodox Church became a symbol of Greek culture and unity. After independence, the Orthodox Church of Greece broke away from the patriarch of Constantinople and became a state church. To be sure, there has been friction between church and state over a variety of issues. However, Greece does not have a severe cleavage like the anticlerical-Catholic split in Italy.

On the other hand, Greece has several types of cleavage that are similar to those found in Italy. Both countries industrialized relatively late; consequently there remains a large gulf between advocates of rapid modernization and those who retain strong attachments to traditional social mores and economic practices. A second cleavage is between urban and rural areas. In Greece, cities offer better educational opportunities and, in turn, greater prospects for upward social mobility. Furthermore, the educated urban elite have generally held rural inhabitants in contempt, and have even flaunted their presumed intellectual superiority by using *Katharevusa* rather than the common demotic form of Greek.[10] Nevertheless, these differences have begun to erode with the spread of urbanization and the rise of internal migration. Finally, a third cleavage that exists in both countries is the chasm between rich and poor.

Perhaps the most important impact of these cleavages on Greek political behavior has been to support fragmented, personalized political parties. Due to the way in which these cleavages are aligned, the rural poor have not been a significant force for changing the status quo. Historically, they have been traditional in outlook, and have joined vertical clientelistic networks rather than horizontal, class-based organizations. Prior to the 1967 coup, Greek parties were loosely organized, nonideological structures created by notable patrons. Following the return to democracy in 1974, many of the old personalistic parties reappeared under new names.

Table 3.3 lists the most prominent political parties to emerge after the fall of the military junta. The primary example of a reorganized personalistic party is the center-right New Democracy (ND) established by Constantine Karamanlis, a charismatic leader who had founded the conservative National Radical Union in 1956. New Democracy's platform stressed the party's commitment to parliamentary democracy, social justice, a free democratic economy, and gradual change. Although these vague ideals broadened the party's appeal, some conservatives felt that ND had moved too far to the left. As a result, the right side of the Greek political spectrum came to be occupied by the more authoritarian National Camp, as well as by such supporters of the military and monarchy as the National Populist Party and the National Democratic Union.

The center of the post-junta political spectrum was held by the Union of the Democratic Center. Though the party made great efforts to emphasize its continuity with the reformist tradition of Eleftherios Venizelos' Liberal Party, it suffered from an identity crisis. Prior to the 1967 coup, the Center Union stood virtually alone as an alternative to the political right and left. After 1974, however, it found much of its old support siphoned off by the center-right ND and the center-left Panhellenic Socialist Movement (PASOK). In addition, it lacked the dynamic leadership possessed by these two rivals.

Unlike the majority of parties that appeared after the junta's fall, the Panhellenic Socialist Movement is not simply a reorganized version of an older party. PASOK is a new entry into Greek electoral politics. Founded in 1974 by the charismatic Andreas Papandreou, it has drawn support from a broad

TABLE 3.3

Greek Political Parties

Major Parties	Ideological Position
National Camp Ethnikon Parataxis (EP)	right
New Democracy Nea Demokratia (ND)	center-right
Union of the Democratic Center Enosis Demokratikou Hellinikou Kentrou (EDHK)	center
Panhellenic Socialist Movement Panellinio Sosialistiko Kinima (PASOK)	center-left
Communist Party of Greece Kommounistiko Komma Ellados (KKE)	left—pro Soviet Union
Significant Minor Parties	
National Populist Party Ethniko Laiko Komma (ELK)	extreme right
National Democratic Union Ethniki Demokratiki Enosis (EDE)	right
Party for Democratic Socialism Komma Demokratikou Sosialismou (Kodeso)	center-left
Socialist Initiative Sosialistiki Protovoulia	center-left
Socialist Course Sosialistiki Poria	center-left
United Democratic Left Eniea Demokratiki Aristera (EDA)	left
Communist Party of Greece—Interior Kommounista Komma Ellados—Esoteriko (KKE—I)	left—Eurocommunist
Revolutionary Communist Party of Greece Espanastatiko Kommounistiko Komma Ellados (EKKE)	left—Maoist

range of groups, including merchants, small industrialists, lower level state employees, engineers, and technicians. According to Papandreou, Greece is an economically dependent country on the periphery of the world capitalist economy. Thus while Greece has a small wealthy elite, its members owe their positions to foreign economic interests. In essence, the Greek upper class is a parasitic comprador class that acts as an agent of foreign imperialists. To attain national independence, PASOK advocates socialization, decentralization, and worker self-management.

Turning next to the left side of the political spectrum, one finds a variety of political parties. First, there are several minor center-left parties that have split from larger parties. Socialist Initiative, for example, consists of indi-

TABLE 3.4

Results from the Greek Parliamentary Elections of 1974, 1977, and 1981

Party	1974 % Vote	Seats	1977 % Vote	Seats	1981 % Votes	Seats
ND	54.4	220	41.8	171	35.9	115
EDHK*	20.5	60	11.9	16	0.4	0
PASOK	13.6	12	25.3	93	48.1	172
EA†	9.5	8	—	—	—	—
KKE	—	—	9.4	11	10.9	13
EP	—	—	6.8	5	—	—
SPAD‡	—	—	2.7	2	—	—
Others	2.0	0	2.1	0	4.7	0

*Prior to the 1977 election, the party was known as the Center Union—New Forces party (EK—ND).

†EA (United Left) was an electoral coalition composed of the EDA, KKE, and KKE—I.

‡SPAD (Alliance of Left and Progressive Forces) was an electoral coalition composed of the EDA, KKE—I, Christian Democracy, Socialist Initiative, and Socialist Course.

viduals who once belonged to the Center Union, and Socialist Course contains dissenters from PASOK. Second, there are a number of Marxist parties, including the pro-Soviet Communist Party of Greece (KKE), the Eurocommunist Communist Party of Greece-Interior, and a former front organization for the KKE known as the United Democratic Left. Finally, there is a welter of small extremist parties, such as the Maoist Revolutionary Communist Party of Greece.

Table 3.4 contains the results of the parliamentary elections that have been held since the end of the military dictatorship. The most notable trend since 1974 has been the emergence of two dominant parties: New Democracy and the Panhellenic Socialist Movement. Another noteworthy trend has been the slow collapse of the Center Union and the gradual polarization of Greek politics between the left and right. Lastly, regardless of the alliances that have been fabricated from one election to the next, the electoral fortunes of the communist left have not improved.

Governmental Institutions and the Policy-Making Process

Italy

The Italian Republic is a unitary state with a highly centralized government and a parliamentary democracy. Regional and local governments owe their existence to the government in Rome, and the laws passed by regional assemblies must not conflict with the interests of the nation or of other regions. The unitary form of government has in certain respects helped to foster a sense of national identity along the peninsula, which has historically been divided by regional antagonisms. On the other hand, many people in the north and especially in the south feel that the central government has been insensitive to their regional needs and aspirations and cannot solve their problems from faraway Rome. In 1970, regional governments were established by authorities in Rome to alleviate some of these problems, but these governments have very limited authority and almost all important decisions concerning regional issues continue to be made in Rome.

Italy's current constitution went into effect on January 1, 1948. The amendment process outlined in the 1948 constitution provides parliament with the determining role in making constitutional changes. An amendment must be passed by two separate votes held at least three months apart in both houses of parliament. On the first vote, a plurality in each house is required for passage. An absolute majority is then required on the second vote. The constitution also stipulates that a national referendum must be held on amendments which do not receive at least a two-thirds majority in both chambers of parliament on the second vote.

The President of the Republic

The President of the Republic is the Italian head of state and enjoys discretionary authority greater than that of most European monarchs, but far less than the powerful president in France. The president symbolizes the unity of the Italian nation and is the protector of the constitution. He is also the commander of the armed forces and may declare war.

Like monarchs in neighboring nations, the Italian president promulgates laws, receives diplomats, confers honors of states, opens national expositions, and carries out many other ceremonial functions. The president also appoints the prime minister and may refuse to accept the recommendation of a prime minister that a government be dissolved. Because of the lack of majority support given to any single party movement since the time of the Christian Democrats' overwhelming victory in 1948, the president can occasionally exercise some discretionary power in the selection of a prime minister and in urging the formation of certain government coalitions. The president also appoints members of the Council of Ministers, but always on the advice of the prime minister.

The president must also authorize government-sponsored legislation before it can be submitted to parliament. If the president refuses to give his authorization, the government can simply introduce the legislation as part of a bill put forward by an individual member of parliament. The president also possesses a weak veto power which can be overridden by a simple plurality of votes in each chamber. In addition to his appointment of the prime minister and the members of the Council of Ministers, the president also selects five judges to the Constitutional Court and nominates up to five lifetime members of the Senate.

The president is selected for a seven-year term by a joint session of parliament and is generally a respected, noncontroversial political figure. A two-thirds majority is required to elect a president on the first three ballots, after which an absolute majority will suffice. If the president is incapacitated and cannot fulfill his duties, the Senate president will assume his responsibilities until he is fit to return to office. If the president dies, a new election will be held to fill the vacancy. Although there are no constitutional limitations on the number of terms served by a president, no one has yet been elected for two successive terms. Upon leaving office, the president is automatically eligible for a lifetime appointment to the Senate.

THE PRIME MINISTER AND THE COUNCIL OF MINISTERS

In Italy, the executive branch is called the "government" and consists of the President of the Council of Ministers and the Council of Ministers itself. The prime minister is the President of the Council of Ministers and is usually the most powerful political figure in Italy. The prime minister leads the government and coordinates the activities of the Council of Ministers, which is the equivalent of the cabinet in Great Britain and Canada. He also selects members of the cabinet who are then approved by the President of the Republic. The prime minister may also dismiss individual members of the cabinet and can submit the collective resignation of the government.

Once a new parliamentary election has been held or a previous government has resigned, the President of the Republic confers with the leaders of the parties in order to determine who should be the new prime minister. This new appointee assumes office immediately and begins to choose his ministers. The new government must then obtain a vote of confidence from the Chamber of Deputies and the Senate within ten days after its formation. Failure to receive a vote of confidence will lead to the immediate resignation of the prime minister and his cabinet.

The size of cabinets varies rather substantially from government to government. For example, the prime minister has the prerogative of appointing deputy prime ministers, usually members of the political parties represented in the coalition, thus helping to give a degree of political balance to the cabinet. Ministers may also be appointed who do not supervise regular departments or agencies of the state. They are called ministers without portfolio and are usually assigned vaguely-described duties or assist the prime minister in fulfilling his own specific assignments. The cabinet as a whole is responsible for approving all government-sponsored bills to be submitted to parliament. Because parliamentary approval is necessary for the survival of the new government, almost all members of the cabinet come from the Chamber of Deputies or the Senate, although in rare cases private citizens have been chosen for special assignments. As is the case in most Western European democracies, the prime minister and the members of the Council of Ministers continue to take an active part in the day-to-day activities of parliament.

THE PARLIAMENT

The Italian parliament is a bicameral legislative body composed of the Chamber of Deputies and the Senate of the Republic. The parliament in Italy is somewhat unique in Europe in that the two chambers have equal powers and similar functions. Because of this feature, some observers insist that the Senate is simply a carbon copy of the Chamber of Deputies and should be either abolished or restructured in order to better represent the interests of the regions. However, there is little likelihood of major structural changes in the foreseeable future.

Parliament is the only national office to which the members are elected by the public. Originally, the constitution stipulated that elections to the Senate should be held at least once every six years and the Chamber of Deputies once every five years. The longer Senate terms and staggered elections would thus allow each house to be more independent of one another and permit the voters to concentrate on choosing members of one chamber at a time. However, the Senate has yet to serve a full six-year term and has always been dissolved at the same time as the Chamber of Deputies.

The 630-member Chamber of Deputies enjoys somewhat more prestige than the Senate, partly because more voters are permitted to elect deputies than senators (age eighteen and above for the Chamber and twenty-five and above for the Senate) and younger people, twenty-five or older, are allowed to run for Chamber seats, whereas the minimum age in the Senate is forty. In addition, a majority of the key party leaders in Italy opt to sit in the Chamber rather than the Senate.

There are 315 members of the Senate who are elected on a regional basis. Generally, a region is assigned senators on the basis of population, but a 1963 law mandates that no region will have less than seven senators with the exception of the smaller regions of Friuli-Venezia Giulia (three senators), Molise (two senators), and Valle d'Aosta (one senator). Moreover, the President of the Republic can nominate up to five people who will become senators for life. These lifetime appointments are reserved for former Presidents of the Republic and for individuals who have offered distinguished service to Italy through their achievements in science, academia, social affairs, the arts, or other fields.

Parliament meets at least twice a year, usually in February and October. In extraordinary circumstances, special sessions may be called by the President of the Republic, the president of either legislative chamber, or by one-third of the members of either house. There is also a provision for secret sessions, but it has never been invoked.

Once bills are introduced in parliament by the government or private members, they may become law by the approval of a simple majority of the senators and deputies present. However, an absolute majority of the membership of each house must be present in order to form a quorum and thereby officially consider legislation. Party affiliation is extremely important as members of parliament almost invariably follow the instructions of their party leaders on how to vote. Once legislation is passed in identical form by the two chambers, it is then sent to the President of the Republic for his signature. If the president refuses to sign, his veto can be negated and the bill will automatically become law if both houses pass the legislation again by simple majority votes.

THE JUDICIARY

The Italian legal system is based on Roman civil law. Because of the unitary nature of the Italian government, all courts are part of a national administration, unlike the United States where federal and state court systems are separate. Also in contrast to the United States, all judges in Italy are appointed to their positions and none elected; furthermore, juries are not used to decide cases. Clearly illustrating the Napoleonic influence, the Italian judicial network is divided into ordinary and administrative courts, with the former dealing with civil and criminal law and the latter with individual grievances against the state. The Constitutional Court, which was created in 1956, deals exclusively with issues linked to the interpretation of the 1948 constitution and its amendments. Officials in the Ministry of Justice and a panel of 24 judges known as the Superior Council of the Judiciary oversee the activities of the judicial branch and with the notable exception of the Constitutional Court, are also empowered to assign judges to the various court benches.

The lowest level in the ordinary court system is the Justice of the Peace who presides over small civil disputes and is to be found in almost every commune. Justices of the Peace rarely have legal training and are chosen because of their educational background and their reputation for honesty and impartiality. They do not receive a salary but do collect fees for hearing cases. The Praetor is at the next level in the ordinary court system and at least one is found in each judicial district. The Praetor is authorized to preside over civil cases and also over criminal cases which may involve a maximum of three years' imprisonment. The next step up the judicial ladder involves the Tribunal and it consists of a panel of three judges who hear more serious cases. A Tribunal court is located in each provincial capital and in some of the larger cities. Next up from the Tribunal is the Court of Appeal which is composed of five judges. This court is restricted to hearing appeals from the lower courts and is situated in each regional capital. The highest ordinary court, the Court of Cassation, is sometimes referred to as Italy's Supreme Court. The Court of Cassation has seven members, and rules on points of law related to the conduct of lower court cases. If this court decides that the law has been applied in a defective or improper manner at the lower court level, it can order a new trial.

The Council of State and the Court of Accounts are the two courts which deal with the administrative system. The Council of State in its judiciary role serves as the court having original jurisdiction over citizen complaints against the Italian state. It hears cases in which individuals consider that they have been wronged by acts of the central government, such as a capricious decision rendered by a regional prefect. The Court of Accounts considers more specialized cases linked directly to the supervision and use of public funds.

The Council of State also provides important consultative services to the government, similar to governmental consultation in the Benelux region and a few other countries in Europe. In its advisory role, the Council of State provides guidance to ministries and executive agencies on the legality of legislation, contracts, and regulations. The government has the right to seek assistance from the Council and although the Council's advice is not binding, the government must inform the public when it chooses to proceed with an action which runs counter to Council recommendations.

Before the creation of the Constitutional Court in 1956, there was no tradition in Italy of judicial review of legislation. The Constitutional Court is composed of fifteen members who serve twelve-year terms. Five are appointed by the President of the Republic, five by a three-fifths majority vote of a joint session of parliament, and five by the judges assigned to the Court of Cassation, the Council of State, and the Court of Accounts.

The Constitutional Court is playing an increasingly important role in Italy's system of government, even though it is weakened by a lack of enforcement powers. The court's most important duty is to decide the constitutionality of new laws, but it is also involved in settling jurisdictional disputes pitting the central state against the regions or one region against another. The Constitutional Court also would be heavily involved if impeachment proceedings were to be initiated against a President of the Republic.

The Constitutional Court flexed its muscles in December 1970, when it voided the law of adultery, claiming that it blatantly discriminated against women. The court has also looked very closely at proposed referendum issues to make sure that they are in accordance with constitutional guidelines. For example, in February 1981, the Constitutional Court gave the green light to a referendum on abortion, but refused to go along with Radical Party demands that a referendum be held on issues concerning the legalization of soft drugs, the demilitarization of the customs police, the banning of nuclear power plant construction, and the prohibition on hunting.

As the Constitutional Court becomes better known to the Italian public and the concept of judicial review gains wider acceptance, this judicial body could become a very important actor in Italy's overall policy-making process. On the other hand, the selection process involving the President of the Republic and the parliament and the limited twelve-year appointment period could introduce an element of political partisanship into the Constitutional Court which would severely compromise its role as the impartial protector of constitutional principles.

REGIONAL, PROVINCIAL, AND LOCAL GOVERNMENT

Although wielding very little power in Italy's highly centralized state system, subnational government units at the regional, provincial, and communal levels have gradually been allocated more responsibilities by Rome since the early 1970s. Italy is divided into twenty regions on the basis of long historical traditions and shared cultural or ethnic identities. The population of the regions varies dramatically from the 100,000 inhabitants in the French-speaking enclave of Valle d'Aosta to the seven million citizens of Lombardy. Five of the regions have been accorded a special status and receive greater policy-making latitude from Rome. Valle d'Aosta, Trentino-Alto Adige, and Friuli-Venezia Giulia have been given greater autonomy because of their distinctive cultural and linguistic communities, while Sicily and Sardinia have received special consideration because they are islands physically separated from the peninsula. Each region has an elected one-chamber council (*consiglio*) and an executive body (*giunta*) chosen from the ranks of the council. The same structure is also used at the provincial and communal levels. However, the main executive power in the region is exercised by the regional commissioners who are representatives of the central government and must approve all regional legislation.

The regions are further subdivided into provinces which are very similar administratively to the departments in neighboring France. Prefects dispatched from the Ministry of the Interior in Rome oversee the activities of each of the ninety-four provinces, including Valle d'Aosta, whereas provincial councils help coordinate certain social services, provide some facilities for secondary schools, and maintain provincial roads. Members of the provincial council are elected by the voters for five-year terms based on a modified single member district-proportional representation electoral system, and council membership varies depending on the province's population base. The council serves as the legislative body of the province, and chooses from its own ranks the executive council. Both institutions are assisted by a permanent bureaucracy headed by a provincial secretary.

The approximately 8,000 communes vary in size from small hamlets to huge metropolitan areas such as Rome and Milan. Communal councils are elected by the local voters and in turn choose an executive council and a mayor from their own ranks. Communes have been assigned the task of providing public health and sanitation services, local roads, and some police protection. Communal officials also regulate zoning provisions, new housing construction, and the operations of certain activities ranging from public transportation to municipal restaurants. Revenues made available to the communes are closely regulated by the central government and the prefects or ministries in Rome can annul decisions made by the communal councils on the basis of illegality or fiscal irresponsibility.

It must be strongly emphasized that all of the subnational governments in Italy clearly are hamstrung because of the overwhelming discretionary power wielded by the central government in Rome. The Christian Democrats especially have been fearful that the creation of regional and other subnational government units would provide the socialists and the communists with an opportunity to build up strength at the grassroots level. Because of Christian Democratic concern, the regional governments were not even created until 1970, when a group of socialists demanded them in return for supporting the Christian Democratic coalition government. As the Christian Democrats feared, the PCI in particular has made some inroads at the subnational level and has shown in several cases that it can provide efficient government services. Over the past decade, bitter disputes have erupted periodically between prefects and local administrations, often based on partisan political issues. For the moment, the central government holds most of the cards and wins the vast majority of the battles, but regionalism is still a strong factor in Italian politics and it is likely that the power base of the subnational governments will gradually increase in the years ahead.

THE POLICY-MAKING PROCESS

Cabinets almost invariably dominate the policy-making process in Western parliamentary democracies, and the prime minister is usually without question the most important single actor in the formulation of public policy. Both of these trends have also been present in Italy, but the roles of the cabinet and prime minister in the policy-making process have generally been weaker than those of their counterparts in other Western European nations. For example, it is true that when the parties in the governing coalition represent a disciplined majority in parliament, those measures approved by the cabinet almost always become law. But this has not usually been the case in Italy. As a concrete illustration, this disciplined majority did not exist during the 1977–1979 period and the cabinet was forced to rely on the unofficial support of the PCI parliamentary party in order to pass legislation. Furthermore, coalitions often include conservatives, moderates, and socialists all at the same time, many with regional, class, and clerical preferences which differ dramatically from one member to the next. As a consequence, the bills considered by the cabinet are often noncontroversial to avoid alienating a coalition partner and thereby breaking up the governing group.

What has occurred in Italy since the early 1950s is in some ways closely akin to what happened in France during the Third and Fourth Republics from 1871 to 1940. In both cases, many parties have been represented in parliament and it has been virtually impossible to form a majority party government or even a stable coalition. Governments in both Italy and France survived for only one year or less and a failure to face up to important issues prompted political stagnation and stalemate. Moreover, it was not uncommon in Third and Fourth Republic France nor has it been unusual in postwar Italy for a coalition partner to deliberately bring down a government in order to secure better cabinet positions and more power in the next government coalition for itself. France eventually turned authority over to strong-willed leaders and the present Fifth Republic gives much more authority to the president at the expense of both the cabinet and the parliament. Italy, on the other hand, continues to tolerate the endless stream of short-lived cabinets and the often chaotic executive decision-making process.

Italy's crisis of executive leadership also extends to the position of prime minister. The prime minister must spend most of his waking hours placating not only the disgruntled coalition partners but members of his own party as well. Even powerful political figures such as Alcide de Gasperi, an early leader of the Christian Democratic Party, suffered numerous headaches in trying to guide coherent proposals through the cabinet. Just imagine the decision-making problems faced by Prime Minister Giovanni Spadolini of the Republican Party, who had only one other Republican colleague in a recent cabinet dominated by Christian Democratic ministers. To complicate matters even further, some of the prime ministers have not even been leaders of their own political movements, which meant they faced additional pressure from their own party hierarchy to toe the party line. In Italy, the prime minister is truly little more than first among equals in the cabinet structure and will remain relatively weak as long as four- or five-party coalition governments remain the order of the day.

As for parliament, the decision-making process is very similar to that in many other neighboring countries, except that the Senate plays a much more critical role than do other upper chambers in Europe. The parliament even has a rather novel way available to it to speed up the lawmaking process. Any of the fourteen standing committees in the Chamber of Deputies or the eleven in the Senate can simply pass legislation without having to send it back to the full chamber for approval. However, the membership of each committee has the same party composition as the legislative chamber as a whole and if 10 percent of the committee members refuse to go along with speeding up the process, the legislation must return to the floor for a vote by the entire chamber.

As long as elections to the two houses of parliament are held at the same time and the voters continue to vote for the same party in each chamber, neither parliamentary unit will serve as an effective check on the other. In particular, the Senate has not been a noteworthy representative of the regions, even though elections to the Senate were structured specifically to represent the regions. On the other hand, if the elections and terms in office of the two chambers were staggered in accordance with the constitution, and if the Senate began to act as an effective body with the interests of the regions in mind, it might become even more difficult to convince the maze of parties to pass meaningful legislation.

Another logjam in the policy process is found within the bureaucracy. The Italian bureaucracy is among the most maligned in the Western world, and generally with good reason. Policies supported by the cabinet, passed by the parliament, and approved by the president are often skewed or even totally ignored by the bureaucracy which is supposed to implement the new laws.

Part of the bureaucracy's problem is linked to staffing. The best and the brightest of young Italian graduates can find the most lucrative and challenging jobs in the private sector, particularly if they have been raised in the north. In the civil service, merit often matters much less than political affiliation and family ties in selection and advancement, and the young people that do opt for government service are usually not motivated by civic pride nor by a keen desire to serve the homeland. Graft and absenteeism are endemic and even the most sincere and dedicated civil servants soon learn that their road to advancement will be blocked if they attempt to rock the boat. The bureaucracy has been notoriously slow in reacting even to highly publicized natural disasters such as villages being decimated by earthquakes. The performance of the public service in implementing day-to-day policies that receive little attention from the public is even shoddier. Fortunately, the bureaucracy at the subnational level seems to be somewhat more efficient, especially in the north, but its areas of jurisdiction are severely limited by the unitary system of government.

The Italian people overwhelmingly resent the bureaucracy, and academic circles have widely condemned it as a major roadblock to effective policy-making. Why then are major steps not taken to revamp the bureaucratic structure and infuse the public service with new blood? For one thing, it is extremely difficult to dismiss incompetent bureaucrats. More importantly, however, the leading parties in the government are able to maintain a semblance of control over the bureaucracy by their power to secure public jobs for the party faithful. Any change in the status quo, especially a major house-cleaning operation, might threaten this party control and therefore has been resisted by the governing political movements.

In sum, Italian governments tend to slither by and postpone difficult decisions to future governments, which, when they come to power, do exactly the same thing. Cabinets and parliamentary parties labor mightily to produce a molehill which will then be skewed or simply ignored by some obscure bureaucratic unit. In order to change this abysmal situation and shake up the status quo, Italy may have to take a sharp turn leftward or rightward, either of which might imperil the fragile democratic structure. Referenda, which are relatively easy to propose and may be spearheaded by interest groups, may also become an increasingly important policy-making tool for passing major controversial proposals. In effect, governments cannot afford to support such proposals for fear of breaking up their coalitions, but cabinets cannot be held directly responsible for what the voters choose to do at the referendum ballot box. However, the earlier referenda upholding liberalized divorce and abortion laws, would seem to indicate that the voters often favor policies opposed by members of the Christian Democrat-led coalition and its major interest group allies. If this is indeed the case, the political parties that have dominated Italy during the postwar period would seem to have a vested interest in cleaning up some of the negative features of the current decision-making system in order to better respond to the demands of the electorate. Unfortunately, there has been thus far little movement in the direction of reforming and streamlining the overall central government policy-making process.

GREECE

During the early morning of April 21, 1967, Greek army armored units surrounded the parliament building and the major government ministries in Athens. Claiming they were not merely conducting a palace coup to replace one set of politicians with another, the military leaders suspended the 1952 constitution and instituted martial law, a curfew, and a ban on private meetings of over five people. According to the junta, its goal was to carry out a revolution to rid Greece of corruption, inefficiency, and political instability. Toward this end, over 6,000 people were arrested, numerous officers and government employees were purged, and, on October 29, 1968, a new constitution was adopted. The new constitution recognized the armed forces as the guardians of the regime, and stipulated that freedoms of the press, assembly, and so on would not be allowed until after the aims of the revolution had been completed.

On June 1, 1973, George Papadopulos, the leader of the junta, unveiled a modified version of the 1968 constitution, one that called for the establishment of a multiparty system by the end of 1974. Five months later, however, preparations for the general elections were scrapped when General Dimitrios Ioannidis overthrew Papadopulos in a coup that he described as a return to the Revolution of 1967. Although this seemed to dash prospects for some form of representative government, the dictatorship came to an abrupt end by the following summer. On July 15, 1974, an attempt was made to annex Cyprus by staging a coup in Nicosia against the government of Archbishop Makarios. To prevent an annexation, Turkey sent troops to Cyprus on July 20, and proceeded to occupy much of the island. Faced with a serious international crisis, the junta convened a meeting of Greece's leading political figures. Based on their recommendation, the 1952 constitution was restored, and Constantine Karamanlis (premier from 1955 to 1963) was brought out of exile to head a caretaker government. Elections were held in November, and on December 8, 1974, 69 percent of the electorate voted in a referendum against the return of the monarchy. Based on the results of the referendum, the new legislature drafted a new constitution to replace the monarchy with a parliamentary republic.

The new constitution of 1975 established a unicameral parliament (*Vouli*) composed of 300 members who are elected directly for four-year terms. Officers are elected at the beginning of each four-year period, and committee composition is based on the proportional strength of the parties in parliament. The leader of the political party with an absolute majority in the parliament is appointed prime minister by the president. Should no absolute majority exist, the leaders of either of those parties with the two largest pluralities may hold the position, subject to a parliamentary vote of confidence.

The president is elected by a two-thirds majority of parliament for a five-year term that is renewable once. As head of state, the president performs various ceremonial functions, appoints the prime minister and, based on the latter's recommendations, appoints individuals to the Council of Ministers (cabinet). In addition, the president has the power to return legislation passed by the parliament. However, if the legislation is passed once again by an absolute majority, the president must accept it within ten days.

The 1975 constitution established a unitary system, with all key decisions being made in Athens. Under this system, Greece is divided into 51 *nomoi* (departments) for administrative purposes. Each department is headed by a *nomarch* who is responsible for coordinating the activities of government ministries within his area of jurisdiction.

The Greek judicial system is organized into two distinct hierarchies. The first hierarchy contains civil and criminal courts. The lowest level of the hierarchy is made up of magistrate and justice of the peace courts, which are designed for minor cases. Directly above them in ascending sequence are courts of first instance for more serious cases, courts of appeal, and the Supreme Court. The second hierarchy contains administrative courts. At the bottom of this hierarchy are a variety of specialized courts, organized into such functional areas as taxation, social security, and labor arbitration. At the top of this hierarchy is the Council of State, which rules on matters sent up from lower courts. Whenever the highest courts in each of the two hierarchies reach contradictory conclusions on a matter of constitutional interpretation, the issue may be brought before the Special High Tribunal for a ruling.

In summary, following the fall of the military junta, Greece acquired a parliamentary form of government with a strong president. Yet as clear as its structures may look on paper, the system still functions somewhat differently in practice from the way its organization charts suggest. In brief, this is due to the continued existence of patron-client networks within the Greek political system. Though clientelism is generally weakened by the emergence of horizontal, class-based organizations in urban areas of Greece, most citizens still prefer informal personalistic ties to either formal associational or nonassociational interest group ties. Indeed, those who lack ties to a patron suffer a serious disadvantage within the Greek political system, regardless of the structures described in the constitution.

Policy Problems and Prospects

ITALY

Italians have been famed for their quest for *La Dolce Vita*, the good life. And indeed, a fair number have now achieved a degree of material prosperity as a result of the economic miracle which transformed parts of Italian society from the 1950s to the present. However, the distribution of societal wealth has been very imbalanced as a small number of people now control a large percentage of the assets while many Italians continue to get by at the subsistence level. The gap in regional prosperity has also widened, with northerners in general enjoying a standard of living at least three times higher than that of the people in the *Mezzogiorno*. Because of these trends, class and regional conflicts will continue to plague Italian decision-makers in the future.

The Italian economic miracle has also been tarnished somewhat in recent years, in spite of the fact that Italy led Western Europe in 1980 in real gross national product growth and continues to make significant gains in certain economic sectors. The peninsula is especially vulnerable to fluctuations in oil prices because it must import 75 percent of its energy needs. Moreover, Italy's inflation rate has been among the highest in Western Europe and the lira has been periodically devalued in an effort to dampen domestic demand for imports (which become more expensive because of the weakened lira) while at the same time improving the competitiveness of Italian exports (which become more attractive to foreign buyers because their currencies are worth more vis-à-vis the devalued lira). However, the recession conditions which have plagued much of the world in recent years have hurt Italy's export markets, and the periodic devaluations of the lira have left many observers wondering whether the Italian currency can remain a part of the European Monetary System (EMS), the European Community's institutional arrangement to keep the value of its currencies within a specified range. Economic woes and pressure on the lira have been further exacerbated by huge deficit spending on the part of the central government, reaching a staggering annual rate of more than 50 billion dollars in 1982.

As long as Italy enjoyed increasing prosperity, many people seemed to tolerate the foibles of the political system. This toleration will dissipate quickly, however, in any lingering period of economic malaise. One must remember that support for Italy's experiment with parliamentary democracy has never been deeply ingrained into the Italian psyche, with most Italians continuing to be very suspicious and distrustful of the governmental apparatus in Rome. Indeed, parliamentary democracy apparently survives by virtue of the fact that it has not threatened the well-being of Italy's major political and interest groups.

There is too much clientelism in Italian governmental circles and too little commitment to rendering effective service to the general public. Several national governments have fallen because of the disclosure of graft and corruption at the highest governmental levels. Even when government officials have been dedicated to serving the people, the proliferation in the number of political parties in parliament and the major policy differences among coalition partners linked to class, regionalism, and clericalism have made it extremely difficult to formulate effective policies. Immobility is plaguing the Italian system of government and, if it persists, the people will eventually abandon the Christian Democrat–dominated coalition which has directed governmental affairs since 1948.

What are the alternatives available for solving Italy's current political and economic problems? Fascism continues to have some support, and, in 1968 and again in 1974, groups of military and paramilitary officers were involved in unsuccessful plots to overthrow the government. Moreover, the P-2 affair of 1981 once again revealed that there is still some support among high ranking government and military officials for right-wing terrorist activities aimed at weakening Italy's democratic framework. On the far left, the Red Brigade has received worldwide publicity for its wave of kidnappings, bombings, and assassinations, including the 1978 execution of former Christian Democrat prime minister, Aldo Moro. An effective crackdown on the Red Brigade following the kidnapping of American General James Dozier has decimated its ranks, but it remains a force to be reckoned with. The goal of the Red Brigade is to bait Italian officials into suspending civil liberties guaranteed by the 1948 constitution, thereby weakening democracy and forcing the polarization of Italy into left-wing and right-wing camps.

Neither the far right nor the far left vendettas against the political system are palatable to most Italians, which leaves the formation of a popular front government of communists and socialists as the major alternative to the perennially dominant centrist-conservative coalitions. Under Enrico Berlinguer, the PCI has shown a willingness to work within the parliamentary system and to cooperate with the parties to its right. Several communist administrations at the communal, provincial, and regional levels have also been widely praised for cutting down corruption and graft and implementing effective policies. Nevertheless, the PCI's internal decision-making system continues to follow Lenin's model of democratic centralism, which means that decisions are made at the top and accepted without question by the mass membership. Furthermore, even though the PCI has shown a tactic acceptance of the European Community and NATO and has been at odds with Moscow over various policy issues, many of the PCI foreign policy stances continue to be more closely aligned with Eastern Europe than with Western Europe. Prior to the 1979 general elections, U.S. officials openly questioned Italy's continued role in NATO if communists were to come to power in Rome. Implicitly, these U.S. representatives doubted the PCI's fervent support for the NATO structure and wondered whether NATO secrets might be forwarded by communist administrators in Rome to their ideological cousins in Moscow. Italy is strategically important to NATO as it guards Western Europe's southern flank and oversees the Mediterranean routes to Europe, North Africa, and the Middle East. Although American fears might be unfounded, NATO would certainly face some unprecedented challenges if communists were to take control of one of its major member governments.

Although support for a republican system of government remains strong, Italy may well be on the verge of a crisis of democracy, and the clientelistic orientation of the party and bureaucratic systems must shoulder much of the blame. Cynicism and suspicion of government practices are higher among the Italian citizenry than anywhere else in the Western industrialized world, and democracy simply cannot flourish under such negative conditions. Italians strongly support their membership in the European Community and NATO, but when they go to the polling booth in the future they will give more credence to domestic concerns than to foreign policy issues. Consequently, frustration with government immobility and a stalemated society could well prompt the electorate to experiment for the first time ever with a PCI-dominated leftist coalition government, a decision which would certainly have profound implications both for Western Europe and the Western alliance in general.

Greece

The victory of PASOK in the 1981 parliamentary elections after almost six years of stability and incremental reform under New Democracy raises two important sets of questions about Greece's immediate future. The first set of questions revolves around the extent to which Greek political development will follow a Gaullist path. In accordance with the constitution of 1975, a presidential election was held in April 1980, five years after Constantine Tsatsos had been elected to the office as the first president of the new republic. After three ballots were taken, Constantine Karamanlis was elected. During the years in which Karamanlis was prime minister, President Tsatsos played primarily a ceremonial role within the Greek political system. However, the constitution provides the president with significant powers, including the ability to dissolve parliament, call for referendums, and rule in emergencies by executive order. A charismatic president with majority support in the parliament could, like de Gaulle, assume the dominant position within the policy-making process. Yet, as Roy Macridis points out, if Karamanlis gives the constitution a Gaullist interpretation and uses the powers of the office against Prime Minister Papandreou of PASOK, "then the old conflict between the prime minister and the crown will reappear as a conflict between the prime minister and the president."[11] Needless to say, such a conflict could jeopardize the stability of the Greek political system.

The second set of questions raised by the PASOK victory pertains to the policies that the new prime minister will attempt to implement. From the establishment of the monarchy after the War of Independence, to the fall of the military junta during the Cyprus crisis in 1974, Greek internal affairs have been influenced by external powers. As mentioned earlier, Papandreou's political outlook is grounded in the belief that popular sovereignty and social liberation are not possible as long as Greece remains a dependent country. Therefore he has called for restructuring the Greek economy to foster what he calls self-supporting development, and has criticized Greek membership in the European Community and the North Atlantic Treaty Organization. But in spite of advocating *allaghi* (change), PASOK has also attempted to shed its Third-World populist image and establish contacts with Western European social democratic parties.

Looking ahead, then, one can suggest two possible scenarios for the Greek political system. According to the first, PASOK and New Democracy will become the dominant parties in a two-party parliamentary system where the president mainly plays a ceremonial role. According to the second, PASOK and New Democracy will eventually splinter, and Greece will possess a multiparty parliamentary system with a Gaullist-style president. Given the history of political factionalism, conflict, and praetorian intervention, movement toward either form of democracy would no doubt be welcomed. As the famous writer Nikos Kazantzakis once put it,

> How pleasant if the Greek could stroll through his country and not hear stern, angry voices beneath the soil! For the Greek, however, a journey through Greece degenerates into a fascinating and exhausting torture.

You stand on a spot of Greek land and you find yourself overcome with anguish. It is a deep tomb with layer upon layer of corpses whose varied voices rise and call you. . . .[12]

Notes

1. Gabriel A. Almond and Sidney Verba, *The Civic Culture* (Boston: Little, Brown, 1965), pp. 37–39, 90–92, 200–202, and 308–310.

2. D. A. Zakythinos, *The Making of Modern Greece*, translated by K. R. Johnstone (Totowa, N.J.: Rowman and Littlefield, 1976), pp. 190–191.

3. Peter F. Sugar, *Southeastern Europe Under Ottoman Rule, 1354–1804* (Seattle: University of Washington Press, 1977), pp. 31–34.

4. Douglas Dakin, *The Greek Struggle For Independence, 1821–1833* (Berkeley and Los Angeles: University of California Press, 1973), p. 78.

5. D. George Kousoulas, *Greece: Uncertain Democracy* (Washington, D.C.: Public Affairs Press, 1973), p. 3.

6. Douglas Dakin, *The Unification of Greece, 1770–1923* (New York: St. Martin's Press, 1972), p. 262.

7. Samuel P. Huntington, *Political Order in Changing Societies* (New Haven: Yale University Press, 1968), pp. 192–198. The term is derived from the Praetorian Guards of the Roman Empire, a unit originally established to protect the emperor but that actually intervened into politics to overthrow certain emperors.

8. *Economist*, 20 February 1982, p. 49.

9. Keith R. Legg, *Politics in Modern Greece* (Stanford, Calif.: Stanford University Press, 1969), p. 36.

10. Until February 1, 1977, when the government adopted the demonic form for all secular purposes, four types of Greek were used. In addition to the common demonic form, *Katharevusa* was spoken by the educated elite, *Koine* was the liturgical language used by the church, and *Kathomiloumeni* was used by the press.

11. Roy C. Macridis, "Elections and Political Modernization in Greece," in *Greece at the Polls: The National Elections of 1974 and 1977*, edited by Howard R. Penniman (Washington, D.C.: American Enterprise Institute for Public Policy Research, 1981), p. 19.

12. Nikos Kazantzakis, *Report to Greco*, translated by P. A. Bien (New York: Simon and Schuster, 1965), p. 164.

Selected Bibliography

Allum, Percy. "Thirty Years of Southern Policy in Italy," *Political Quarterly* 52 (July 1981): 314–323.

Athinaios, Andreas, and McHale, Vincent. "Community Characteristics and Voting Patterns in Urban Greece," *European Journal of Political Research* 7 (September 1979): 235–252.

Campbell, John C., and Sherrard, Phillip. *Modern Greece*. New York: Praeger, 1968.

Carey, Jane, and Carey, Andrew. *The Web of Modern Greek Politics*. New York: Columbia University Press, 1968.

Clogg, Richard. *A Short History of Modern Greece*. Cambridge: Cambridge University Press, 1979.

Clogg, Richard, and Yannopoulos, George, eds. *Greece Under Military Rule*. New York: Basic Books, 1972.

Couloumbis, Theodore A. "Post World War II Greece: A Political Review," *East European Quarterly* 7 (Fall 1973): 285–310.

Couloumbis, Theodore A. "The Greek Junta Phenomenon," *Polity* 6 (Spring 1974): 345–374.

Couloumbis, Theodore A., Petropulous, John A., and Psomiades, Harry J. *Foreign Interference in Greek Politics*. New York: Pella, 1976.

Dakin, Douglas. *The Greek Struggle for Independence, 1821–1833*. Berkeley and Los Angeles: University of California Press, 1973.

Danopaulos, Constantine, and Patel, Kant. "Military Professionals as Political Governors: A Case Study of Contemporary Greece," *West European Politics* 3 (May 1980): 188–202.

Di Palma, Giuseppe. *Surviving Without Governing: Italian Parties in Parliament*. Berkeley: University of California Press, 1977.

Graziano, Luigi. "On Political Compromise: Italy After the 1979 Elections," *Government and Opposition* 15 (Spring 1980): 190–207.

Kertzer, David I. *Comrades and Christians: Religion and Political Struggle in Communist Italy*. Cambridge: Cambridge University Press, 1980.

Kogan, Norman. *A Political History of Postwar Italy*. New York: Praeger, 1981.

Kousoulas, D. George. *Revolution and Defeat: The Story of the Greek Communist Party*. London: Oxford University Press, 1965.

Lange, Peter, and Tarrow, Sidney, eds. *Italy in Transition*. London: Frank Cass, 1980.

Legg, Keith R. "Political Change in a Clientelistic Polity: The Failure of Democracy in Greece," *Journal of Political and Military Sociology* 1 (Fall 1973): 231–246.

Legg, Keith R. *Politics in Modern Greece*. Stanford, Calif.: Stanford University Press, 1969.

Mouzelis, Nicos. "Capitalism and the Development of the Greek State." In *The State in Western Europe*. Edited by Richard Scase. New York: St. Martin's Press, 1980.

Mouzelis, Nicos. "Class and Clientelistic Politics: The Case of Greece," *Sociological Review* 26 (August 1978): 471–497.

Penniman, Howard R., ed. *Greece at the Polls: The National Elections of 1974 and 1977*. Washington, D.C.: American Enterprise Institute, 1981.

Penniman, Howard R., ed. *Italy at the Polls: The Parliamentary Elections of 1976*. Washington, D.C.: American Enterprise Institute, 1977.

Petropulos, John A. *Politics and Statecraft in the Kingdom of Greece*. Princeton: Princeton University Press, 1968.

Pridham, Geoffrey. *The Nature of the Italian Party System*. New York: St. Martin's Press, 1981.

Sani, Giacomo. "The Political Culture of Italy: Continuity and Change." In *The Civic Culture Revisited*. Edited by Gabriel A. Almond and Sidney Verba. Boston: Little, Brown, 1980, pp. 273–324.

Tsoucalas, Constantine. *The Greek Tragedy*. Baltimore: Penguin, 1969.

Vatikiotis, Panayiotios J. "Greece: A Political Essay." In *The Washington Papers, II*. Beverly Hills, Calif.: Sage Publications, 1974.

Weinberg, Leonard B. *After Mussolini: Italian Neo-Fascism and the Nature of Fascism*. Washington, D.C.: University Press of America, 1979.

Woodhouse, C. M. *Modern Greece: A Short History*. London: Faber and Faber, 1977.

Xydis, Stephen G. "Coups and Countercoups in Greece, 1967–1973 (with postscript)," *Political Science Quarterly* 89 (Fall 1974): 507–538.

Xydis, Stephen G. "Modern Greek Nationalism." In *Nationalism in Eastern Europe*. Edited by Peter F. Sugar and Ivo J. Lederer. Seattle: University of Washington Press, 1969.

Zariski, Raphael. *Italy: The Politics of Uneven Development*. Hinsdale, Ill.: Dryden Press, 1972.

4.

The Benelux Region: The Politics of Consociational Democracies

The Historical Setting

An Overview

The Netherlands, Belgium, and Luxembourg are among the smaller nations of Western Europe, a characteristic which has not escaped the attention of would-be punsters. David Frost once quipped that Luxembourg is so small that every time a person rolls over in bed he has to show his passport. Indeed, the Grand Duchy of Luxembourg, fondly referred to at times as the "mighty dwarf" of Europe, sports a rather miniscule population of 358,000 in an area covering 2,500 square kilometers, appreciably smaller than America's tiniest state, Rhode Island. Even in the case of Belgium, Britons have frequently commented that the entire width of that nation can be traversed by rail in the short period between "lunch and tea. "

Quite often, of course, size can be deceiving. For example, the Netherlands and Belgium once possessed vast empires which spanned several continents. And perhaps even more important in terms of contemporary affairs, the Benelux nations have been in the forefront of efforts to achieve European integration in the post–World War II era.

The destinies of the three Benelux nations have crossed paths repeatedly during the past several centuries. In particular, one historical tendency has punctuated the development of all three nations—foreign intrusion. Starting with the conquests of Caesar's legions in 57 B.C. and ending with the German onslaught in World War II, much of the history of the Netherlands, Belgium, and Luxembourg has been characterized by foreign invasion and domination. The Franks, Burgundians, Hapsburgs, Spanish, French, and several other non-indigenous groups have, at one time or another, laid claim to the Benelux region.

As a result of these persistent incursions and the nationalist extremism which helped to plunge Europe into two catastrophic conflicts in the twentieth century, the Benelux leaders have vigorously supported efforts to bring some semblance of unity and order to the devastated European continent in the post-1945 period. Belgium and Luxembourg consummated an economic union as far back as 1922, and pursuant to an agreement signed by the respective governments-in-exile during World War II and ratified in 1947, both nations joined with the Netherlands in creating a modified economic union. This Benelux Customs Union, which went into operation in the late 1940s and which was further strengthened in 1960, was an important milestone in the eventual establishment of the European Economic Community (EEC).

Moreover, because of the Nazi occupation and the advent of the Cold War, the Benelux nations abandoned their traditional neutrality and opted for both a Western European and an Atlantic defense alliance. The three nations were all signatories to the Brussels Treaty of 1948 and were charter members of the North Atlantic Treaty Organization (NATO), which was formed one year later in Washington.

In a concerted effort to foster greater intergovernmental and transnational cooperation in postwar Western Europe, the Benelux nations joined the Western European Union in 1948, the Council of Europe in 1949, the European Coal and Steel Community in 1952, the European Atomic Energy Community in 1958, and the European Economic Community in 1958. Even today, the citizens of the Benelux countries are considered to be among the most ardent supporters of a supranational-oriented United States of Europe.

In addition, the three Benelux nations may be categorized by what Arend Lijphart has referred to as "consociational democracies." In effect, these nations are fragmented into various subcultures but have fairly stable democratic political systems. However, in order to maintain this stability, Lijphart insists that the leaders of the major subcultures must (1) have the ability to accommodate the divergent demands of their subcultures, (2) be able to transcend traditional points of difference and join in fruitful discussions with each other, (3) be committed to preserving the political system and improving its stability and cohesiveness, and (4) clearly understand the perils of political fragmentation. As will be illustrated later on, the Netherlands and Luxembourg have fairly well satisfied these conditions, but Belgium continues to be plagued by periodic political instability directly linked to sharp subcultural differences.

The Netherlands

The 14.1 million inhabitants of the Netherlands live in an area approximately two-thirds the size of the state of West Virginia, but with a population density which ranks among the highest in the world, twelve times higher than that of West Virginia and almost fifteen times greater than that of the United States as a whole.

The Netherlands once possessed an expansive empire with colonial possessions spanning the globe in such diverse places as Europe, Asia, Africa, North America, and South America. However, following the granting of independence to the South American country of Suriname in November 1975, the "Kingdom of the Netherlands" has been reduced in size and consists only of the Netherlands proper and a Caribbean island chain known as the Netherlands Antilles.

For 1600 years after the Roman invasion of 57 B.C., the area now constituting the Netherlands was dominated by a succession of foreign rulers, culminating with the leadership of the Hapsburgs. In 1555, the Emperor Charles V abdicated his position as ruler of the Low Countries in favor of his son, who was soon anointed Philip II, King of the Spanish Empire. To the dismay of many in the Low Countries, Philip began to treat the Northern European provinces as a minor appendage of Spain. Tensions were further aggravated because of the inroads made by the Calvinists in the Low Countries, a situation which alarmed both Philip and the Catholic church hierarchy. As a result, a concerted effort was made by Philip to root out this Protestant influence, with the king authorizing measures which included at times the wanton execution of Calvinists. This reign of terror, coupled with Philip's proclivity toward absolutism in other spheres, evoked widespread criticism and discontent among the inhabitants of the northern provinces of the empire.

Sporadic outbreaks of violence protesting Philip's policies occurred in various northern regions in the 1560s. By 1576, many of the northern provinces were united in their opposition to Spanish rule. Seven regions, led by the province of Holland, formed the Union of Utrecht in 1579 and soon called for the complete independence of the Low Countries. With little doubt, the destruction of the Spanish Armada by the English and Spain's continual problems with Henry IV of France greatly assisted the northern provinces in their efforts to achieve victory.

Although the Spanish troops were eventually forced out of the Netherlands, Spanish garrisons continued to control much of what is now Belgium and Luxembourg. The Spaniards refused to formally recognize the independence of the Netherlands until the signing of the historic Treaty of Westphalia in 1648, but in the interim period the Dutch had already made rapid strides toward becoming a world power. Justifiably renowned for their maritime skills and mercantile acumen, the Dutch were soon establishing colonial outposts in many sectors of the globe. And in spite of periodic wars with France and England and the eventual relinquishment of New Amsterdam (later called New York) to the English, the seventeenth century stands out as the high mark of Dutch colonial power.

In marked contrast, the eighteenth century was a rather turbulent period in Dutch history culminating in the demise of the independent Dutch Republic and the institution of French control in 1795. Napoleon temporarily incorporated the Low Countries region into his vast empire, but following his exile in 1814, the Congress of Vienna established the Kingdom of the Netherlands as a buffer zone between the major European powers. Although frequently revised, the Constitution of 1814, which delineated the powers of the new kingdom, remains in effect today. The constitution originally stipulated that the Netherlands was to be a unitary state with central power divided between a constitutional monarch and a parliamentary chamber known as the States-General. Unfortunately, the kingdom established by the major powers which had assembled at the Congress of Vienna was apparently predestined to suffer from irreparable cleavages.

The Vienna Congress had added Belgium, an industrial region with a significant French-speaking Catholic population, to the new Kingdom of the Netherlands, a mercantile-oriented area with a large Dutch-speaking Protestant population. William I, Prince of Orange, was named ruler of the Kingdom of the Netherlands, but was soon challenged by disgruntled Catholics in Belgium, who perceived him as ignoring their aspirations. Finally in 1830, a year noted for upheavals in Europe, the southern Catholic provinces revolted against the monarch and proclaimed a separate Kingdom of the Belgians. The British, in particular, stood by the Belgian separatists and thus helped guarantee the independence of the new nation.

By 1850, the power of the monarchy in the Netherlands had begun to wane considerably, with greater policy-making latitude being assumed by the parliamentary States-General. In foreign affairs, the Dutch adopted a stance of strict neutrality and in spite of stringent pressure placed on them by both contending sides, they were able to remain neutral even during World War I.

The Dutch continued to advocate a position of neutrality during the turbulent period leading up to the Second World War, but were not spared this time from German invasion. German aerial bombings decimated the center of Rotterdam and Nazi troops eventually overran the country, bringing about the occupation of the entire nation until 1945. During this tragic period, Dutch Jews were particularly singled out for persecution and even liquidation. Among those killed by the Nazis was a young Jewish girl from Amsterdam, Anne Frank, who left for posterity a diary which poignantly describes the plight of her people during the occupation.

Naturally disturbed by the events which transpired during World War II, as well as the emergence of the Cold War in the latter half of the 1940s, the Dutch finally abandoned their traditional stance of neutrality by joining various regional and international organizations, including NATO. The Dutch also relinquished many of their remaining overseas possessions after World War II. In particular, Indonesia was finally granted independence after some bitter confrontations between Dutch troops and Indonesian nationalists.

The Kingdom of the Netherlands is now primarily limited to the European mainland, and although the nation is officially a constitutional monarchy, almost all governmental authority is centered in the cabinet and the States-General. Moreover, even though the country is geographically small, its citizens are among the most prosperous people in the world. The Dutch have created an extensive welfare system which provides "cradle to grave" security for the citizenry and, on a per capita GNP basis, they contribute almost as much aid to third world countries as the Scandinavian nations and much more than the United States. Dutch officials also continue to push strenuously for European integration, enthusiastically endorsing the recommendations made in such documents as the Tindemans report and their own Spierenburg paper, both of which advocate greater policy-making latitude for the supranational-oriented European Parliament and Commission.

As will be discussed later, the Dutch currently face several onerous challenges, some indigenous to their own society and some common to all Western advanced industrial societies. On the other hand, the Dutch spirit has been tempered by the legacy of foreign invasion and by the constant onslaught of the sea to reclaim an area that is two-fifths under sea level. In comparison to these traditional challenges to Dutch survival, the contemporary problems faced by the Netherlands may appear somewhat mundane, a characteristic which, unfortunately, cannot be attributed to present-day Belgium.

Belgium

Belgium's surface area of 30,519 square kilometers is somewhat larger than that of Maryland, which ranks among the ten smallest states in the United States. On the other hand, Belgium has a population of 9.9 million as compared to Maryland's 4.1 million, resulting in Belgium having a population density of 321 per square kilometer, among the highest of any nation in the world and fourteen times larger than that of the United States.

The linguistic frontier which is still quite evident in modern Belgium may be traced as far back as the fifth century A.D. Whereas the Roman language and customs endured in the southern part of what is now Belgium well beyond the fifth century, the northern region was subjugated by the Franks, who introduced a Germanic language. Even today, many of Belgium's most serious problems may be linked to tensions between its two major linguistic communities, the Flemings, who speak a Germanic language, and the Walloons, who speak the Latin-derived French language.

At the beginning of the ninth century, the Emperor Charlemagne consolidated a vast European area, including what is now Belgium, into the Holy Roman Empire. After his death, this massive empire was divided among three descendants of Charlemagne, one of whom took control of French territory, a second of German lands, and the third, Lothair, of an area which included the Low Countries region of modern-day Belgium, Luxembourg, and the Netherlands. Tragically, this third area, "Lotharingia," was highly coveted by the leaders of the other two territories, and was frequently relegated to battlefield status as the competing sides fought to dominate it.

Through treaties, conquests, and propitious intermarriages, the dukes of Bergundy were able to seize control over the Low Countries in the latter part of the fourteenth century. The marriage of Mary of Burgundy to Maximilian of Austria formally united the House of Burgundy with the Hapsburgs. The son of Mary and Maximilian, Charles V, was born in the Belgian city of Ghent and through his own marriage to Jeanne of Castile, became leader of the Spanish Empire in 1516.

Embittered by what they considered to be the discriminatory policies of Philip II, Charles's son, certain northern provinces split away from Spanish domination and formed the Netherlands. Meanwhile, the predominately Catholic population in the Belgian area did not join with the northern independence movement and thus remained under Spanish domination.

With the exception of the episcopal principality of Liège, which at times enjoyed some degree of autonomy, the Belgian region continued to be a pawn of the European powers. With the signing of the Treaty of Utrecht in 1713, the Austrian Hapsburgs replaced the Spaniards as the rulers of Belgium. In 1789, a portion of the Belgian populace rebelled against Austrian domination and declared the independence of the United Belgian States. The independence was short-lived, however, as the Austrians soon reasserted their domination, only to be replaced a few years later by the French.

Following the Emperor Napoleon's final defeat in 1815 at Waterloo, only a few miles from Brussels, Belgium was reunited with the Netherlands. Thus the period of French domination was relatively short, but French constitutional, legal, and administrative codes were to have a dramatic impact on the Belgian governmental and legal processes and are still largely in effect today.

Widespread discontent with the rule of the Protestant King of the Netherlands, William I, finally precipitated a movement for complete Belgian independence in 1830. The revolution began in Brussels in August 1830, and a provisional government was instituted that October. The following year, Belgian notables astutely decided to name Prince Leopold as their monarch. Leopold, aside from his own leadership qualities, was the uncle of Queen Victoria of England and the soon-to-be son-in-law of the king of France. Both France and England later guaranteed the territorial integrity of the new Kingdom of Belgium, a proclamation which dampened any Dutch zeal to reconquer the region. The independence of Belgium was formally recognized by the major European powers in 1839.

In spite of sporadic efforts by the Prussians and the French to annex Belgian territories, the Kingdom of Belgium remained independent and began to prosper industrially. The young nation also began to seek colonies abroad and was particularly successful in gaining a foothold in Africa. The Congo became an official colony of Belgium in 1908 and following World War I, the Belgians were given a mandate over the African regions of Rwanda and Burundi. These colonies proved to be a valuable source of raw materials which helped to keep Belgian industry at full tilt and made various Belgian entrepreneurs extremely wealthy. The major Belgian possession in Africa, the Congo (now Zaire), was finally granted independence in 1960.

Until World War I, Belgium retained a strict policy of neutrality vis-à-vis international and regional affairs. In 1914, the Germans demanded free passage through Belgium in order to wage war with the French and the British. The Belgian government refused this request and in spite of its official neutrality, the Belgian people suffered another territorial incursion. The resistance to the invasion was intense, with 35 percent of the Belgian army being destroyed and tens of thousands of troops and civilians killed. The Germans eventually occupied a large portion of the nation and many of the key battles of World War I were fought on Belgian soil.

Neutrality was cast aside after the war as the Belgian government hastened to form an alliance with the French and the British. Unfortunately, this strategy also proved unsuccessful, as Hitler's troops swarmed over Belgium in May 1940 and forced an unconditional surrender. The bitter occupation continued until September 1944, with the Germans treating Belgium virtually as a colony. Thousands of Belgian workers were transported to Germany during the war to perform forced labor and by war's end, 70,000 of Belgium's 7,000,000 people had been killed.

In an effort to achieve a modicum of security in the post–World War II era, the Belgians joined with their Dutch and Luxembourgeois neighbors in pushing for economic unity and military cooperation. Belgium was a founding member of NATO, the EEC, and several other regional and international organizations. Several of Belgium's leading statesmen, from Paul-Henri Spaak to Leo Tindemans, have actively pursued greater international cooperation and more extensive European integration. Spaak was the first president of the United Nations General Assembly, president of the Organization of European Economic Cooperation and the Consultative Assembly of the Council of Europe, and secretary-general of NATO. Tindemans was the author of a much-publicized report which called for greater supranational authority to be transferred to European institutions such as the EEC Commission and the

European Parliament. Not too surprisingly, Brussels is currently the home of many of the European institutions as well as the European headquarters for many of the world's major multinational corporations. Several of the other European organizations are located nearby in neighboring Luxembourg.

Luxembourg

The Grand Duchy of Luxembourg has a population of 358,000, far smaller than many European cities and comparable to that of Alaska, America's least populated state. Its population density of 132 per square kilometer is far less than that of the Netherlands and Belgium and is comparable to the density of the state of New York.

This ministate nestled between Belgium, France, and Germany first emerged as a distinct entity in the tenth century as a fiefdom within the German Empire. In 1308, Henry, Count of Luxembourg, ascended to the German throne and eventually became Holy Roman Emperor. Henry's descendants upgraded Luxembourg from the status of a province to a duchy, but the small region later suffered the fate of its Dutch and Belgian neighbors by falling under the control of the Burgundians and then the Hapsburgs.

Both Belgium and Luxembourg remained under the control of the Spanish branch of the Hapsburgs even after the Netherlands had achieved its independence. The Austrians took control of the area in 1713 and were later replaced by the French, who governed the Luxembourg region at the turn of the nineteenth century. Finally in 1815, the Congress of Vienna incorporated Luxembourg into the new Kingdom of the Netherlands.

Luxembourg later joined with Belgium in breaking away from the Netherlands in 1830. The French-speaking area of Luxembourg was then incorporated into the Kingdom of Belgium, whereas the German-speaking region became known as the Grand Duchy of Luxembourg, with King William I of the Netherlands becoming the Grand Duke. Luxembourg eventually joined the German Confederation, but with dissolution of the confederation in 1866, the Grand Duchy became an independent state. The royal family of the Netherlands continued to formally preside over the country until control was transferred to the house of Nassau-Weilburg, a family line closely related to the Dutch royalty. The Nassau royal family continues to preside over the Luxembourgeois today.

The independence of Luxembourg was enhanced when the major European powers signed the Treaty of London of 1867, which guaranteed Luxembourg's existence as a neutral state and possibly thwarted the ambitions of Napoleon III to absorb the tiny state into France. But sharing the same fate as its neighbors, Belgium and the Netherlands, Luxembourg continued to suffer frequent invasions and onerous occupations. This unwelcome trend was carried forth into the present century, when in spite of its declaration of strict neutrality, the country was invaded by the Germans in both World War I and

World War II. Following its liberation from German occupation in September 1944, Luxembourg abandoned its traditional position of neutrality and joined the same regional and international organizations as the Netherlands and Belgium.

Luxembourg's current influence in the Western European arena certainly belies its small size. For example, Luxembourg was able to delay the formation of the European Economic Community until it received what it considered to be appropriate compensation for the loss of the High Authority of the Coal and Steel Community, a supranational organization which predated the establishment of the EEC. In addition, Luxembourg was originally given a disproportionate number of seats in the European Parliament and is the home of the European Community's Court of Justice and Office of Statistics, and the Secretariat of the European Parliament. Furthermore, Gaston Thorn, a former Luxembourg prime minister, has served as president of the United Nations General Assembly and of the European Commission. Top Luxembourg officials have frequently visited the United States, and in June 1975, Grand Duke Jean and Gaston Thorn spent a week in the Soviet Union as the guests of Kremlin officials. Despite its lilliputian dimensions, Luxembourg perhaps best typifies the resolve shared by many Western Europeans who favor the creation of some form of a United States of Europe and a large European voice in world affairs.

Political Culture and Socialization

The Netherlands

Dutch society is socially compartmentalized, yet politically accommodating. Perhaps this apparent paradox can best be illustrated by briefly explaining the political party configuration in the mid-1970s. Keep in mind, of course, that the United States, with a population fifteen times as great as the Netherlands', has traditionally had a two-party "catch-all" system, with the Democrats and the Republicans divvying up almost all of the seats in Congress as well as vying for the coveted White House oval office. In contrast, fourteen distinct political parties were seated in the Dutch parliament in 1976, an indication of the great social and ideological divergencies in Dutch society. Moreover, five separate parties had to join together before a governing coalition could be formed. Nonetheless, the coalition proved fairly stable and significant legislation was passed by this montage of parties in the parliament. Consequently, political stability and vitality remain intact in the midst of a societal structure which is highly compartmentalized.

Dutch children are raised in a system characterized by *verzuiling* ("columnization"). The three traditional pillars of Dutch society have been the Roman Catholic, Protestant, and secular social groupings. Each group has its own distinct political party (or parties), schools, labor unions, mass media facilities, and employer organizations. It is entirely conceivable for a person to receive an education from kindergarten through the doctorate, marry, and then work and fraternize almost totally within his own clearly delineated social group sphere. Indeed, the separate subculture communities have spawned their own social and political institutions and there is a minimum of interaction and communication across subcultural boundaries.

Over a century ago, three out of every four students attended public schools in the Netherlands. Today, only a quarter of the primary and secondary students are enrolled in public schools, while the other three-fourths attend Catholic, Protestant, and non-denominational schools. University education is still predominately public, with nine of the twelve Dutch universities being run by the state and over 70 percent of the university students attending public institutions. Nonetheless, the student is still permitted the prerogative of attending either the one Protestant university or one of the two Catholic institutions of higher learning. Even if the student chooses to attend a public university, there will be several social organizations in the university community reflecting his social group leanings.

Illiteracy has been almost completely eradicated in the Netherlands and children are required to attend school full-time until at least the age of fifteen, with two years of part-time schooling beyond fifteen for those who choose to work. Education currently represents the largest chunk of the government budget, consuming about 28 percent of the total allocation.

The issue of educating the young people has been hotly contested in the Netherlands for well over a century. In 1806, the state assumed a virtual monopoly over the education system and very few private schools were allowed to function. State control was relaxed somewhat in 1857, when organized religious groups clamored for greater access to private education. A provision was made for the establishment of more private schools but no state financial support was to be permitted. In 1889, token financial funding from the state was extended to certain private institutions. The compromise which is currently in effect allows the state to set certain minimum standards for all schools, public and private. In return, the state provides funding for both educational sectors and allows the parochial schools to propagate some of the values of their own particular subcultures.

Historically, Dutch Catholics have at times suffered the brunt of discriminatory practices emanating from Dutch officialdom. The war of independence against Catholic Spain caused some harsh feelings toward those Dutch Catholics who were reluctant to break ties with King Philip. In 1573, Catholic services were banned in the Dutch provinces and later on Catholic schools were closed and practicing Catholics were forbidden to run for public office. In particular, the predominately Catholic provinces of Brabant and Limburg, which were not included in the original unification of the Netherlands, were singled out for special discriminatory measures. These two provinces were taken over by the seven northern provinces early in the seventeenth century and were ruled as "dependent territories" with limited privileges for the next 150 years. Part of the rationale for this subservient status was the allegedly questionable loyalty of the Catholic population to the Dutch union.

These discriminatory practices directed toward the Catholic subculture were eventually eradicated, but even as late as 1871, only 6 percent of the top civil servants were Catholics and the first Catholic prime minister was not selected until 1918. In 1900, only 7 percent of Dutch university students were Catholic and only 2 of the 220 Dutch professors in state universities were identified with Catholicism. In the late 1950s, Catholics held 22 percent of the professorships, 27 percent of the university student positions, and 12 percent of the civil service posts. These figures were still somewhat disappointing because Catholics represent 40 percent of the entire work force and 40 percent of the college-age cohort.

Dutch social groups stick fairly much to themselves and even one's perspective of Dutch political development may differ dramatically depending on the subculture's values. For example, Catholic schools still somewhat downplay the absolutist tendencies of Philip (including his role in the Spanish Inquisition) which helped to precipitate the Dutch War of Independence. Protestant schools, on the other hand, still accentuate the negative features of both Philip's conduct and the actions of the Catholic church hierarchy during the independence struggle. Protestants also proclaim the virtues of William of Orange and revere him as a national hero, whereas Catholic views of this staunch Protestant supporter are much more subdued.

In essence, a Dutch person might well live his life quite comfortably within his own social sphere with few forays into the outside world. Census reports from 1960 indicate that 95 percent of married Catholics have Catholic spouses, 90 percent of Dutch Reformed (Protestant) members have Dutch Reformed spouses, and 87 percent of those professing no religious affiliation have spouses similarly unaffiliated.

Instead of actively combatting this social compartmentalization, Dutch state authorities have deemed it wise to tacitly support the policy of *verzuilung*, and not without certain justification. Nationalism and loyalty to the governmental framework and process actually predate the pattern of structural compartmentalization which really came into vogue during the nineteenth century. In addition, the heritage of foreign invasion and domination has poignantly illustrated the need for all groups to work toward political stability and national unity. As a result, the Catholics, Protestants, liberals, socialists, and other groupings have almost always been willing to compromise *within the political sphere*, while continuing to articulate and propagate the basic values of their respective subcultures. Within this framework, the state functions as a neutral arbiter.

Even though these subcultures stress group distinctiveness and even "purity," no single subcultural group has been able to dominate the political process, as is readily indicated by the fact that all post–World War II governments have been coalitions. Consequently, the major subcultures must be willing to accommodate other viewpoints within the political sphere in order to maintain governmental stability. Thus, socialization in Dutch society continues to be segmented, but there is an underlying consensus of opinion which stipulates that the groups, though separated societally, must meet, exchange views, and, if necessary, compromise within the political sphere in order to achieve national harmony. Moreover, the monarchy has helped to facilitate political cooperation by serving as a symbol of national unity for most segments of society, regardless of subcultural affinities.

The Dutch have thus molded a viable and stable political system based on collegial-style governing and proportionality, rather than simple majority policy-making. At the same time, the Dutch have been able to perpetuate a highly pluralistic and compartmentalized social and cultural structure. Neighboring Belgium, on the other hand, is also characterized by a high degree of cultural diversity and compartmentalization, but has not been as successful as the Netherlands in accommodating the demands of the various competing groups within the political sphere.

Belgium

Belgium differs quite dramatically from the Netherlands in that it does not have the religious compartmentalization which characterizes Dutch society. Approximately 8 million of the 9.8 million Belgians are Catholics, with the Protestant-Evangelical, Anglican, Jewish, and Islamic faiths all receiving subsidies for their programs but all having relatively small memberships.

On the other hand, the Belgian people have not been nearly as accommodating as the Dutch in the political sphere, leading to the persistent linguistic problems having an overbearing effect at times on both the political culture and the governmental system.

For many years, French-speaking Walloons dominated the Belgian political and social spheres, even though they were numerically inferior to the Dutch-speaking Flemings. The Flemings have continued to outdistance the Walloons in population growth, and today enjoy majorities in the representative governmental institutions. Fifty-six percent of the Belgian population now lives in Flemish-speaking areas, 32 percent in French-speaking Walloon areas, 11 percent in the officially bilingual area of Brussels (even though most of the Bruxellois are, in reality, French-speaking), and 0.6 percent in German-speaking areas nestled along the border with West Germany.

This eventual shift in favor in the Flemings in the representative institutions has greatly worried the French-speaking Walloons, and their frustrations have been further exacerbated by the fact that economically the Flemish areas have noticeably outpaced the Walloon regions in recent years.

The polarization of attitudes between the two major linguistic communities continues almost unabated today, with the opportunity being afforded zealots on each side to fairly well avoid any relations with people from the other linguistic grouping. Parents normally have the option of sending their children to a school which teaches in the language of their choice. In addition, parents may pick either state schools or private schools. Currently, 57 percent of the children attend the predominately Catholic private schools, while the remaining 43 percent go to state institutions. At the university level, students have a choice of four state schools or four private institutions of higher learning. Once again, the linguistic barriers have a profound impact on the choice of universities. Two of the state schools are in Flemish-speaking areas and two in French-speaking provinces. The two major private universities, the Catholic University of Louvain and the Free University of Brussels, have had to establish separate autonomous units for French-speaking and Flemish-speaking students. The Louvain University attempted to set up a separate French-language section in Flemish territory, but this effort precipitated intense rioting in 1968 and eventually led to the downfall of the government. As a result of the bitter protests from segments of the Flemish community, the French-language section of the university was transferred to a Walloon area.

The state controls radio and television networks in Belgium, but separate programs are beamed to the Flemish and Walloon provinces. In addition, each linguistic group has its own newspapers, periodicals, social groups, and political parties. The problem of establishing any sort of meaningful dialogue between the groups has been further complicated by the strong emphasis on individualism and the inherent distrust of centralized authority. Perhaps because the centralized governmental apparatus was for so many years dominated by outside powers, the Belgian people have strongly stressed local and regional rights and values. As is the case in neighboring France, representatives to the Belgian Parliament may simultaneously hold local positions, such as memberships on municipal or regional councils. As a result, the parliamentary deputy is viewed more as a protector of local rights than as a representative of the national government, a trait which occasionally introduces a strong element of parochialism at the expense of national consensus-building. In addition, the governor or prefect of each province is viewed by the Belgian populace as primarily a defender of regional rights rather than as a representative of the central government. It is even a common practice for the local people to attempt to avoid paying taxes to the central government.

Consequently, even though Belgium has a modified unitary governmental system, parochialism remains a prevalent trend in the country, a parochialism essentially delineated along linguistic lines. The family, schools, and even the mass media act as socializing agents which may well entrench linguistic differences rather than work toward ameliorating the problem. In addition, the problems have been carried over into the political arena, with certain political parties representing the exclusive interests of a specific linguistic group. Voting is compulsory in Belgium and a significant portion of both linguistic communities cast their ballots in line with their own parochial tendencies. In essence, the Belgian political culture is permeated even today by the pervasive linguistic differences, and the governmental system has in turn been prone to institutionalize many of these differences. Ironically, a nation which stands at the forefront of European integration efforts and serves as the headquarters for more than one hundred international agencies and organizations continues to face severe problems in molding its own population into a national community. In contrast, little Luxembourg has three official languages, but has thus far avoided the linguistic-related problems associated with Belgium.

Luxembourg

The Luxembourg people are among the best educated in Europe and enjoy one of the highest per capita income levels on the continent. The Luxembourgeois can also take some comfort in having virtual cradle to grave security with liberal health and accident insurance coverage, unemployment benefits, and old-age pensions.

The vast majority of the Luxembourgeois speak Letzeburgesch, a Germanic language. The tiny duchy also has two other official languages, French and German. French is the language of state administration and the secondary school system, but it is not uncommon to find Luxembourg newspapers printing articles in all three languages on the same page. Yet even with this mixture of three languages, the Luxembourgeois have normally mastered all three tongues and have not experienced the problems faced by the Belgians. German is initially taught in the school system, at the primary level, and French is gradually added to the course curriculum as the student progresses, eventually becoming the dominant language of instruction at the secondary level. In this way, the Luxembourgeois are versatile in these two major languages as well as conversant in the Letzeburgesch dialect.

The various competing groups in Luxembourg society have had little difficulty in reaching a consensus in the political sphere. Part of this facility for political accommodation is attributable to the rather homogenous nature of this small, predominately Catholic populace of 350,000. In addition, the desire to survive as a distinct nation is keenly ingrained in the Luxembourgeois, who have experienced great adversity caused by foreign interference. Moreover, the fact that Luxembourg has usually had a miniscule unemployment rate has contributed to the willingness of most elements in society to attain a political consensus. The major problem in this sphere has been Luxembourg's need to import more than 80,000 foreign workers in order to keep the steel and iron industries going. These thousands of foreigners represent almost one-quarter of the work force, a situation which has precipitated occasional xenophobic outbursts on the part of certain native-born Luxembourgeois.

Internal Cleavages, Political Competition, and Citizen Participation

The Netherlands

CLEAVAGES

The traditional divisions among Catholic, Protestant, and secularist elements in Dutch society are reflected quite strongly in the political arena. With the addition of class-related and narrow interest group movements, the present Dutch party system has been transformed into a veritable kaleidoscope of political tendencies. As was mentioned previously, no less than fourteen parties were represented in the 1976 Dutch parliament and five of these were participating in the coalition government of then Prime Minister Joop den Uyl.

Theoretically, the political parties are not directly linked to the preparation of electoral candidate lists, but the lists are, nevertheless, closely identified with a particular party movement. Each party has an electoral committee which recommends the names of people to be placed on the candidate list. Consequently, the central party organizations have a dominant say in the rank ordering of candidates for election, an important factor in determining who will be elected to parliament. These candidate lists are rather easy to submit, needing only twenty-five signatures of eligible voters and an accompanying deposit, which is held by the Dutch Treasury. This deposit is returned only if the list receives at least 75 percent of the "quota," an electoral computation which will be explained shortly. The deposit provision is designed to deter frivolous groups from competing in the electoral system by attaching a penalty if a certain number of votes are not received.

The entire nation is considered as one gigantic constituency area, although separate electoral lists may be submitted in any of the eighteen designated electoral districts. Consequently, major parties will often emphasize the names of candidates who are popular in a given electoral district in the hopes of attracting additional votes for the overall candidate list.

There are 150 seats at stake in elections to the Second Chamber of the States-General, the most important legislative body in the nation. Deputies are elected for four-year terms, and elections are normally held in May of the fourth year, unless the monarch formally dissolves the Second Chamber prematurely, an action which rarely occurs in the Netherlands. In the United States candidates are elected to Congress in single-member districts, with the one candidate winning the most votes in the district being elected. In contrast, the Dutch employ a proportional representation system which has been in effect since 1917 and which partially explains why so many Dutch governments have been coalitions. In fact, all of the post–World War II governments have consisted of more than one political party, a situation almost unheard of in the United States.

The Dutch proportional representation system involves dividing the total number of votes by the 150 seats at stake in the Second Chamber. The figure derived from this equation is called the "quota." For example, in 1972, 7,394,045 votes were cast. By dividing this number by 150, a quota of 49,293 is derived. The total number of votes received by a party nationally is then divided by the quota to determine the number of seats to be allotted to that party in the Second Chamber. On the other hand, if a party in 1972 did not receive 36,970 votes, which represents 75 percent of the quota, its electoral deposit was automatically forfeited.

Elections are supervised by the Electoral Council, which renders a final verdict on all electoral disputes. Dutch campaigns last little more than forty days, far short of the many months involved in American electioneering. During this period, parties are allocated time on state-run television and radio in order to explain their positions, and party-linked newspapers and periodicals are also used to disseminate voting information to the public.

Until 1970, voting was compulsory in the Netherlands, but currently anyone eighteen years or older can exercise the option of casting a ballot or abstaining. Polling booths are open from 8:00 a.m. until 7:00 p.m. on election day, with the voters casting secret ballots for individual candidates, not parties. Nonetheless, each candidate is identified with a party and a vote will be added to the party's national tally. Once the polling booths close, the ballots are sent along to the central polling station, where votes are tabulated for individual candidates and parties. The final results are then transmitted to the Electoral Council. Even after mandatory voting was eliminated, the percentage of Dutch adults casting valid ballots was 82.9 percent in 1972, 86.5 percent in 1977, 86.1 percent in 1981, and 80.6 percent in 1982. In the United States, the turnout of eligible voters was 53.3 percent in the 1976 presidential election and 53.9 percent in 1980.

POLITICAL COMPETITION AND CITIZEN PARTICIPATION

The granddaddy of Dutch political parties is the Calvinistic Anti-Revolutionary Party (ARP), a partner in the CDA movement. When a liberal-dominated cabinet decreed in 1878 that parents sending children to parochial schools would have to pay taxes for public schools as well as pay the fees for private education, irate Catholics and Protestants denounced the decision. Three hundred thousand people out of a total population of four million signed a petition demanding a change in the government's policy. As a result of this crisis, the ARP was formed. Thirty years later, another Protestant party, the Christian Historical Union (CHU), was created as an offshoot of the ARP. Members of the CHU come mainly from among conservatives in the Netherlands' largest Protestant group, the Dutch Reformed church. A smaller Protestant political movement, the Calvinist-linked Political Reformed Party (SGP), has also garnered a few seats in recent elections.

In 1976, the Anti-Revolutionary Party, Christian Historical Union, and Catholic People's Party joined together to form the Christian Democratic Appeal (CDA), a political movement which has enjoyed a major influence over the governmental decision-making process in the Netherlands. The CDA joined with the Liberal Party to form a center-right coalition government in 1977 and, following the parliamentary elections of 1981, the CDA became the senior coalition partner in a center-left government. Another center-right coalition spearheaded by the CDA was formed after the September 1982 general elections. The CDA is basically middle-of-the-road in its political orientation and favors expanding the private economic sector while at the same time limiting the growth of the Netherlands' extensive social welfare system. Most of the CDA leadership also strongly favors the Netherlands' continued participation in NATO, although there is substantial disagreement concerning the deployment of missiles with nuclear warheads on Dutch soil.

Roman Catholics now form the single largest church group in the Netherlands and are primarily represented by the Catholic People's Party (KVP), which was established in 1926. The KVP's close identification with Dutch Catholics, as well as its rather moderate political stances, have made it an almost indispensable member of government coalitions. The KVP, in fact, has participated in every government coalition since the end of World War II. Its electoral strength has waned somewhat in recent years, perhaps a harbinger of decreasing religious-based electoral support and increasing nonreligious ideological leanings. Nonetheless, the KVP remains a pivotal partner in the CDA movement. A more extremist Catholic-oriented movement, the Radical Political Party (PPR), broke off from the KVP in 1968 and has controlled a few seats in recent parliaments.

The People's Party for Freedom and Democracy (VVD) is the traditional liberal party of the Netherlands and draws most of its support from middle- and upper-income groups, moderate secularists, and certain sectors of the civil service. This party generally supports the perpetuation of free enterprise and has been critical at times of Dutch welfare legislation. It agreed to form a coalition government with the CDA in 1982.

The Labor Party (PVDA) is the main socialist movement and had the second largest parliamentary delegation following the elections of 1982, but was unsuccessful in its efforts to form a new government. This party has been critical of the compartmentalization of Dutch social life and has spearheaded efforts to pass welfare-related legislation. In recent years, a more militant wing of the party has asserted greater influence over party affairs, questioning the wisdom of the Netherlands remaining in NATO and advocating greater nationalization in the economic sphere. The Pacifist-Socialist Party (PSP) split off from the Labor Party in 1957 and has generally been more extremist than the parent movement. Another splinter party, the Democratic Socialists 1970

TABLE 4.1

The Major Dutch Political Parties

CDA	Christian Democratic Appeal (coalition of KVP, ARP, and CHU formed in December 1976)
KVP	Catholic People's Party
ARP	Anti-Revolutionary Party
CHU	Christian Historical Union
PVDA	Labor Party
VVD	People's Party for Freedom and Democracy
PPR	Radical Political Party
CPN	Netherlands Communist Party
D '66	Democrats 1966
DS '70	Democratic Socialists 1970
SGP	Political Reformed Party
BP	Farmers' Party
GPV	National Reformed Political Association
PSP	Pacifist-Socialist Party
RPF	Reformed Political Federation

(DS '70), garnered one seat in the Second Chamber in 1977 but none in the 1982 parliament. It is composed of moderate socialists who were alarmed by the growing militancy in the PVDA and were thus prompted to establish a separate movement.

The Communist Party of the Netherlands (CPN) held three Second Chamber seats in 1982, drawing most of its support from industrial workers and Amsterdam dockworkers. With the decreasing tensions between East and West in the era of detente, the Dutch Communists had been able to achieve modest gains in the early 1970s, increasing their share of the vote from 3.6 percent in 1967 to 4.5 percent in 1972. Moreover, the CPN has followed the trend of several other Western European communist movements in recent years by declaring its independence from the Communist Party of the Soviet Union. However, in the 1982 parliamentary elections, the CPN's percentage of the overall electoral vote was only 1.8 percent.

Certain intellectual circles banded together in 1966 to form the leftist-oriented Democrats '66 (D '66) movement, which currently advocates greater popular control over cabinet appointments and more government concern toward environmental and consumer issues. The movement's development has been sporadic at best, winning 11 parliamentary seats in 1971, falling to 6 in 1972, and rebounding to 8 in 1977. In 1981, it captured an all-time high of 17 seats and became a partner in the new government coalition, but then suffered a major setback in 1982, winning only 6 seats in parliament.

In addition to the trend in recent years toward a slight decrease in religious party voting, especially among younger people, there also seemed to be developing in the 1960s and early 1970s a pattern of ever greater party diversity. Traditionally, the five major parties in the Netherlands have been the Labor,

Catholic People's, Liberal, Anti-Revolutionary, and Christian Historical Union movements. In 1959, these five parties accounted for 142 of the 150 seats in the major chamber of the parliament. In ensuing elections, the total number of seats garnered by the five parties was 135 (1963), 123 (1967), 113 (1971), and 113 (1972). Moreover, the aggregate voting percentage of the five major parties fell from 91.5 percent in 1956 to 63.1 percent in 1972. Apparently, a growing number of Dutch voters became disenchanted with the performance of the major parties and thus sought out alternatives. For example, only eight parties gained parliamentary representation in 1959, as compared to fourteen in 1972.

However, the 1977, 1981, and 1982 parliamentary contests seem to indicate that Dutch voters are once again slowly turning away from the smaller splinter groups in favor of the larger national parties. This tendency has most assuredly been helped along by the decision of the Catholic People's Party, Anti-Revolutionary Party, and the Christian Historical Union to join together to form an electoral alliance. Thus, in 1977 eleven party movements were represented in parliament, nine in 1981, and twelve in 1982, with only four parties having more than six seats following the 1982 elections. Some of the smaller political movements, such as the Pacifist-Socialist Party, the Communist Party, the Farmers' Party, and Democratic Socialists 1970, have done very poorly in terms of garnering seats in parliament.

Prior to the 1977 parliamentary elections, the Dutch did not seem to be distressed by the large number of parties which had been able to surpass the quota and gain at least one seat in the Second Chamber. This seemingly quiescent attitude was at least partially attributable to the fact that the governmental system had generally been quite stable in spite of the proliferation of party movements. With few exceptions, the parliament had remained in session for the full four years and government coalitions had been able to pass significant legislative packages. This situation differs dramatically from the French Third and Fourth Republics and the German Weimar Republic, which all suffered from widespread governmental stagnation or *immobilisme* because of the proliferation of political parties and the inability of coalitions to cooperate for long periods of time.

However, following the 1977 elections, the Netherlands was shaken by the longest political deadlock in Dutch parliamentary history. For seven long months, no party or group of parties was able to step forward and form a new government, and the impasse was not broken until the liberals agreed to join with the confessional parties to put together a rather shaky coalition under the leadership of Andreas van Agt. In 1981, a less serious but nonetheless worrisome stalemate also occurred before Andries van Agt and his CDA supporters were able to put together a new coalition government. This coalition lasted little more than a year, and new elections were called in 1982. Because of these unusually long periods of political uncertainty and governmental immo-

TABLE 4.2

Party Representation in the Dutch Second Chamber

| | May 1981 | | September 1982 | |
	% Vote	Seats	% Vote	Seats
PVDA	28.3	44	30.4	47
CDA*	30.8	48	29.3	45
VVD	17.3	26	23.1	36
PPR	1.7	3	1.6	2
CPN	2.1	3	1.8	3
D '66	11.1	17	4.3	6
DS '70	0.6	0	0.4	0
SGP	2.0	3	1.9	3
BP	0.2	0	—	—
GPV	0.8	1	0.8	1
PSP	2.1	3	2.3	3
RPF	1.2	2	1.5	2
Others	1.5	0	2.6	2

*The KVP, ARP, and CHU formed the Christian Democratic Appeal (CDA) electoral alliance in December 1976.

bility, Dutch voters may indeed have second thoughts in the future about selecting such a large smorgasbord of diverse political movements to represent their interests at the national level.

Nevertheless, Dutch society remains noticeably compartmentalized, with religious and certain secular groups practicing a mild form of social apartheid. For example, the Catholic hierarchy condemned liberal, socialist, and communist practices in 1954 and forbade Catholics to join left-wing trade unions or read left-wing publications on penalty of exclusion from the sacrament. In 1958, the Catholic bishops decreed that only architects, contractors, and laborers allied with Catholic trade and social organizations would be permitted to work on Church-sponsored building projects. Certain Protestant groups have also voiced a deep aversion toward left-wing movements.

On the other hand, the hostilities between religious and secular groups have subsided somewhat in recent years, with ecumenism helping to dissipate some of the barriers between Protestants and Catholics. Moreover, the major social groups have almost invariably been willing to sit down in the political arena and reach some form of political accommodation. For example, the Labor Party was in coalition in 1976 with the Catholic People's Party, the Protestant-linked Anti-Revolutionary Party, the Radical Political Party, and the Democrats '66 movement, representing a mosaic of diverse political and ideological persuasions.

There has also been a fairly stable consensus in the Netherlands concerning the basic structure of the socioeconomic system as well as foreign policy priorities. And even though religious cleavages do exist, they are not divided along class lines, a situation which helps to mitigate the intensity of differences among the religious and class-related secular movements. In other words, both Catholics and Protestants draw support from most income and occupational groups and are not identified closely with any one distinct class orientation, a characteristic which is not found among their religious counterparts in Northern Ireland.

The Dutch have also been able to avoid serious linguistic and racial turmoil. Unlike their Belgian neighbors, the Dutch are linguistically homogeneous, speaking the Dutch language, which has Germanic origins. In addition, the Netherlands has been able to absorb and fairly well assimilate immigrant groups from former Dutch colonies. In contrast, a portion of the British populace has occasionally experienced great difficulty in accepting so-called coloureds from former British colonial possessions. Until 1968, 14,000 of a total 202,000 immigrants in the Netherlands were Indonesian, with the remainder being primarily of European stock. With the granting of independence to the nation of Suriname in late 1975, the Dutch have now opened the door to any residents of Suriname who desire to move to the Netherlands. Thus far, there have been few problems in absorbing these South American residents into the Dutch socioeconomic structure.

Unlike federal systems which divide governmental authority among a national government and regional governments (such as the United States and West Germany) or primarily among regional governments (such as Switzerland), the Netherlands is a unitary system which concentrates authority in the central government at The Hague. This unitary system may be traced back to the French occupation period of the late eighteenth and early nineteenth centuries, as well as the post-Napoleonic era, when the Congress of Vienna reinstituted a monarchy in the Netherlands with significant centralized authority.

Yet in spite of the unitary nature of the governmental structure, the Dutch remain profoundly suspicious of concentrating too much authority in the hands of one individual or one group. Consequently, there is a definite balance of executive and legislative authority and implicit checks have been built into the system to guarantee against the blatant abuse of political power.

Keeping in mind this distrust of centralized authority and the pluralistic nature of Dutch society, one might now better understand why the Dutch tolerate a multiparty system and perhaps even encourage the formation of coalition governments. With the major exception of the 1977 stalemate, the political system has remained stable even with governing coalitions, and the essence of coalition-making is to exact concessions and make sure no individual or group completely dominates. Moreover, even though *verzuiling* or compartmentalization remains in vogue in the social sphere, the major religious and secular groups have agreed to interact and compromise in the political arena to ensure national harmony and to guarantee that no social or interest group becomes all-powerful in the governmental sector. As a result of this spirit of political accommodation, the Dutch multiparty system, which exists within a framework of major societal cleavages, has been one of the most stable and productive party systems in the world, an enviable achievement which has largely escaped its Belgian counterpart. However, because of the recent governmental crises in the late 1970s and early 1980s, the Dutch may be persuaded in the future to pare down the number of parties represented in parliament to a dozen or even fewer.

Belgium

CLEAVAGES

Several nations in the world have more than one official language, including Switzerland, Canada, and Belgium. Yet perhaps to a greater extent than in any other country, multilingualism in Belgium has caused deep fissures in the societal framework. Cleavages related to French-speaking and Flemish-speaking antagonisms have made consensus and accommodation within the political sphere much more difficult to achieve in Belgium than, for example, in the neighboring Netherlands.

In Switzerland, the language for the canton must be used as the principal language in the schools of that community, based on the premise that the use of a conflicting language might jeopardize both communal and national harmony. The Belgian government has recently instituted changes which will bring a great deal of language conformity to certain regions, but traditionally, Belgian parents have had the right to educate their children in the language of their choice, a situation which enhances individual prerogatives but at the same time exacerbates efforts to overcome linguistic differences. The government has attempted to ameliorate the situation by making it mandatory for each side to learn the other's tongue as a second language, but this program has only been mildly successful.

In essence, the more militant elements in both linguistic communities view relations between the two sides in zero-sum terms. In other words, they are constantly involved in a head-to-head poker game in which there will always be one winner and one loser, and anything which is perceived as benefitting one side will be viewed as a loss by the other side. Thus it is very difficult for some extremists to conceive of anything that could be done by the government for the betterment of *both* linguistic communities, other than complete separation or, at the least, a devolution plan which would lead to separate federations.

The language difficulties go back generations. At the time of Belgian independence in 1830, French was the language of the educated class and eventually became the language of the state administration, even though Flemish-speaking people were in the majority. Even as late as World War I, the vast majority of military officers were French-speaking, forcing most Flemish soldiers to take their orders in French. This situation was not rectified until the 1930s, when separate Flemish- and French-speaking military units were formed. During this same period, Flemish finally became the official language of state administration in Flanders.

Thus for many years, the Flemish people considered themselves treated as second-class citizens, with some degree of justification. Presently, however, the Walloons are worried about their own fate. The Flemish population has continued to increase in relation to the Walloons, with over six million Flemish people living in Belgium compared to four million Walloons. In addition, Wallonia was far more industrialized than the Flemish area at the turn of the twentieth century, mainly because of its coal, steel, and textile industries. In recent decades, however, these key industries have declined somewhat in Wallonia, while many multinational enterprises have decided to set up shop in Flanders. During the 1960s, the GNP grew an average of 8.4 percent annually in Flanders and only 6.1 percent in Wallonia. In 1978, the per capita income was 18 percent higher in Flanders than in Wallonia. Various sectors of the French-speaking community now complain that they have not been fairly dealt with in terms of state investment and spending, attributing this imbalance to the fact that they are outnumbered by the Flemings in Parliament.

The Belgian government has introduced several proposals in recent years to attempt to defuse the volatile language problem. With few exceptions, however, the governmental initiatives have been in the direction of further segregating the communities rather than in implementing a major program to better integrate the groups into a national society. In the 1960s, Brussels was officially proclaimed bilingual in the hopes of establishing a kind of buffer zone between the Flemish region in the north and the Walloon area in the south. Some Walloons have complained that this artificial creation discriminates against them because Brussels and its suburbs are 80 percent French-speaking. On the other hand, certain Flemings have complained that Brussels remains a French-speaking enclave and not enough has been done to achieve de facto bilingualism in the capital area.

Another traditional cleavage, which has seemingly lost momentum in the past decade, is the religious-secular argument. During the nineteenth century, Belgian liberals pushed for more expansive individual rights, greater secularization of education, and the separation of church and state. In particular, this dispute carried over into the twentieth century in the form of the merits or demerits of Catholic-based parochial education. Finally in 1958, the major political parties agreed to support the Schools Pact, a document which provided state financial support for both public and private schools and formulated certain guidelines which had to be satisfied by the parochial schools in order to qualify for state financial assistance. Currently, a majority of schoolchildren attend private institutions.

The problems of the working class were not given much attention by Parliament until after World War I. At this time, the Belgian government finally recognized the right of workers to join unions and to vote. The socialist movement, which has traditionally been identified with the working class, remains strong in Belgium and the communists have also received a fair share of votes in certain industrial areas. On the other hand, class-related problems have not been as serious in Belgium as in certain other Western European nations, partially because the linguistic differences have not been closely identified with underlying class imperatives.

POLITICAL COMPETITION AND CITIZEN PARTICIPATION

The Belgian political party system noticeably reflects the regional and ideological cleavages in the nation. For example, strictly linguistic-based political movements have achieved representation in Parliament, and even those movements which claim to be national parties have had to make concessions to the two linguistic communities. Until recently, the Belgian Socialist Party was a national movement which conceded that language divisions were important by stipulating that the president and vice-president of the party had to be from different language groups, that the executive bureau of the party had to be divided along linguistic lines, and that the Walloon and Flemish sectors of the party reserved the privilege, under certain circumstances, to meet in separate conferences. In addition, the nominees for political office were almost invariably selected by the party organizations in the separate language communities. In spite of these concessions to the two major language groups, the Socialist Party still claimed to be a federation of French- and Flemish-speaking units which spoke for the working class throughout Belgium. Moreover, the party insisted that there was an indivisibility of class interests, regardless of what language community was involved. However, even this movement finally succumbed to the siren song of linguistic separatism when in October 1978, the French-speaking federation voted to go its own way and form the entirely autonomous francophone Socialist Party Conference.

The Socialist Party, Social Christian Party, and the Party of Liberty and Progress have traditionally been the dominant political movements in Belgium and usually control at least three-quarters of the seats in Parliament. The Social Christian Party is somewhat comparable to the Christian Democratic movements in neighboring Northern European countries and generally supports moderate free enterprise and social welfare programs. It consists of autonomous organizations in each linguistic region which support certain common policies, while agreeing to disagree on language priorities. The National Committee of the party fulfills the role of a collective executive and fairly evenly represents both linguistic groups, even though most successful party candidates come from the Flemish region. The president of the party supervises the activities of the National Committee and often emerges as the leader of the government when the Social Christian Party participates in a governing coalition, which has been frequently.

The Party of Liberty and Progress is an alliance of distinct political movements in Flanders, Wallonia, and Brussels. It is a fairly traditional liberal party movement which still supports a quasi-laissez-faire economic system and remains suspicious of religious influence on state activities. In 1965, francophone members from the Wallonia and Brussels districts actually engaged in a virulent anti-Flemish campaign, hoping in the process to stir up passions and thus attract greater electoral support from the Catholic middle class in the south. This factionalism within the movement has recently subsided somewhat but each side continues to reflect many of the values of its linguistic community.

Strictly linguistic-based parties also exist within the Belgian party network. The *Volksunie* (People's Union) movement runs candidates exclusively in Flanders and is a strong supporter of Flemish nationalist issues. The *Rassemblement Wallon* is the major regional party in the French-speaking region and has recently joined forces with the *Front Démocratique des Francophones* (French-Speaking Front) in the Brussels area. Above all, these political movements attempt to enhance the position of the francophone population of Belgium.

Electoral campaigns are relatively short in Belgium, lasting a maximum of forty days for parliamentary elections. Voting is compulsory, thus everyone over the age of eighteen is required to cast a ballot in one of the thirty electoral districts into which Belgium is divided, although the voter is permitted to submit a blank or spoiled ballot as a means of protest against the compulsory voting system or the government system in general. In the 1981 elections, 7.4 percent of the ballots were blank or otherwise invalid. Women were not allowed to vote in parliamentary elections until 1949, but now are entitled to full voting rights. Belgium has essentially adopted a proportional representation system, thus each party submits a list of candidates in each electoral district and the key to winning a parliamentary seat is how far up the list a candidate's name appears. For example, the party list, which must first be nominated by from two hundred to five hundred voters before it will appear on the electoral district ballot, will usually have the same number of candidates as parliamentary seats available in that district. If under the proportional representation system the party qualifies for three seats, then the first three names appearing on the party's list will be elected. Consequently, the closer a candidate is to the top of the list, the better his chances of being elected.

The voter may choose either to cast his ballot for a party list or cast preferential votes for specific candidates. This second tactic permits the voter to voice his support for a candidate who may be well down the party list and

TABLE 4.3

Party Representation in Belgium's
Chamber of Representatives

Party	December 1978		November 1981	
	% Vote	Seats	% Vote	Seats
Social Christian Party	36.3	82	26.4	61
Belgian Socialist Party*	25.4	58	25.1	61
Liberty and Progress Party	16.3	37	21.5	52
People's Union	7.0	14	9.8	20
French-Speaking Front, Rassemblement Wallon, and allies	7.1	15	4.2	8
Communist Party and allies	3.2	4	3.3	2
Ecologist Movement	0.8	0	4.8	4
Others	3.9	2	4.9	4

*The Belgian Socialist Party split into independent Flemish and Walloon groups prior to the 1978 elections.

thus will not be elected unless enough people state a specific preference for him. Through the proportional representation system, the Belgian electorate chooses the entire membership of the Chamber of Representatives and 60 percent of the Senate seats. The remaining seats in the Senate are filled partly by the Provincial Councils and partly by cooptation (which means those who have already been elected will decide among themselves who will be selected for the unfilled vacancies).

The Belgian parties are actually a synthesis of regional views. On the whole, there is very little respect for politicians per se in Belgium and most citizens place their greatest trust in local authorities as the defenders of their rights. The genesis of this viewpoint may be traced to the many centuries when Belgium was under foreign domination, during which time foreigners set national priorities while at the same time allowing local officials some latitude in running the affairs of the commune. Thus, the local leaders were viewed by the populace as the only ones who understood the needs and aspirations of the Belgian people. This trust of local authorities and a concomitant suspicion of centralized control has persisted through time and has been reinforced by the linguistic antagonisms. Thus the notion of a unitary political system, which is basically a French import dating from the Napoleonic occupation, has not been thoroughly accepted by many in the Belgian populace. In addition, the communes emerged as the center of resistance during the Nazi occupation from 1940 to 1944, a situation which helped to reinforce the local loyalties in the postwar era. Even today, there are over 2,600 communes in Belgium, two-thirds of which have fewer than 2,000 people. Efforts to consolidate some of the communes in order to provide more efficient services and avoid duplication of tasks have thus far been strongly resisted. Consequently, in view of the persistent linguistic cleavages, local loyalties, and widespread antipathy toward centralized authority, governing the relatively small country of Belgium from the capital city of Brussels has not been an easy task.

To alleviate some of the chronic problems associated with linguistic animosities, successive Belgian governments in the 1970s pushed for regional devolution. Under a plan formulated by Leo Tindemans, Flanders, Wallonia, and Brussels would all become semiautonomous administrative regions with directly elected regional parliaments exercising extensive authority in the economic and social policy domains. Moreover, the members of the regional parliaments would also join together and form a revamped Senate at the national parliamentary level. In effect, Belgium would be transformed into a federal system, with the central government continuing to be responsible for foreign and defense policy and other "national" concerns.

Some optimists expressed the hope that the devolution wagon could begin to roll before the 1980s, and the government's regionalization plan was approved in principle by the necessary two-thirds majorities in both chambers of Parliament in March 1978. However, major differences of opinion continue to persist, particularly in terms of the new regional status to be accorded to the Brussels district. The 1978 and 1981 election results were generally indecisive, but it is clear that a majority of the Belgian electorate wants to see some form of devolution implemented in the near future. In essence, the Belgian populace now considers regionalization a partial panacea for the immobility which has plagued the governmental system in recent years.

Luxembourg

The Luxembourg electoral system is somewhat more complicated than Belgium's and ranks as one of the most unusual in Europe. Voting is compulsory and the approximately 200,000 voters are divided among four electoral districts. The parliamentary seats at stake are distributed among the four districts along population lines, with the smallest district having seven seats at stake and the largest twenty-three. Each deputy represents approximately 5,500 people.

Luxembourg political parties are permitted to submit candidate lists in each district equal to the number of seats at stake in that district. As is the case with Belgium and the Netherlands, the tiny duchy has a proportional representation system, but Luxembourg voters are allowed to cast as many votes as seats available in their electoral district (in other words, from seven to twenty-three votes). Further complicating the process is the fact that a citizen may also express a preference for individual candidates on the party list, casting one or even two weighted votes for individuals, even if their names appear on

TABLE 4.4

Party Representation in Luxembourg's
Chamber of Deputies

Party	May 1974		June 1979	
	% Vote	Seats	% Vote	Seats
Christian Social Party	28.0	18	34.5	24
Socialist Party	29.0	17	24.3	14
Democratic Party ("Liberals")	22.1	14	21.3	15
Communist Party	10.4	5	5.8	2
Social Democratic Party	9.1	5	6.0	2
Enrôlés de Force	—	0	4.4	1
Independent Socialists	—	0	2.2	1
Others	1.4	0	1.4	0

different party lists. However, parliamentary representation is ultimately determined by the number of votes garnered by each party.

There are no cataclysmic cleavages in Luxembourg society and the predominant political parties have been able to work together reasonably well in ironing out any problems that have arisen. For example, almost all agree on the virtues of being in the European Community and in NATO. In the post–World War II period, the Christian Social Party has consistently been the top vote-getter and has participated in every government from 1919 through 1974. This party is moderate in its orientation, generally supports free enterprise proposals, and is fairly closely linked to the Catholic church in a nation which is overwhelmingly Catholic.

The Socialist Party was formed at the turn of the century and has emerged in recent years as a major political movement. Furthermore, it has been the most common coalition partner of the Christian Social Party in the post–World War II period. Its support is derived mainly from industrial circles, and in a nation which depends heavily on its iron and steel concerns, any serious problems occurring in the industrial sector may eventually work to the advantage of socialists.

The third major political movement in Luxembourg is the Democratic Party, which has been a pivotal coalition partner in recent governments. This party is liberal and in the past has been known for its anticlericalism and its staunch stand in favor of separation of church and state. Much of its support is derived from the more secular oriented people in the middle class. Following the elections of May 1974, the Democratic Party joined with the Socialist Party to form a coalition led by Prime Minister Gaston Thorn of the Democratic Party. After the 1979 elections, the Democratic Party abandoned the Socialist Party and agreed to form a right-of-center government with the Christian Social Party.

Two other minor political movements are the Social Democratic and Communist Parties, each of which won five seats in 1974. The Communists have remained fairly close to the Soviet movement, and even followed the Kremlin line in denouncing NATO and the EEC and in praising the invasion of Czechoslovakia in 1968. At best, the Communist Party remains on the fringe of the Luxembourg political spectrum, with the three major parties consistently accounting for more than 80 percent of the parliamentary seats. What voting strength the Communists do have is centered in the coal-mining regions and in certain working-class districts of the city of Luxembourg. The Social Democrats, on the other hand, are moderate socialists who made significant gains in the 1974 elections but only reelected two members to parliament in 1979. In the 1979 parliamentary elections, the Independent Socialist movement, which had accused the Socialist Party of compromising socialist principles while in office, managed to elect one representative. Enrôlés de Force, a pressure group claiming compensation from the West German government for the enforced recruitment of 12,000 Luxembourg soldiers into the German army during World War II, also ran candidates and won one parliamentary seat.

Governmental Institutions and the Policy-Making Process

The Netherlands

The Kingdom of the Netherlands is a constitutional monarchy with a unitary system of government. The capital is Amsterdam but the seat of government is The Hague. The Dutch constitution dates from 1814 but has been revised rather substantially over the years. Major revisions were made as recently as 1972, when provisions such as voting age, church-state financial relations, and freedom of education were amended. These constitutional revisions are not made easily, as both chambers of parliament must first pass a bill stating that constitutional changes are necessary. Once this bill is passed and signed by the monarch, both parliamentary chambers are dissolved and new general elections are held to choose members of the powerful Second Chamber. The two new legislative bodies must then pass the proposed constitutional amendments by a two-thirds majority and royal approval must be given before the revisions are formally put into effect.

THE MONARCHY

As is the case with almost all other Western European monarchs, the Dutch royal leader has little substantive political power. Even though the Congress of Vienna established a powerful monarchial leadership in the Netherlands in 1814, it was not long before the monarch's authority began to wane. Parliamentary supremacy was firmly entrenched in 1868, when the monarch was refused the right to select a cabinet against the wishes of a parliamentary majority.

Only members of the House of Orange, which has reigned over the Netherlands for four hundred years with only sporadic interruptions, are eligible to ascend to the throne. Monarchial succession is hereditary but a woman will become leader of the royal family only in the absence of a qualified male heir. In spite of this rule, women have been on the throne throughout the twentieth century, and when Queen Juliana retired in 1980, she was succeeded by her daughter, Beatrix.

The monarch formally chooses the prime minister and the cabinet, but generally heeds the advice of the top political leaders in the country, particularly those who will participate in the coalition government. The monarch initially chooses a "formateur" who will attempt to form a cabinet and who will most likely become the new prime minister if he can piece together a solid coalition. If prospects are dim for forming a new cabinet, then the queen might appoint an "informateur" who will try to bring likely coalition leaders together in order to work out some solution. Once the "informateur" is successful in his endeavors, the "formateur" will be selected. Either way, the queen will abide by the counsel offered by possible coalition leaders rather than going ahead and naming her own preferences.

The monarch may also dissolve the parliament before the end of the four-year term, but this is only done when a coalition disintegrates, no substitute coalition can be formed, and the governing of the nation is jeopardized. In addition, the monarch must sign all legislation passed by parliament, but the royal assent is considered a foregone conclusion.

The monarch's primary role is to act as chief of state and to symbolize Dutch national unity. In essence, the royal family is to be dignified and to remain "above politics." Until recently, the monarch has adroitly fulfilled this function. During World War II, Queen Wilhelmina and her family fled the country and set up a government-in-exile in London. The queen sent messages of encouragement to her people over Radio London and urged them to resist the Nazi occupation forces. After the war, she returned a national hero and was viewed quite favorably by all sectors of society, including the Catholics, even though the leaders of the House of Orange have traditionally been members of the Dutch Reformed Church.

In 1976, however, the integrity of the royal family was seriously shaken, which led to some speculation about the continued usefulness of the monarch as a symbol of national unity. After an extensive investigation, a three-member commission chosen by the prime minister determined in the fall of 1976 that Prince Bernhard, the husband of Queen Juliana, had accepted bribes from the Lockheed Corporation. This revelation reverberated throughout the country and precipitated some outcries for the abolition of the monarchy. Nonetheless, this explosive situation was defused somewhat when Prime Minister Joop den Uyl concluded that Bernhard's conduct was extremely imprudent but decided not to prosecute because of possible repercussions for the queen. The prime minister's decision has apparently received the approbation of most Dutch citizens, particularly after Bernhard resigned from most of his important posts. However, the Socialist Party national congress passed a resolution in 1977 calling for the establishment of a republican form of government, and some fairly vocal sectors of Dutch society continue to advocate an end to the monarchial system.

THE PRIME MINISTER AND THE COUNCIL OF MINISTERS

The prime minister and the cabinet, along with the minister plenipotentiary of the Netherlands Antilles, form the Council of Ministers of the Kingdom of the Netherlands and are responsible for coordinating the activities of the government and approving all government bills which will be submittd to the parliament. The Dutch prime minister probably does not exercise as much discretionary power over the cabinet as his British counterpart, for example, because of the fact that the Dutch government is invariably a coalition and the prime minister must make certain concessions to the other parties in the government. In particular, the cabinet posts must be allocated among the coalition parties in such a manner that all the parties are relatively satisfied with the composition of the government. Moreover, certain issues will be stressed by the prime minister and others played down, depending on the makeup of the government. For example, the coalition government in 1976 was directed by a socialist, but he was obviously not going to get involved in certain touchy religious-related disputes because two of the partners of the socialists in the coalition were the major Catholic and Protestant parties.

Once the cabinet is formed, it is not necessary to go directly to the parliament for a vote of confidence nor is it necessary to submit an initial government program for approval by the parliamentary chambers. Nonetheless, great pressure is on the cabinet to resign at any juncture during its term in office when the parliament rejects a key bill submitted by the government or adds an important amendment which is not supported by the prime minister and his cabinet officers. The resignation of the cabinet is even more clearly sanctioned if the parliament adopts a vote of no confidence, which is tantamount to saying that the legislature no longer supports the cabinet as then constituted. If this occurs, the monarch may attempt to form a new coalition government or, if this fails, may call for new parliamentary elections which must take place no later than forty days after the dissolution of the legislature.

As is the case in Fifth Republic France and certain other Western European nations, a cabinet minister cannot simultaneously hold a seat in the parliament. Aside from the prime minister, the most important cabinet position is that of finance minister. The finance minister functions as a watchdog in the government and can even veto monetary requests from ministers of other departments. In terms of expenditures, the finance minister can openly question the sagacity of certain ministerial actions and may refuse to grant special credits to certain departments. At times, bitter disputes have broken out between the finance minister and other ministers, especially if they are from different parties. When this occurs, the entire cabinet may be forced to intervene and to mediate the dispute.

The cabinet minister is assisted in his departmental duties by a state secretary, who is normally chosen by the minister and must resign if the minister gives up his post. The Council of Ministers normally meets once a week and its proceedings are private except for any information it may choose to relay to the mass media after the session has concluded. Each minister proposes pieces of legislation emanating from his department and the council as a whole decides if the proposal will be sent to the parliament. The Dutch have adopted a system of collective cabinet responsibility, and if a particular minister cannot abide by a decision made in the Council of Ministers, he is expected to resign. In addition, if the parliament attaches an amendment to a piece of legislation over the vociferous objections of the minister who initially sponsored the bill, he may be pressured to step down unless the entire cabinet comes to his aid and makes the issue a matter of governmental confidence. The disputed bill may then be withdrawn altogether, with the sovereign's permission, or it may lead to a vote of no confidence against the government. This scenario will rarely occur, however, because if the coalition is supportive of the measure in the Council of Ministers and if it retains majority support in the Second Chamber, the proposed bill should be passed with little trouble. Potentially controversial issues are normally ferreted out in the council proceedings and thus are not sent to the parliament unless some substantive compromise has been reached in advance among all of the coalition partners.

THE COUNCIL OF STATE

The Council of State functions as an advisory body to the monarch and to the Council of Ministers. The monarch presides over its sessions and its membership is comprised of certain members of the royal family as well as approximately twenty other individuals who represent a broad spectrum of expertise.

Before any bill is submitted to the States-General, the Council of State first examines it to determine both its functionality and its constitutionality. In addition, the council can recommend to the prime minister that legislation be prepared to deal with a certain area of concern. The council also recommends preferable courses of action to the monarch and to the government when decisions regarding administrative appeals must be handed down.

THE PARLIAMENT

The parliament, or States-General, is composed of two legislative bodies, with the Second Chamber clearly ascendant. The 150 members of the Second

Chamber must be at least twenty-five years old and are elected through universal suffrage for four-year terms.

Once the Council of State has approved a proposed bill from the Council of Ministers, it is sent directly to the Second Chamber, which then transmits it to the appropriate standing committee. Debates within the Second Chamber are normally open to the public unless the presiding officer or one-tenth of the deputies decree that the proceedings should take place behind closed doors. The members of the Second Chamber can pass, defeat, or amend bills submitted by the cabinet or they may propose their own pieces of legislation.

If the bill is passed by the Second Chamber, it is sent along to the First Chamber, which can either pass or reject the measure, but cannot amend it. The seventy-five members of this legislative body must be at least twenty-five years old and are selected by the Dutch Provincial Councils for six-year terms, one-half of which are up for renewal every three years. Even though its authority is definitely subordinate to that of the Second Chamber, the First Chamber, with its regional bodies, functions as an important safeguard against any blatant misuse of centralized power. Unless this chamber approves proposed legislation, the bill cannot become law.

Selected members of the States-General also fulfill an important function by representing the Netherlands and their own specific political movements in various international organizations such as the European Parliament, the Benelux Inter-Parliamentary Consulative Council, the North Atlantic Assembly, the Council of Europe, and the Assembly of the Western European Union. In this way, the Dutch parliamentarians, who generally favor greater European integration, are able to contribute to federalist tendencies in Western Europe (see Chapter 7 for an examination of European integration efforts).

THE JUDICIARY

In contrast to its American counterpart, the Dutch judicial system cannot exercise judicial review, which is the power to declare an action of the executive or legislative branches unconstitutional. Consequently, the Dutch courts do not act as a substantial check on centralized power.

The court system consists essentially of sixty-two magistrate courts, nineteen district courts, five courts of appeal, and one Supreme Court, located in The Hague. The approximately six hundred judges are appointed by the monarch on the advice of the political leadership (in the case of the Supreme Court, the monarch makes the appointment from a list prepared by the Second Chamber) and serve for life unless removed by the Supreme Court. These professional judges try civil and criminal cases and there are no jury trials.

The magistrate and district courts have original jurisdiction in a variety of areas, with the appeals courts only exercising original jurisdiction in tax cases. The Supreme Court is divided into several sections, most notably civil, criminal, and tax, with five justices presiding in each section. Unlike the tendency in the United States, the principle of *stare decisis* ("let precedence guide") is not closely followed in the Netherlands, even though lower courts do pay close attention to decisions rendered by the highest court. Sectors of the Supreme Court may also try civil servants, government officials, and members of the parliament under certain circumstances, somewhat akin to the American impeachment process which is carried out by the U.S. Congress.

PROVINCIAL AND LOCAL GOVERNMENT

Because of the unitary nature of the Dutch political system, most power is concentrated at the national level. Nevertheless, the Netherlands is divided into eleven provinces, which have almost identical governmental structures. Citizens of each province are represented by a Provincial Council, which consists of from forty-seven to eighty-three members, depending on the population of the area. Members of these councils are elected through direct universal suffrage under the Dutch proportional representation system. They must be at least twenty-five years old and serve for renewable four-year terms.

The daily activities of the council are carried out by the Provincial Executive, consisting of six members chosen from the ranks of the Provincial Council. This executive organization implements provisional ordinances and may recommend that the central government either initiate certain policies which will help the province or desist from certain actions which are perceived as injurious to the provincial populace.

The central government is represented in each province by the Queen's Commissioner, a position somewhat equivalent to that of prefect in the French system. The commissioner functions as the chairperson of the Provincial Council and the Provincial Executive. The queen's representative is the highest authority in the province and is responsible for guaranteeing that orders from The Hague are faithfully carried out.

At the local level, Municipal Councils are selected by universal suffrage through the proportional representation system and are entitled to convene for up to four years. Once again, the number of members on the Municipal Councils varies, depending on the population of the area. Currently, council sizes range from seven to forty-five members. The council is directed by a burgomaster, or mayor, who is appointed by the central government for a six-year term and who represents the interests of The Hague in each municipality.

The burgomaster is rarely from the city where he presides, but serves as the chairperson of the Municipal Council and as the leader of the Municipal Executive, which consists of from two to six aldermen, depending on the population of the municipality. This executive body implements the decisions of the council and regulates revenues and expenditures. Its activities are subject to close supervision by the provincial authorities and, ultimately, by the central government, especially in the preparation of the municipality's annual budget.

In sharp contrast to federal systems, in the Dutch unitary system the central government located in The Hague is responsible for governmental actions at all levels of Dutch society. The municipal and provincial organizations perform certain policy-making tasks and provide valuable feedback to The Hague in terms of local needs and aspirations. However, The Hague controls the purse strings and has veto power at its disposal if it is unhappy with policies or actions emanating from the localities. In order to exact additional concessions from the central apparatus, the cities formed the Union of Netherlands Municipalities in 1912 for the purpose of articulating their demands in The Hague. This organization has been successful in placing added pressure on central authorities to grant certain concessions to the cities, but overall, the local and provincial authorities remain quite dependent on the goodwill and generosity of the central administration.

Even though the Dutch have a highly centralized structure, there are various safeguards built into the system to make sure no sector completely dominates the policy-making process. Of course, as long as there is agreement among the party leaders comprising the coalition government, and as long as the coalition retains disciplined majority support in both parliamentary chambers, the prime minister can be fairly assured of passing whatever legislation he desires. On the other hand, prime ministerial discretionary power may be difficult to attain. First of all, the cabinet is not composed of people who are exclusively from the prime minister's party, thus the prime minister must be very careful not to propose legislation which might alienate some cabinet ministers and perhaps lead to the demise of the coalition. Second, party discipline in the Netherlands is significantly stronger than in the United States but not as strong as in Great Britain. Consequently, even if the Council of Ministers agrees to support a controversial bill, there is always the danger of party defections in the parliament, a situation which might again precipitate the downfall of the coalition. Third, the political party lineup in the Second Chamber may differ substantially from that in the First Chamber. This may be explained by the fact that Second Chamber members are elected by the general populace, whereas First Chamber members are selected by the Provincial Councils. Consequently, even if the coalition government were assured of sufficient support in the Second Chamber, it could not be certain that the First Chamber would automatically give its approval.

If the issue were of such paramount importance as to necessitate a constitutional amendment, the government would face the strenuous step-by-step process of first convincing the two parliamentary chambers to agree that such drastic changes were indeed necessary, of then asking the monarch to dissolve the parliament and set a date for new elections, and finally of persuading the new parliamentary bodies to enact the proposed constitutional amendment by two-thirds majorities. However, this arduous process should not be construed as making the passage of significant legislation unlikely. On the contrary, landmark passage of significant legislation has been introduced and passed, but mainly because there has been a widespread consensus in Dutch political circles and in Dutch society as a whole that such changes were desirable at that particular time. On the other hand, a prime minister who is convinced of an urgent need to pass a bold legislative package without significant societal support risks the disintegration of his coalition and a poor showing at the ballot box by his party and by those movements closely aligned with his party.

As for overseeing the day-to-day operations of the cabinet in particular and the central apparatus in general, most parliamentary systems, including those in the Netherlands and Belgium, provide certain checks to the legislative body. In effect, the Dutch States-General can limit the policy parameters available to the cabinet because the Dutch parliament (1) must approve all pieces of legislation submitted by the Council of Ministers, (2) must sanction all international agreements and commitments, (3) may drastically amend or even reject the government's budget, thus exercising substantial control over the purse strings, (4) may order government officials to publicly account for their actions and policies, (5) may conduct independent investigations pertaining to the conduct of the government, the civil service, or the royal family, (6) may formulate its own legislative package by working through members of the Second Chamber, who are entitled to submit bills independent of the Council of Ministers, and (7) may act, if deemed necessary, to remove the governing coalition by the introduction of a vote of no confidence in the Second Chamber.

Belgium

THE MONARCHY

The Belgian Constitution dates from 1831 but was significantly modified in 1893, when universal male suffrage was introduced, in 1921, when women were granted the right to vote, and in 1971, when certain differences between the linguistic communities were formally recognized. The constitution provides for a constitutional monarchy, with monarchial power definitely subordinated to parliamentary authority. Among other duties, the monarch may dissolve Parliament, appoint and dismiss ministers, and command the armed forces. All of these prerogatives, however, are highly dependent on the desires of the political party or coalition which controls the government. The monarch must also sign all bills passed by Parliament, but his approval is considered automatic. In addition, all of the decrees he signs must be countersigned by the responsible minister in the cabinet.

The present king, Baudouin, is the fifth Belgian monarch and is a direct descendant of the first monarch, Leopold I. Belgium has a hereditary monarchy with succession based on the male lineage. If no male heir is available, the reigning king nominates a successor who must first be approved by Parliament.

The monarchy serves as a symbol of unity for the nation and is generally respected by the major linguistic communities. At times, however, the Belgian monarchy has been a source of controversy, unlike the royal leadership in the Netherlands until the Lockheed scandal. Baudouin's father, Leopold III, used his power as commander-in-chief to order the surrender of Belgian troops to the Germans after eighteen days of fighting during World War II. Leopold took this action without the approval of the Belgian cabinet and without prior consultations with the British or French allies. Leopold also chose to remain in Belgium during the occupation instead of joining the exiled government in London. Although Leopold's cooperation with the Nazis was not at all synonymous with the actions of the Vichy government in France, some Belgians did question his desire to resist the foreign intruders. Leopold defended his actions by insisting that if his country were to be occupied, he should remain with his people. Nonetheless, after the war, Leopold was temporarily relieved of his duties and highly vocal forces in the Walloon and French-speaking Brussels regions pushed for his dethronement. In 1949, a national vote was taken on whether or not to remove Leopold from his position. Fifty-eight percent of the populace voted to keep him as monarch, but negative majorities were recorded in both Wallonia and Brussels.

Baudouin ascended to the throne in 1951 and has proved a popular leader, with support emanating from most sectors of Belgian society. Moreover, his marriage to Fabiola, a Spanish noblewoman, has apparently met with the approval of the Belgian citizenry. As a result, much of the integrity once associated with the monarchy has been restored and even though the king lacks political clout, the fact that he serves as a national unifier is important in a country so divided by linguistic cleavages.

THE EXECUTIVE

Executive authority in Belgium is formally shared by the monarch, the prime minister, and the cabinet, but in actuality the great bulk of the authority is in the hands of the prime minister, the cabinet, and the party or coalition of parties which they represent.

After a parliamentary election has been held, the monarch may appoint an "informateur," who will talk with the various parties represented in Parliament to find out which party or coalition of parties will be able to form a government. Once the "informateur's" task is completed, the king will designate a "formateur," who will put together a ruling coalition and conclude an agreement on a common governmental program. This "formateur" will normally become the new prime minister. Once the common program is enunciated, the prime minister will submit a list of prospective cabinet ministers to the monarch for his approval. The common program of the new government must then be sent to Parliament for a positive vote of confidence before the government can begin its work.

In direct contrast to the Netherlands and to France, cabinet ministers may retain their seats in Parliament. Cabinets are normally composed of from twenty to thirty ministers, with an executive committee, consisting of the prime minister and approximately seven other ministers, usually screening all proposals before they are submitted to the cabinet as a whole.

The prime minister officially designates the members of his cabinet, but is usually constrained in the choices he may make. Between 1830 and 1983, there were seventy-three different governments in Belgium, twenty-four of which were one-party dominated, twenty-five two-party dominated, sixteen three-party dominated, six four-party dominated, and one each with five and six parties forming coalitions. A vast majority of the governments have been coalitions and consequently the prime minister must make concessions to the other parties in the cabinet in order to retain governmental stability. In particular, he must settle upon a common legislative program and upon people to hold specific cabinet positions so that his new government will receive the initial approval of Parliament. In addition, because the leading parties are normally composed of federations from the linguistic regions, the prime minister has to be quite careful in his own party's selections to cabinet posts and in the legislative priorities he espouses. The prime minister's task may have been even further complicated by a 1971 constitutional revision which requires that the cabinet have an equal number of Flemish-speaking and French-speaking ministers, regardless of ideological orientation.

The cabinet is responsible for submitting the vast majority of legislation which will be considered by the Belgian Parliament. Because the overall cabinet membership is so large, much of the work of the ministers is performed in smaller communities. For example, the executive committee or "restricted cabinet" is composed of the prime minister and a few other ministers, who basically monitor the proposals being sent to the cabinet for its approval. Specific committees, such as Economic and Social Coordination, Budget Management and the Civil Service, and Scientific Policy, also exist within the framework of the cabinet structure. These committees consider proposed legislation within their particular spheres of confidence before the program is presented to the whole cabinet for approval.

THE COUNCIL OF STATE

The Council of State was created in 1946 and is primarily responsible for performing certain duties within the judicial sector. In particular, the administrative sector of the council, whose members are appointed by Parliament, are responsible for ensuring that the rights of the citizens are protected in their dealings with the government.

The council also has a legislative sector, composed of people selected by the monarch with the prior approval of the cabinet. This sector provides technical advice concerning proposed decrees and pieces of legislation. In addition, this advisory body counsels on the legality and constitutionality of proposed legislation or proposed actions by the monarch or the government.

PARLIAMENT

The Belgian Parliament consists of the 212-member Chamber of Representatives and the 182-member Senate. A parliamentary session lasts for four years, unless a cabinet crisis occurs and the monarch is forced to call new elections prematurely. Members of the chamber must be at least twenty-five years old and are elected by universal suffrage under the Belgian proportional representation system. Except for male members of the royal family, senators must be at least forty years old and have distinguished themselves in the political sphere, business field, or some other occupational endeavor. Sixty percent of the senators are chosen by universal suffrage, with the remainder selected by the Provincial Councils and by cooptation.

Both chambers have the right to initiate legislation, but remain almost totally dependent on cabinet proposals. Once a bill is submitted by the cabinet, it is assigned to a legislative committee, perhaps amended, then voted on, and if passed, sent along to the other chamber for its approval. Legislative committees fairly well parallel ministerial assignments and thus the committee, or the chamber as a whole, has the right to question the responsible minister concerning various features of the proposed legislation.

The Chamber of Representatives is the dominant legislative body, even though both chambers must pass the proposed legislation before it is sent along for the monarch's signature. All bills relating to defense and finance must first be voted on by the Chamber of Representatives, and the Senate rarely sends more than 10 percent of all bills back to the Chamber of Representatives for reconsideration. In essence, the Senate is intended to represent provincial interests more fully than the chamber and serves as a check on the Chamber of Representatives' activities. Most of the time, however, there is not a great deal of difference in the political makeup of the two legislative chambers, and members of the Chamber of Representatives are normally cognizant of the desires of the regions they represent.

THE JUDICIARY

The Belgian judicial system is somewhat comparable to the Dutch system, and due to the unitary nature of the political system, there is no separate state and federal court apparatus such as is found in the United States. Moreover, the Belgian judiciary does not exercise judicial review, and thus does not check legislative or executive actions.

Judges are appointed for life and cannot be transferred without their approval nor removed unless serious violations have been determined by the Court of Cassation, the Belgian Supreme Court. Justices of the Peace, numbering 230, represent the primary judicial level and deal with minor civil and criminal cases. Twenty-six Tribunals of First Instance, each composed of three judges, have original jurisdiction in moderately important criminal and civil cases. The most serious cases are heard initially by the Superior Courts, which are composed of three judges and which meet once every three months in each of the nine provincial capitals. Juries are used only at this level, but if the professional judges and the jury are not in agreement on the verdict, the judges may overturn the jury's decision.

Five judges sit on each of the five Courts of Appeal, two located in French-speaking areas, two in Flemish-speaking regions, and one in the officially bilingual Brussels district. These courts hear appeals on points of law from the lower courts and only exercise original jurisdiction in trials of high government officials.

The Court of Cassation is the top Belgian court and has separate civil and criminal tribunals, each composed of seven judges. This court determines jurisdictional disputes between the civil and administrative courts and hears appeals, based only on legal technicalities, from the lower court systems.

REGIONAL AND LOCAL GOVERNMENT

Belgium's unitary system stipulates that most governmental authority must emanate from the central government in Brussels. Nonetheless, as of 1983, Belgium was divided into 9 provinces, 44 arrondissements, and about 590 communes, each of which has some governmental prerogatives.

Each of the provinces has a Provincial Council, which is composed of from fifty to ninety members, depending on the population of the province, who are elected by universal suffrage for four-year terms. These councils are the chief legislative bodies for the provinces but can only meet for a maximum of four weeks per year. Consequently, most of the work is carried on by a permanent council of six people who are chosen from the ranks of the larger Provincial Council and who meet regularly throughout the year. The central government is represented in the province by a governor, who is nominated by the cabinet with the monarch's approval and given life tenure. Many people in the provinces view the governor as representing provincial interests above all, but if the central government orders the governor to carry out a certain decision, he is duty-bound to do so. Consequently, the provincial representatives essentially plead their case to the central government and provide technical advice to the government and Parliament on matters affecting the province, but they exercise very little discretionary authority on their own part.

Depending on the population of the commune, Communal Councils composed of from seven to forty-five members are elected directly by the voters for six-year terms. The council serves as the chief legislative body at the local level and votes on such matters as the budget, the local constabulary, public services, and education. The Communal Council is linked to Brussels by virtue of the monarch's appointment of a burgomaster, someone who is usually already a member of the council. Six aldermen are also selected by the council from among its ranks to serve as the daily executive which oversees the activities of the commune.

Communal decisions must be made within the parameters of the guidelines established by the central government in Brussels. If these guidelines are ignored, the council's decision may be abrogated. In addition, the commune remains almost totally dependent on financial assistance from Brussels and communal budgets must be approved by the provincial governor and the monarch before they can go into effect.

Although communal authority is sharply limited within the Belgian unitary structure, most people still attach their greatest loyalty to the commune. Recently, the number of communes has been reduced by a process of amalgamation from almost 2,400 to approximately 590. Similar programs have been adopted in the Netherlands and in West Germany with a fair degree of success. The argument in favor of communal fusion is to cut down on the costly duplication of tasks and to increase coordination between districts in providing necessary public services. For example, the quality of roads and public utility services have differed rather dramatically depending on the communal authority involved. Thus, the amalgamation plan would seem to have many economic merits, but attachments to the traditional communal structures and a concomitant fear that the new process will increase the central government's control over the individual have fomented some opposition to the fusion plan.

The Policy-Making Process

The central government continues to dominate the policy-making process in Belgium, in spite of the individual citizen's distrust of centralized authority and his repugnance toward politicians in general. However, the constitutional revisions of 1971, which transferred some policy-making latitude to the linguistic regions, and certain constitutional amendments now being considered by Parliament may drastically alter the traditional policy-making hegemony enjoyed by the central government.

There is no formal separation of powers in Belgium and as long as the cabinet can be assured of disciplined party support in Parliament, it can fairly well implement what it pleases. Thus, almost all legislative proposals emanate from the cabinet, are approved by the parliamentary majorities aligned with the government in each chamber, and then sent along to the monarch for his automatic approval. The central administration is then responsible for implementing the new law.

On the other hand, the governments are usually coalitions and the prime minister must take into account the desires of the other party or parties represented in the cabinet. If the prime minister were to alienate any of these cabinet ministers, he might precipitate the demise of the coalition. In addition, the prime minister and his closest advisers must be very wary of incurring the wrath of any of the linguistic communities. Cabinets are now composed of equal numbers of French-speaking and Flemish-speaking ministers, and any issue which might be perceived as benefitting one side at the expense of the other would almost invariably foment a great deal of turmoil. For this precise reason, it has been very difficult to initiate any proposals which would lead to the integration of the linguistic communities.

With the major exception of matters pertaining directly to the linguistic groupings, the Belgian governments have been fairly successful in passing important legislation. The major political parties have traditionally emphasized the need for a modicum of unity within the nation and have therefore been willing to compromise on many vital issues, such as the establishment of a dual system of education. In essence, the Belgians have not been as willing to compromise in the political arena as their Dutch counterparts, particularly in terms of issues related to the onerous language antagonisms, but the major political leaders have been accommodating enough to ensure the passage of important legislation needed to retain the vitality of Belgian society.

Luxembourg

THE MONARCHY

The Luxembourg Constitution of 1868 provides for a constitutional monarchy, with succession to the throne based on hereditary lines within the House of Nassau. Grand Duke Jean has reigned over the country since 1964, succeeding his mother Charlotte, who had served as monarch for forty-five years. The Nassau family is related to the Dutch royalty and Jean is married to the sister of King Baudouin of Belgium, thus integrally linking the three Low Countries together.

There is a great deal of support within Luxembourg for the perpetuation of the monarchy. In a 1919 referendum, four-fifths of the voters proclaimed their desire to retain the monarchial institution. The royal family also evinced a great deal of courage during World War II, which helped to solidify its already strong support from the Luxembourgeois. Charlotte was on the throne when the Germans invaded, but she fled the country and established a government-in-exile in London. She frequently transmitted words of encouragement to her people and was instrumental in making sure that the Allies recognized that Luxembourg wanted to retain its independence after the war and not be absorbed by one of the victorious powers. Meanwhile, Jean enlisted with the Irish Guard and took part in the fighting which eventually led to Luxembourg's liberation in 1944.

The monarch's power is quite limited, even though Jean has taken a substantial interest in the governing of Luxembourg society. The monarch does have the power to designate a prime minister and must give his royal assent before any piece of legislation becomes law. Nonetheless, the parties which form the ruling coalition essentially dictate who will be the new prime minister and the royal assent is considered automatic once the parliament has approved a bill. Moreover, any decree emanating from the throne must be counter-signed by an appropriate minister in the cabinet before it can go into effect.

THE EXECUTIVE

There has been a great deal of governmental stability in Luxembourg, with almost every cabinet lasting the maximum five years in office. The prime minister heads the government and is responsible for selecting the members of his cabinet. All of the ministers meet weekly in the Council of Ministers, which is the collective policy-making body endowed with the power to make governmental decisions. The council is quite small by European standards, with only six or seven people selected for ministerial positions. On the other hand, each minister is normally assigned at least two "portfolios," in other words, administrative areas of responsibility. The prime minister personally heads the Ministry of State, which oversees the activities of the twenty or so other ministries. The cabinet is responsible to the parliament for its actions and may be removed at any time by a vote of no confidence. Each minister is also legally responsible for the actions which he orders or undertakes while serving in the cabinet.

With the exception of the 1974–1979 period, all of the post–World War II governments have been coalitions of the Christian Social Party and either the Socialist Party or the Democratic Party. Again, with one exception, all prime ministers in the postwar period have been Social Christians, but the leader of the cabinet has been limited in his choices for ministerial posts and policy priorities by the fact that he must respect the wishes of his coalition partners in order to keep the government together. In addition, parliamentary deputies who are chosen to positions in the cabinet must forfeit their seats in the

Chamber of Deputies, a situation which approximates the French Fifth Republic policy.

THE COUNCIL OF STATE

The Luxembourg Council of State exercises more power than its counterparts in other Western European countries. The Council of State functions as an administrative court, a consultative body to the monarch, and as a form of constitutional tribunal which rules on the legality of proposed legislation before it is submitted to the parliament. In addition, the council also has a quasi-legislative function in the Luxembourg unicameral system. The parliamentary chamber must pass a bill twice before it goes into effect, with at least a three-month interval between the two motions of approval. However, this three-month waiting period can be waived by the Council of State, a rule which provides the council with a limited suspensive veto power.

A person is selected to serve on the twenty-one-member council by the Grand Duke on the recommendation of the cabinet, the parliament, and the other council members. Eleven of the members deal specifically with administrative matters, while the entire membership participates in rulings concerning the legal technicalities of bills and the waiver of the three-month legislative waiting period.

THE PARLIAMENT

In the European Community, only Luxembourg and Denmark have unicameral legislatures. The Chamber of Deputies in Luxembourg has fifty-nine members and has been granted a maximum term of five years before new elections must be held. Most postwar parliamentary bodies have met for the full five-year period.

Deputies may initiate legislation, but actually remain highly dependent on the cabinet for legislative proposals. Once a bill is sent to the Chamber, it is assigned to a permanent committee or, in special cases, to an ad hoc committee specifically formed to review the bill. The Chamber of Deputies can amend proposed legislation, but as long as the government enjoys majority support in the parliament, there is very little opposition deputies can add to or delete from bills without the approbation of the prime minister and his cabinet. Deputies may also initiate motions of no confidence against the government, but unless the governing coalition is in the process of dissipation, the motion will inevitably prove futile. On the other hand, the deputies may exercise some latitude over the government by requiring ministers to account for their actions and by forming investigatory committees to scrutinize alleged problems within the central government administration.

The constitution is amended in Luxembourg in much the same way as in Belgium. The Chamber of Deputies must first decide that an amendment is desirable and then the Chamber is dissolved and new parliamentary elections held. Once the new membership is seated, the deputies work out the exact wording of the new amendment and then vote on it. For this crucial vote, at least three-quarters of the deputies must be in attendance and a two-thirds majority is needed for passage.

THE JUDICIARY

The Luxembourg judicial system fairly well parallels the Belgian structure with Justices of the Peace resolving minor civil and criminal cases, intermediate courts hearing appeals from the local level and exercising original jurisdiction over more serious criminal and civil disputes, and the High Court of Justice acting as the ultimate judicial authority. Judges are appointed for life by the crown and can only be removed by the High Court. Trials are presided over by professional judges and juries are not used. In addition, the Luxembourg judicial system does not exercise judicial review over the actions of the executive or of the legislature.

LOCAL GOVERNMENT

Because Luxembourg is so small, only the central government and local communal governments exist, with no stipulation being made for provincial authorities. Municipal Council members in the 126 communes are elected directly by the people for six-year terms, through a proportional representation system. The executive body within the council is composed of a college of aldermen and a burgomaster who is appointed by the crown and who is normally a member of the council in the first place. These local authorities do exercise some decision-making power in such areas as minor road construction, protective services, and construction codes. They may also levy a special tax to defray their operating costs.

THE POLICY-MAKING PROCESS

The prime minister and his cabinet dominate the policy-making process, even though the leader of the government must avoid actions which might alienate his coalition partners and thus foment instability in the governing apparatus. As long as the prime minister can depend on the support of the deputies from the parties forming the governing coalition, his policies which have already been cleared by the Council of Ministers will almost invariably be passed by the Chamber of Deputies.

The usual policy-making process is for a proposed bill to emanate from one of the ministries, be approved by the Council of Ministers, be sent to the Grand Duke and to the Council of State for their approbation, be passed by the Council of Deputies, and then if the Council of State does not issue a waiver, be passed for a second time by the Chamber of Deputies three months later. The Grand Duke will then sign the bill and a sector of the 7,000-member civil service will be charged with implementing it. Organized interest groups, such as business, labor, trade, and agriculture, are normally consulted when the proposed bill is first considered by the Council of Ministers. On matters of primary importance, the electorate will occasionally be consulted directly through a referendum, a technique which is also used sporadically in neighboring France.

Luxembourg has a unitary system of government, with most authority emanating from the capital city of Luxembourg. Consequently, the prerogatives of the communal leadership are severely limited. The burgomaster represents the central government at the local level and any major disputes between local and central authorities could conceivably result in the dismembering of the Municipal Council. Conversely, the Luxembourg central government might be more in touch and more empathetic with the needs of the communes than central authorities in other countries simply because of the diminutiveness in terms of population size and geographical area. Because of this characteristic, there might well be a greater rapport between central government and local government officials in Luxembourg than is to be found in neighboring European countries.

Policy Problems and Prospects

The Common Fear of Recession

All three Benelux nations have been hurt by the worldwide recession of the early 1980s. In particular, both inflation and unemployment have dramatically increased. Belgium currently has one of the highest unemployment rates in the Western world and has been forced to resort to emergency measures in order to provide additional jobs. Unfortunately, the nation has been caught in a vicious circle of sorts; in order to combat its double-digit inflation rate an economic austerity package was implemented, including temporary wage and price controls. These measures, of course, do little to stimulate job production in the private economic sector.

The Netherlands has also been plagued by economic problems, in spite of the fact that it has natural gas reserves and is not as dependent as Belgium and Luxembourg on foreign petroleum imports. In the early 1980s, its unemployment rate topped 10 percent and the government deficit was close to 10 percent of its overall gross domestic product.

Luxembourg is highly dependent on the production of its steel industry, which has been adversely affected by the world recession. The steel industry provides 20 percent of the national product, employs 40 percent of the overall work force, and produces 60 percent of the exports. With world demand down, however, the large Luxembourg steel conglomerate, Arbed, has only been operating at 60 percent capacity. Even though only several thousand people have been laid off or put on part-time shifts, this represents the worst economic situation since the Great Depression and has produced significant consternation in this small nation which has traditionally prided itself on almost zero unemployment.

The Netherlands

In spite of the worrisome economic difficulties, the Netherlands is not presently confronted with a problem of such magnitude that it threatens the stability of the entire governmental system. Just the same, the jobs issue does represent a formidable challenge to the governing coalition. Some university graduates are now experiencing great difficulty in securing jobs commensurate with their training. The problem is further complicated by the fact that more women than ever before are casting aside the traditional homemaker role in favor of full-time employment outside of the home. In view of the recent economic recession which has gripped the nation, the problem of accommodating the demands of these new entries into the labor force has been greatly accentuated.

Malaise within the labor force has also increased significantly in certain sectors. On a given work day, more than 15 percent of Dutch workers are absent from their jobs, up nearly 100 percent in just five years. Regional industrial development and employment have also been uneven, with too much industry concentrated in the Rotterdam area and not nearly enough in the northern and southeastern provinces. The government has attempted to persuade companies to either relocate or establish subsidiaries in these relatively underdeveloped areas, but if it applies too much pressure, the companies might decide to move to neighboring Germany or Belgium, the latter having tax rates approximately 10 percent below those in the Netherlands. Because of the free movement of goods within the Common Market, a company which relocates to another EEC country would still have access to the Dutch market but Dutch workers would no longer benefit from producing the goods. Consequently, this governmental effort to promote regional industrial development has only been marginally successful.

Business circles have also been somewhat disgruntled with the large government expenditures earmarked for the public sector, as well as the minimum wage of over 500 dollars per month, which ranks among the highest in the world. As of 1982, the Dutch public sector accounted for more than 60 percent of the nation's total domestic product. These business interests contend that the government has neglected its needs and has not been adequately supportive of expansion in the private economic sector. The problem has become even more acute with the slowdown of industrial production during the worldwide recession which followed the precipitous rise in OPEC oil prices. As a result of the September 1982 elections, a moderate-conservative coalition of Christian Democrats and Liberals came to power, pledging to curb government spending and facilitate greater productivity in the private sector. Whether or not such tactics will shake the Netherlands out of its economic doldrums remains to be seen.

On the whole, however, the political outlook remains fairly optimistic. The Prince Bernhard affair shook the nation for a while but has not caused any permanent damage to the integrity of the Dutch political system. Moreover, in spite of the fact that some sectors of Dutch society are disillusioned with the monarchical system, it is highly unlikely that the monarchy will be abolished and replaced by a republican form of government.

The South Moluccan problem remains a thorn in the side of officials in The Hague, but there is little that they can reasonably do to satiate the demands of these nationalists who now reside in the Netherlands but who originally came from the Molucca Sea region near Indonesia. In effect, South Moluccan extremists have demanded official Dutch support for the creation of an autonomous South Moluccan republic on an island once under the colonial direction of the Netherlands but which is now fully controlled by the Indonesian government. In order to dramatize their cause, some of the extremists forcibly seized a train, a schoolhouse, and a government building. Government troops eventually captured the terrorists, but not before several innocent hostages had been killed. The perpetrators of these crimes are now behind prison walls, but sporadic incidents involving South Moluccan nationalists are bound to occur in the future and the major task facing the government in The Hague is to ensure that the Dutch populace as a whole does not turn against the South Moluccan community. Although easily forgotten because of the extremist actions of a few, the fact remains that the vast majority of South Moluccans living in the Netherlands are law abiding and have not condoned the terrorist activities carried out by a few nationalists.

The inability of Dutch parties to form a stable governing coalition during the seven months following the 1977 national elections, the four months following the 1981 elections, and the calling of new elections in September 1982, may convince Dutch voters to cut down on the number of political movements represented in the parliament. Traditionally, the Dutch multiparty system has functioned remarkably well, and governing coalitions composed of three, four, or even five distinct parties have been able in the past to formulate and pass significant legislation. However, the recent governmental uncertainty attributable to the recent deadlocks may temper the electorate's enthusiasm for a parliament which contains more than a dozen separate political movements.

If the inability to form a stable coalition government were to be repeated in the near future, the Dutch might give serious consideration to the implementation of a threshold law similar to that now used in West Germany and Sweden. Under the threshold provisions, a party must be able to garner a certain percentage of the national vote (5 percent in Germany and 4 percent in Sweden), or do well in individual electoral districts, before it can be represented in the parliament. The aim of the threshold law is to weed out the fringe parties, encourage electoral alliances among parties, and increase the likelihood of the formation of stable governing coalitions. If the Netherlands had implemented a 4 percent threshold barrier in the 1977, 1981, and 1982 elections, only six distinct political movements (including the three confessional parties joined together in the CDA alliance) would have gained seats in the parliament, even though thirty or so parties ran candidates for parliamentary office. In essence, the challenge facing Dutch society is to safeguard the political representation of its subcultures while ensuring that stable governing coalitions can be formed. In spite of recent problems, the politics of accommodation continues to be a hallmark of the Dutch system of government, and the introduction of some variation of the threshold concept might well engender even greater accommodation in Dutch society as a whole.

Belgium

Primarily as a result of the persistent disputes between the two major linguistic communities, Belgium's prospects for the future are somewhat dimmer than those of the Netherlands and Luxembourg. The Flemings and the Walloons have made little headway in resolving their differences and the areas of contention continue to polarize the political sector, even though the problems do not represent a dire threat to overall systemic stability. In essence, the governing coalitions are perennially forced to walk a political tightrope as they attempt to avoid alienating either language community.

The problem is further aggravated by the fact that Belgium, just like Great Britain, was industrialized quite early in the nineteenth century. As a result, some sectors of the economy continue to rely on outmoded facilities and techniques, whereas nations which industrialized later have found it much easier to adopt technologically advanced production systems. In the nineteenth and well into the twentieth century, this early industrialization, based primarily on iron and steel production and located primarily in the southern part of the nation, benefitted the then-dominant Walloon class. The tide has now turned in favor of the Flemish populace, which not only has the larger representation in Parliament, but has also attracted many multinational corporations to its territory. Thus, even during the recent recession period, the Flemish region to the north has been much more prosperous, economically, than the rather comatose areas of the south. The Walloons believe that the government must do more to aid their region, but think that the Flemish-speaking majority in Parliament has worked against the interests of the French-speaking minority.

Thus, the economic problems which have continued to plague Belgium, accompanied by high unemployment, have tended to exacerbate the traditional linguistic disputes. Many observers felt that as a result of negotiations directed by then-Prime Minister Leo Tindemans some of the most abrasive side effects of the linguistic cleavages could be relieved by as early as the

1980s. The perceived panacea for the problem was the Egmont Pact, an agreement reached among the major parties in 1977 to establish three semi-autonomous regions, Flanders, Wallonia, and Brussels. More than four-fifths of the members of Parliament supported in principle this devolution formula, which would provide each of these regions significant policy-making authority over social and economic issues. However, some of the Flemish politicians began to raise objections, complaining that an independent Brussels district would give the French-speaking minority in Belgium control over two regions, whereas the Flemish-speaking majority would control only one. The momentum which Tindemans had built up in support of the agreement soon dissipated and the prime minister eventually resigned in protest. Parliament was later dissolved after having convened for only eighteen months, and new nationwide elections were held in December 1978. Tindemans and the supporters of the devolution plan hoped that the Belgian electorate would vote overwhelmingly for the parties which had strongly backed the Egmont Pact. However, the Belgian voters did not heed this advice and the newly elected parliament was almost a mirror image of the previous one. Consequently, the linguistic-linked problems and the accompanying governmental immobility remain unresolved.

The linguistic dualism has even been extended at times to regional Benelux concerns. For example, a report commissioned in 1976 recommended the merger of the three major airlines of Belgium, the Netherlands, and Luxembourg. Sabena, the Belgian national airlines, has incurred record losses in recent years and would probably benefit substantially from such a merger. Many Walloons, however, have adamantly opposed the proposal, fearing that the Dutch and the Flemings would dominate the new air transportation arrangement. Consequently, in spite of the economic advantages associated with the airline merger which would accrue to Belgium and the two other Benelux nations, the linguistic concerns thwarted the finalizing of any agreement.

Because of Belgium's severe economic problems, the government of Wilfred Martens pushed forward in 1982 with a major austerity program which included the devaluation of the Belgian franc, a cut in public spending, a limit on wage increases, and a diminution in government aid to troubled economic sectors such as the steel industry. Riots ensued in some of the steel-making centers of Wallonia, partly as a result of the new government policies which stated that the industry would have to survive on fewer government subsidies, and partly because the Martens coalition had been primarily voted into office by the Flemings. In spite of linguistically-based suspicions, many Belgian citizens from Flanders and Wallonia believe that such tough measures are needed to restore the nation's economic vitality. Nevertheless, the fragile nature of government coalitions in Belgium and the constant need to placate the demands of coalition partners will severely strain the government's ability to stick with such a bold and controversial program for the period needed to attain tangible economic progress.

Luxembourg

In contrast to Belgium, the Grand Duchy does not face any extremely onerous problems in the immediate future. Indeed, Luxembourg continues to enjoy a great deal of governmental stability and is not plagued by any major cleavages.

Perhaps the most serious task to be completed in the near future is the diversification of the economy. Almost 80 percent of the goods produced in Luxembourg are exported, leaving the economy somewhat at the mercy of world market conditions. The steel industry continues to dominate the Luxembourg economy and has particularly been hurt by the decreasing demands for its products during the world recession.

On the other hand, Luxembourg has already taken several constructive steps toward diversifying its economic structure. Lenient tax laws have been implemented for the purpose of attracting foreign capital and industries. Foreign institutions are currently exempt from local and national income taxes, paying instead a modest capital subscription tax at the time of their arrival and an annual subscription tax based on capital, stocks, and transaction volume. As a result of these liberal tax policies, many financial institutions have settled in Luxembourg, making this small nation one of the foremost money markets in Europe. In addition, such large multinational corporations as Dupont, Monsanto, General Motors, and Royal Tires have constructed new facilities in the country.

Another potential problem area is linked to the relatively high percentage of foreigners who reside in Luxembourg. Foreigners represent almost one-fourth of the entire population, with 33 percent of the steel industry, 60 percent of the handicrafts sector, and 85 percent of the building trades work forces composed of foreign nationals. Some xenophobic outbursts have emanated from a segment of the indigenous population which fears that certain cultural values and traditions are being jeopardized by the influx of foreign customs. On the other hand, the Luxembourg economy is largely dependent on the services rendered by these foreign workers and it is very unlikely that any anti-foreigner movement will gain enough of a following to upset the tranquility of the Grand Duchy.

Selected Bibliography

Beck, Barbara. "Holland: Too Good to Be True?" *The Economist* (May 29, 1976): S1–S31.

Cook, Chris, and Paxton, John. *European Political Facts, 1918–73.* New York: St. Martin's Press, 1975.

Daalder, Hans. "On Building Consociational Nations: The Cases of the Netherlands and Switzerland," *International Social Science Journal* 23, no. 3 (1971): 355–370.

Daalder, Hans, and Irwin, Galen. "Interests and Institutions in the Netherlands: An Assessment by the People and by Parliament," *Annals of the American Academy of Political and Social Science* 413 (May 1974): 58–71.

Griffiths, Richard, T., ed. The Economy and Politics of the Netherlands Since 1945. The Hague: M. Nijhoff, 1980.

Heisler, Martin O. "Managing Ethnic Conflict in Belgium," *Annals of the American Academy of Political and Social Science* 433 (September 1977): 32–46.

Henig, Stanley, ed. *European Political Parties: A Handbook.* New York: Praeger, 1970.

"Holland." *The Economist* (January 1982): S3–S26.

Holt, Stephen. *Six European States.* London: Hamish Hamilton, 1970.

Huggett, Frank E. *The Modern Netherlands.* New York: Praeger, 1971.

Hury, Carlo, and Christophory, Jules, ed. *Luxembourg.* Santa Barbara: ABC-Clio, 1981.

Lijphart, Arend. "Consociational Democracy," *Comparative Political Studies* 1 (April 1968): 3–33.

Lijphart, Arend. *The Politics of Accommodation: Pluralism and Democracy in the Netherlands.* Berkeley and Los Angeles: University of California Press, 1968.

Netherlands' Ministry of Foreign Affairs. *The Kingdom of the Netherlands: Constitution, Justice.* The Hague: Government Printing Office, 1974.

Weil, Gordon L. *The Benelux Nations: The Politics of Small-Country Democracies.* New York: Holt, Rinehart & Winston, 1970.

5.

The Alpine Region: Diversity and Stability within a Federalist Framework

David E. Bohn

The Historical Setting

An Overview

For more than two thousand years, the countries now known as Switzerland and Austria have been the crossroads between both Northern and Southern and Eastern and Western Europe. While this geographic centrality has influenced the historical development of these two mountainous states differently, they nonetheless have come to share various traits which are of considerable interest to students of comparative politics. Both countries base their government systems on democracy and federalism; both have adopted a foreign policy of neutrality and both are small in population and size. Furthermore, in the years following World War II, both the Swiss and the Austrians have enjoyed political stability and economic prosperity. It is no wonder, then, that many individuals look for an explanation of these achievements in the political attributes which the two states appear to have in common. However similar these two states may appear to be, it is clear that they arrived at their present condition by very different routes. A more complete understanding will therefore require an explanation of how democracy, federation and neutrality have evolved in each state.

Switzerland

Switzerland is about the size of Massachusetts and Connecticut combined— situated in the mountainous center ground of Western Europe. It borders

France to the west, Germany to the north, Austria to the east, and Italy to the south. Its many landforms and waterways create an astonishing variety of terrain and divide Switzerland into numerous regions. The Jura Mountains, which separate Switzerland from France, extend to Basel and then taper off into undulating terrain which continues to Lake Constance, where the elevation again begins to rise in anticipation of the Austrian Alps. To the immediate south, extending from Geneva on the east to Zurich on the west, lies the flatter lowland where the vast majority of the Swiss live. Here fertile farmlands and productive concentrations of industry secure the wealth of the Swiss economy. But even this land is rippled with rolling hills and laced with numerous rivers and lakes. Further south, the twin backbones of the Alps rise abruptly, knotting into a cluster of peaks which are crisscrossed by numerous valleys and gorges, at the bottom of which are often deep running lakes and roaring rivers.

Swiss cultural, social, and political forms were largely established before the industrial revolution. Consequently, the physical heterogeneity of Switzerland has left a distinct imprint upon Swiss institutions. In view of the inconvenience of travel and the localized nature of economic structures linked to a variety of soil and climate conditions, Switzerland perhaps more than any other European country maintained the high level of decentralization characteristic of the Middle Ages. Compatible with this decentralization has been the persistence of a rich diversity of cultural, social, and political life. The Swiss speak at least four languages, with multiple dialects; and this great variety of language and dialect portrays the corresponding variety of culture, which seems to differ from commune to commune, canton to canton, and region to region. There is no such thing as the French or Swiss-German culture, but rather the French and Swiss-German cultures—the language only describes a variety of subcultures, each with its own distinct characteristics. There are two major religions, Catholicism and Protestantism, but a variety of subcultures and practices exist within each. The economics of the various regions of Switzerland differ widely with mountain agriculture, tourism, the generation of hydroelectric power, truck farming, cereal and grain production, the raising of livestock, milk production, the manufacture of watches, jewelry, fine instruments, heavy machinery and high quality textiles, the processing of foods, tool and dye fabrication, chemical and pharmaceutical production, and banking and insurance representing the gamut. But it is in tracing the evolution of Switzerland's governmental structures that one gains a comprehensive understanding of the rich mixture of cultural, social, and political institutions which exist in this country.

Historically, one must distinguish between the Old Switzerland and the New Switzerland, between the institutions of the Old Confederation and those of the New Confederation. The historical roots of the Old Confederation reach back to at least 1291, when the three original cantons, Uri, Schwyz, and Unterwalden, signed the Eternal Alliance. This alliance lasted until 1789, by which time its membership had increased to thirteen cantons and its subject territories encompassed almost all of what is now modern Switzerland. When one speaks of the New Switzerland, one is referring to the state which was formally established in 1847 with some twenty-five cantons and half cantons.

The Old Switzerland was in fact not truly a state, it was more of a military alliance designed to protect various independent cantons from their common enemy, Austria. Unlike most alliances, the Eternal Alliance became more complex and more vigorous as centuries passed. Even the ravages of the Thirty Years' War, with its poisonous religious fanaticism, failed to destroy the Confederation. The evolution of Switzerland from a group of allies to a near state occurred for at least three reasons.

First, Austria was a long-term enemy and no alliance against her could be of short duration. In fact, for the first three centuries of the alliance, the Confederation's military capability was so great that not only did it defeat Austria in numerous encounters, but it substantially expanded the subject regions, which the cantons controlled either individually or collectively.

Second, the alliance was cemented by common economic interests. Internal trade became important to many areas, but in particular it was the Gotthard Pass which bound the Confederation during its first two hundred years. This was the principal Alpine trade route between Northern and Southern Europe and along it grew commercial and productive centers such as Zurich and Lucerne. The pass was central to the livelihood of most of the early cantons and sustained their alliance against the Austrian Empire, which sought to annex the area.

Finally, the political and economic foundation of the Confederation was reinforced by the growth of an overarching Swiss identity. Slowly, but visibly, the populations of the various cantons began to consider themselves more than simply citizens of their home canton—they were citizens of Switzerland. Legends grew of the triumphs of the Confederation and of the Swiss armies' heroic defeats of the Austrians, and the stories reinforced the belief that the freedom and prosperity of Switzerland depended upon a common willingness to cooperate in opposing the invader.

It is particularly important to see the growth of the Old Confederation as a piecemeal affair, where isolated and often very heterogeneous political entities—sometimes cities sometimes Alpine cantons, sometimes Catholic sometimes Protestant, sometimes democratic sometimes autocratic, sometimes populous and sometimes scarcely populated—came together in muddling fashion to form a larger political jurisdiction. Important too is that in the process no single canton succeeded in dominating the others. While there were disparities of power and substantial intercantonal conflict, the balance of power within the Confederation maintained a certain equality among the cantons and guaranteed the independence to which each canton could nominally lay claim.

However, this was not the case for the subject cantons. In order to control access to the Gotthard, it was necessary to control the area known as Ticino, the Italian-speaking part of Switzerland. In addition, as a result of old feudal claims and conquests, the cantons or the Confederation as a whole ruled over the remaining area, which presently constitutes modern Switzerland with the exception of Geneva, a city-state bound to the Confederation by treaty, and the Jura, which came to the Confederation as a result of a decision made by the Congress of Vienna in 1815. The subject cantons did not suffer because of their status. The concept of individual freedom had yet to gain wide currency and ethnic consciousness was low. Furthermore, as long as the inhabitants of these areas paid their taxes and accepted the nominal authority of the ruling canton or cantons, they were allowed substantial local autonomy and received in return competent political administration and long-term protection from invasion and plunder by external enemies. At the very least they could console themselves with the fact that the vast majority of the inhabitants of the countryside of the member cantons were ruled by the cities and in some cases enjoyed even less autonomy than the inhabitants of the subject cantons.

By the seventeenth century, political and economic interdependence, as well as a sense of community, had increased to the point that it was possible to create a diet or parliament to mediate conflicts between cantons and to make binding decisions on questions of common military action. The parliament also provided a forum in which Swiss problems could be discussed in general and the elites from the various cantons could meet and exchange ideas. Even this further institutionalization of the Confederation fell short of furnishing the basis for a nation-state. In almost every area except military action, the cantons remained sovereign and even in the area of foreign affairs they conducted, with some proscriptions, their own relations with other cantons and other states.

By the outbreak of the French Revolution, the geographic entity known as Switzerland could claim a five-hundred-year history. Despite the great cultural and institutional differences which existed in the Switzerland of that day and the decentralized nature of its economic and political structures, the solidarity of the Confederation was unquestioned and its legitimacy strong in the eyes of all the Swiss. One proof of the binding strength of this legitimacy is the behavior of the subject areas of Switzerland after the French Revolution liberated them from the authority of their former rulers. These areas included almost all of the French and Italian cantons of modern-day Switzerland, some of which had subsequently been annexed by France. With the final defeat of Napoleon and during the Congress of Vienna, these areas did not request annexation by the states of northern Italy or by France, but rather preferred to remain part of Switzerland as full-fledged members of the Confederation. In addition to granting this wish, the Congress of Vienna gave to the canton of

Bern a border area called the Jura in order to compensate the once powerful canton for the loss of its French territories.

It was the objective of the Congress of Vienna to return Europe to the status quo of the Old Regime, a return to the privileges and institutions of monarchial Europe. In Switzerland this meant restoring to the cantons the economic and political privileges that Napoleon had abolished. Yet the restoration achieved this purpose in appearance only. The old medieval trade restrictions were ignored, the political power of the old ruling families and guilds never regained its former legitimacy, and the cities found it difficult to reestablish their control over the countryside. In Switzerland, as in many European countries, radical politics took hold. It began at the local level, the level of the commune and the canton, where the liberal reforms of the revolutionary period were reinstituted, and spread to the Confederation. Eventually, demands arose for the creation of a sovereign federal government which could implement liberal reforms nationally.

This nationalist-liberal movement was opposed by a coalition of Catholic cantons which feared that the liberals, who were largely Protestant, would use the power of the federal government to oppress the Catholic church. They were particularly offended by the demands of liberals that public administrative functions which had for centuries been performed by the church be assumed by the local or national government. The threat that the educational activities of the church might be hampered and that the new state might even intervene in the strictly religious observances of the church seemed very real to the inhabitants of the Catholic cantons. On the other hand, the Protestants accused the Catholics of being unpatriotic and pointed to the subversive political activities of foreign monks as proof.

The confrontation between the Protestant radicals and the Catholic conservatives climaxed in a short civil war called the *Sonderbundskrieg*. The Catholic cantons were easily defeated with very few deaths. The radicals proceeded to create sovereign federal institutions with the Constitution of 1848, which was later revised by the Constitutional Convention of 1874. The administrative functions which the church had performed for the communes and the cantons were secularized, but the structure of the New Confederation was a compromise which fell far short of the unitary state the Catholic's feared. The vast majority of political power was still located in the cantons, and the religious prerogatives of the Catholic church were protected except for the expulsion of the Jesuits from Switzerland.

The subordination of the cantons to the power of the central government created for the first time a national citizenship, which allowed citizens of one canton to migrate to another and maintain the same privileges and immunities of the original residents of the canton. Perhaps this reform more than any other signaled the emergence of modern Switzerland as a complex alliance of cantons. These legal conditions and the subsequent industrialization of Switzerland would stimulate an almost unprecedented internal migration. Whereas in 1847 only 7 percent of the Swiss lived outside of their canton of family origin, by 1960 more than 42 percent had established residence in a canton other than that of their family. Thus, the New Confederation of 1847 would come to be bound not only by interest and by the legitimacy of common institutions, but also by demography.

Austria

In contrast to Switzerland, present-day Austria is but a remnant of the once vast Austrian and later Austro-Hungarian Empire, which extended from the Balkans deep into Central Europe. For centuries this empire played a major role in European politics and served as a center for cultural grandeur and intellectual achievment. However, it stood on feet of clay. In the nineteenth century, the jarring impact of modernity created social, economic, and political pressures which the empire's anachronistic and ill-adapted political institutions—themselves a loosely woven patchwork of historical compromise—could scarcely contain. Political instability threatened from many quarters; ethnic minorities demanded political independence; the growing working class demanded an international socialist revolution; the nationalists demanded a patriotic and aggressive pan-German foreign policy as well as strong anti-Jewish, anticapitalist, anticommunist, and anticlerical initiatives; and the privileged and peasant classes demanded a continuation of traditional rule.

The actual abolition of the Austro-Hungarian Empire came as a consequence of World War I. The conflict was ignited when a Serbian nationalist assassinated Archduke Franz Ferdinand, heir to the throne of the empire. Four years of bloody trench warfare brought the defeat of the imperial army and the collapse of the monarchy. The victorious and rancorous Allies formally dismembered the empire in the Treaty of St. Germain, reducing Austria to a small country not much larger than the original holdings of the House of Hapsburg.

The new Austria faced grave problems. Its very integrity was threatened by separatist movements in the southern Tyrol and Voralberg. Its economy was in shambles and there was no stable government. Recognizing the inviability of the new state, socialists, conservatives, and nationalists sought an *Anschluss* or union with Germany. When the Allies refused, the democratic forces of the center and left proceeded, despite intense class conflict, to create the First Republic. It survived until 1934, when after a short but brutal civil war the republic was replaced by a dictatorship. In 1938, Hitler absorbed Austria into the Third Reich only for it to reemerge at the end of World War II with the same boundaries.

The Allies allowed a partial return to local rule as early as 1945 and 1946. The Second Republic was proclaimed with essentially the same constitution as the First Republic. However, the government of Austria faced a perilous international situation. The great victors of the war, the United States and the Soviet Union, had divided the continent into two great power spheres, with Austria standing in the middle somewhat as a no-man's-land. Choosing a policy of neutrality, Austria sought to extract itself from Cold War politics and regain full political control from the occupation forces. Domestically, the Nazi political movement had been dismantled, nationalism as an ideology was discredited, and the pan-German dream had lost its appeal. The leaders of Austria's various political parties had to face the irreversible reality that the boundaries of Austria were unlikely to change in the foreseeable future and that survival would require a type of cooperation which had previously been impossible.

Political Culture and Socialization

Switzerland

Creating a democratic political process which could manage both Switzerland's and Austria's domestic cleavages while steering clear of dangerous international shoals is both the challenge and the achievement of these two countries. To understand how this has been accomplished, we must analyze their changing political cultures.

An extended analysis of political culture would focus upon the agents of political socialization and the structures which perpetuate and alter the political values of the Swiss and Austrian people. This study will, however, limit itself to the level of ideas, beliefs, attitudes, values, and skills which condition their political behavior and expectations. Switzerland has long been recognized as one of the most heterogeneous cultures in the Western world. We have discussed how geography promoted heterogeneity, but there are also social and political reasons for the rich diversity of Swiss society.

LANGUAGE

Swiss culture is marked by three major and one minor language. Approximately 74 percent of the Swiss speak Swiss-German as their mother tongue, 20 percent French, 4 percent Italian and 1 percent Romansh. These figures have remained approximately the same since 1848. Three cantons are historically French-speaking, three mixed, with both French and German as historical languages, one mixed, with German, Italian and Romansh, one Italian, and the remaining speaking predominately Swiss-German. However, as was pointed out earlier, dialects abound, especially in Swiss-German cantons, and some of them are so obscure that an inhabitant of a larger city who travels to the countryside may experience some difficulty in communicating with the local people. This means that Swiss-German is the medium of many different cantonal cultures. The fact that the Swiss refer to Basel German, Bern German, Zurich German, etc., reflects the decentralized and parochial nature of the Swiss-German culture.

Switzerland has long been celebrated as a country where the inhabitants, who speak many different languages, have had the good sense to get along. Although historically true, this does not mean that there have been no tensions or conflicts over ethnic and lingual issues. Interestingly enough, during the period of the Old Confederation, when the Swiss-German cantons ruled over most of the French and Italian-speaking cantons in aristocratic fashion, there was very little conflict. It was the French Revolution which awakened throughout Europe the passion of nationalism and with it the ethnic consciousness of the subject peoples of the Old Confederation. Their demands were modest—equal partnership in the Confederation. This they received except in the mixed cantons, where during the Restoration the French-speaking inhabitants of the cantons of Bern, Fribourg, and Valais continued to be ruled by the old Swiss-German aristocracy. The Constitution of 1848 and its revised version of 1874 divested the old ruling elite of its power once and for all, and the new cantonal constitutions established various forms of democracy. This did not completely solve the problem, however, because even within democratic institutions the French-speaking population in the canton of Bern was in the minority, and the French-speaking population of Fribourg, which had formerly been oppressed, sought to turn the tables on the German-speaking minority.

During the last half of the nineteenth and the first half of the twentieth centuries the flame of nationalism continued to burn, igniting latent energies in Central Europe. It was in 1870 that Germany achieved the status of nation-state, radiating a cultural nationalism designed to draw the sympathies if not the alliance of all Germans living outside of the Second Reich. Switzerland was strongly affected by this pan-German nationalism and some German-speaking groups became hostile toward the non-German-speaking populations, in particular the French-speaking inhabitants in the Bernese Jura.

With the outbreak of World War I, ethnic tensions in Switzerland reached a crescendo. Only Swiss neutrality saved Switzerland from a highly destructive internal struggle, for quite naturally the Swiss-Germans, French, and Italians identified strongly with the cause of their ethnic counterparts in Germany, France, and Italy. Ironically, this was not the case in World War II. The Swiss-Germans failed to identify in any great numbers with the Nazi cause, thus the many years of sacrifice that the war occasioned actually strengthened Swiss ethnic solidarity.

Ethnic relations have also been strained by the very success of the dominant Swiss-Germans. The poor Swiss-Germans have tended to migrate to other cantons, many going to French- and Italian-speaking areas. In the French-speaking cantons they were generally absorbed, but in Ticino, the Italian-speaking canton, the Swiss-Germans were slow to assimilate. Furthermore, the climate of the area attracted many wealthy Germans as well as Swiss-Germans, who began to buy up choice land and by their economic importance began to alter the cultural practices of the canton.

At this point, the important overarching Swiss cultural tolerance played a crucial role. In general, nationalism in Switzerland incarnated not one people but clusters of ethnic groups. Thus, diversity is looked upon as an essential part of Switzerland's identity. The *territorial principle* is an expression of this value. This principle, guaranteed by the central government, recognizes the right of any area at the cantonal or even communal level to protect its lingual and cultural heritage against the influx of residents who cannot speak the local language. This prevailing value of intercultural tolerance has allowed Swiss-Italians to take strong measures to protect their culture; requiring that public signs be written in Italian, and if translated, the translation be of smaller type; requiring all schools to teach Italian as the first language; and prohibiting the sale of land to foreigners. Similar measures, although generally not as far-reaching, have been taken in the French-speaking cantons. The problems of those speaking Romansh, an obscure language tracing its roots to Latin, are much greater because this small population is unable to generate the economic, cultural, or political resources to make Romansh a relevant language in the modern world. Increasingly, the Romansh-speaking inhabitants must rely on one of Switzerland's other languages as their functional language in education, business, and administration.

Another lingering language conflict which over the years was not resolved by Switzerland's existing institutions pitted the French-speaking inhabitants of the North Jura against the rest of the canton of Bern, which is predominantly Swiss-German. This persistent conflict, and the national referendum which was recently held to attempt to resolve it, will be discussed in greater detail later.

RELIGION

Language and related ethnic sentiments are not the only expression of culture. Religious values also play a significant role in cultural development. In Switzerland, religion has been the root cause of some of the most violent conflicts. One need only reflect upon the battles which were fought between Protestant and Catholic cantons during the Reformation and the tenuous peace during the Thirty Years' War. It has already been pointed out that a short civil war, the *Sonderbundskrieg*, was fought between Catholics and Protestants over the creation of new federal institutions. It is surprising, however, that religion has not been more of a source of conflict. Indeed, one must return to the period of the Reformation to discover truly doctrinally motivated conflicts. The *Sonderbundskrieg* was fought primarily over a political issue—the separation of church and state. In fact, not all of the Catholic cantons were in favor of the military action, and a strong case could be made that the economic and political interests of the militant mountain cantons were as much a cause as religion.

In twentieth-century Switzerland, religious issues have declined in intensity. Doctrinal conflicts seem of little interest to anyone, the political question has largely been settled, and secularization and materialism have reduced the influence of religion in the daily lives of the average citizen. Still, religion remains one of the most far-reaching cultural elements around which social and political organizations coalesce, and therefore must be considered an important political and moral force.

Switzerland enjoys a very mixed political heritage. In the Old Confederation, Switzerland had both aristocratic and democratic forms of government. While the patrician families and the urban oligarchies tended to predominate, the democratic tradition was maintained in legends such as the story of William Tell and national histories which highlight the constitutions of the founding cantons of the Confederation. The unique feature of these stories is that they are almost devoid of any reference to local aristocratic families or great leaders. The imagery of the Swiss past is equalitarian, celebrating simple but courageous farmers who leave their fields to take up arms against ambitious tyrants. Here it should be noted that even though many of the cantons were ruled by aristocratic families, there was no ruling family or monarch over the whole of Switzerland. Thus the doctrines of the Enlightenment and the militant ideology of the French Revolution found many adherents in Switzerland. Their dislike of Napoleon arose out of opposition to the highly centralized regime he established rather than its liberal nature. It is therefore not surprising that in establishing the New Confederation the Swiss would design one of the world's most democratic constitutions.

Accompanying the widespread legitimacy of liberal political doctrines is the complementary principle of decentralization and local autonomy. In fact, the Swiss identify freedom with the degree of local autonomy they enjoy. The national histories of Switzerland focus upon the local cantons' struggle to maintain their freedom against the centralizing ambitions of Austria. In the Old Confederation, citizens of the various cantons clearly considered their canton the most important political entity. This cantonal and communal loyalty carried on after the collapse of the Old Confederation, when Napoleon tried and failed to impose a highly centralized regime on the Swiss and even plunged the country into civil war when the Catholics refused to accept an expansion of the power and jurisdiction of the national government in 1847. Although the defenders of local autonomy lost the war, the victorious cantons cautiously designed a federal system which included provisions for both a senate and a referendum (requiring a majority of cantons for passage of any proposition), intended to maintain the integrity of the cantons.

The strong legitimacy enjoyed by the principle of decentralization and local autonomy is not limited to the political sphere, but extends to the social and economic sectors. It has already been pointed out that the territorial principle and religious tolerance corresponded to the geographic distribution of ethnic and religious populations and helped limit religious and ethnic conflict by allowing local control of these matters—not only at the level of the canton but often at the level of the commune. It is also clear that the principles of territoriality and religious tolerance are linked very closely to the overarching Swiss national identity. In other words, to be Swiss is to accept the coexistence of a variety of cultures, lingual communities, and religions as legitimate and desirable, and to see the very diversity of Swiss culture as the secret of its richness.

Switzerland's economy evolved in the same decentralized pattern as did its political institutions. It is thus characterized by two hallmarks: great variety and multiple centers of development. The Swiss economy grew from the bottom up, as there was no central government capable of stimulating growth or creating grand designs. Thus, responding to local conditions, resources, skills, and needs, industries were established, agricultural exploitation organized, financial liquidity created, and foreign markets secured by the inhabitants of the various communes and cantons. Zurich, Basel, Bern, and Geneva all became important core areas for regional economic development. Given this pattern of growth, it is not surprising that capitalism should have been a popular political doctrine or that today Switzerland is Europe's most capitalist country. Even monetary control and welfare state functions are largely effectuated in coordination with private banks and companies rather than imposed by a centralized bureaucracy. Again, for the Swiss, decentralization means freedom, the right to be different, and the right to develop one's talents, unobstructed by centralized authority.

One might well ask, in view of such obstinate localism, how necessary cooperation at higher levels is sustained and how Switzerland keeps from falling into outright anarchy? Here a contradictory and yet compatible tradition checks the excesses which might otherwise arise. If in Switzerland there exists a cult of local autonomy, there also exists the cult of order. At the base of this cult of order are the norms of cooperation and hard work. One might be tempted to attribute this concern for order and industry to the effects of the Protestant Reformation and the Protestant ethic, if one were not already acquainted with the sober and frugal enterprise of the Catholic farmers living in the mountain cantons of central Switzerland.

Historically, life in Switzerland was always hard. The forests had to be cleared in order to cultivate the land, most of which was hilly or mountainous. The soil was not terribly rich and the growing season in many areas was limited. Switzerland has few mineral resources of any importance. When population pressures bore upon the already fragile traditional economy, the inhabitants were threatened with impoverishment and even starvation. The Swiss have reacted to these conditions in many ways: they have developed skills which allow them to transform imported raw materials into high-priced items which can be re-exported, such as watches, jewelry, precision instruments, heavy machinery, pharmaceutical and chemical products, textiles; they have used their central position in Western Europe to maximize their importance as a commercial and banking center, using their political and economic stability to expand Switzerland's international banking and insurance industry to worldwide proportions; and they have profited from the one natural resource Switzerland does have, its natural beauty, producing a multibillion dollar tourist industry.

Even today, despite the fact that Switzerland has one of the highest per capita incomes in the world, its people take life very seriously. In school, they learn that their economic wealth is precarious because Switzerland is poor in natural resources, and that if the Swiss do not compensate for this lack of materials by hard work, their standard of living will drop. They learn in their families, at school, through the media, and in numerous voluntary associations that all must produce what they can and that if all do not cooperate there will be less for everyone. This ethic of cooperation and work has attenuated the tensions arising out of the vertical and horizontal divisions of the society. No canton can survive alone; each must cooperate with the others or else all will suffer. No economic class can selfishly pursue its interests at the expense of the others or prosperity will decline. This is why the wealthy in Switzerland seem to be much more reserved and inconspicuous than in other countries. Frugality and moderation are considered public virtues and a violation of this code is sharply criticized at all levels of the society. It is even said that in contrast to the nouveau riche in America and Europe, the first great industrial magnates of Switzerland would return to their homes at night on the tram rather than in private coaches. This attitude also accounts for the fact that labor and management disputes have long since been worked out within a framework of compromise and reason, since both sides know that prolonged strikes and antagonisms can reduce Swiss exports and bring disastrous results.

This same type of quiet, orderly, and efficient behavior is required of Switzerland's government. Interest groups and parties seek to stir up support at election time, as they do in all democracies, but excessively inflammatory rhetoric weakens rather than strengthens a party's case. Once elected, the people expect their representatives to efficiently and quietly handle the business at hand with compromise and moderation. The same is true of the bureaucracy. The degree of self-effacing behavior among politicians and public servants and the degree of seriousness with which they take their responsibility of managing the people's business is amazing. In many ways, Swiss government is more like administration than politics.

The ideal of cooperation and joint enterprise is found in another dimension of Swiss life—the military. Historically, Switzerland owes its existence to its success at defending itself from the aggressive hegemonic designs of the Hapsburgs. In the nineteenth century it became increasingly clear that only a policy of neutrality, which was in the interest of all of the competing European powers which were its neighbors, could secure the independent survival of Switzerland. But this was not enough, for Switzerland would have to be an armed neutral, a nation guarded by an army which was expert at defending its difficult terrain and which could, in a defensive encounter, inflict serious losses upon an invading enemy. In short, the army must be sufficiently strong to make an attack on Switzerland not worth the cost.

In Switzerland, therefore, military service is obligatory for all male citizens. After basic training the citizen soldier must return every year for three weeks of training. The army is highly democratic; all, including officers, are citizen soldiers exercising a civilian profession. The military is a socializing agency which continually reminds the Swiss that their independence is precarious and that only their cooperation has kept them free from external domination.

Associated with neutrality and citizen militias and of great cultural importance are Switzerland's ethic of service to the victims of war and natural disaster and its image of promoter of world peace. Serving as home base for the International Red Cross and meeting place for the resolution of world problems such as arms control and Middle East tensions, Switzerland has long been perceived by its people as playing a positive and influential role in global affairs.

In summary, it is true that Switzerland is a very heterogeneous country, but linguistic, religious, economic, and regional differences have been mitigated because of the presence of a pervasive Swiss culture rooted in almost seven hundred years of common history with all its inherited images. This overarching Swiss culture is rooted in the legitimacy of cultural diversity and the right of historical minorities to maintain their identity. Cultural freedom is largely secured through compatible political values favoring decentralized government, with democracy and liberal constitutional guarantees protecting individual and minority rights and liberties. Nevertheless, the values of localism are moderated by the historical consciousness of the necessity of voluntary cooperation among all local jurisdictions, ethnic groups, religions, classes, and political persuasions in order to maintain the benefits of prosperity and order. Thus the values of compromise and mutual give-and-take, of hard work and a serious attitude toward one's social responsibilities, have left an indelible imprint on Switzerland's political, economic, and social institutions. While the ideas, values, and images presented thus far in this study may not always coincide with the facts of Swiss history, they nevertheless exert a tremendous influence upon how Switzerland's institutions function and how the Swiss currently respond to the political dimensions of their everyday lives.

Austria

In marked contrast to Switzerland's political development, Austria's political heritage is a mixture of recent contradictory and often-times traumatic transformation of values, customs, beliefs, and practices. This should not be surprising, for the infant Austrian Republic had to generate a new national identity and a new popular commitment to democratic values. Nevertheless, changes in values, beliefs, attitudes, and skills are seldom a clean-cut operation. Inevitably, they are achieved by grafting the new to the old in order to create continuity and maintain social cohesion.

NATIONAL IDENTITY

Without a symbolic linkage between national identity and existing democratic institutions, long-term political stability cannot be attained. In times of crisis this linkage justifies collective sacrifice and sustains the government until the problems can be resolved. Without it, leaders are tempted to abandon democratic institutions for dictatorship.

Clearly, a major defect of the First Republic was the lack of consensus on what it meant to be Austrian. There was no transfer of identity between the empire and the republic, no congruence between the authoritarian political culture of the former and the democratic requirements of the latter. The First Republic was born in crisis, crisis continued during the twenties, and the Great Depression deepened crisis into disaster. The retreat to dictatorship in 1934 and the acceptance of *Anschluss* in 1938 seemed the natural consequence of discontinuity in Austria's political culture.

The Second Republic faced this same identity crisis: What did it mean to be Austrian and how were Austrians different from Germans? As late as 1956, a public opinion poll showed that 46 percent of Austrians surveyed believed that Austria belonged to the German nation and was not a nation in its own right. Time, an effective political and economic system, and an emphasis upon civic training have contributed to the resolution of this identity crisis. A similar survey conducted in 1971 revealed that 92 percent of Austrians surveyed believed that Austria was, or was becoming, a nation. However, the real depth and strength of this identity is unknown and it would not be unfair to expect that at least one more generation will have to pass before the feeling of belonging to an Austrian *Volk* will become an independent stabilizing factor in Austrian politics.

Democratic Values

In addition to the problem of creating a strong national identity linked to national political institutions, Austria has faced the challenge of creating an equally strong commitment to democratic values. The new national identity had to incorporate democratic values to be fully supportive of Austria's new form of government. This has been a major challenge because of Austria's traditional authoritarian political culture. From medieval times, Hapsburg rule in Austria was authoritarian and centralized. During the Enlightenment, the degree of centralized authority increased with the creation of a modern bureaucracy, which has since grown to enormous proportions. As a consequence, the centralized bureaucratic and political structures sapped local political institutions of their jurisdiction and resources, thereby transforming them into primarily administsrative bodies. As a result, the democratic values of local control and individual participation failed to achieve widespread acceptance. One might correctly demand that the government function justly and that public policy not be formulated or applied in an arbitrary manner, but one could not demand the right to equal participation in the formulation of that policy.

The authoritarian political culture was further reinforced by the conservative political and social policies of the Catholic church. In exchange for favorable governmental programs in the area of education, morals, and other church-related issues, the Catholic church lent its support to the monarchy, denounced liberalism, and opposed social reform. It inculcated in the faithful a sense of moral obligation to not question but rather to obey traditional authority, be it that of the father, priest, or emperor.

Finally, democratic values have historically been weak because Austria never experienced a liberal revolution. The transition from the corporate economy of the Middle Ages to the capitalist economy of the nineteenth century was uneven and incomplete. The capitalist economy required the abolition of corporate restrictions on production and distribution, the proclamation of individual freedom to make contracts and own private property, and a substructure of laws designed to maintain the free market. This generally meant the dissolution of the political and economic privileges that the aristocratic classes had so long enjoyed and the creation of at least semidemocratic political institutions dominated by the capitalist class.

However, as will be explained in greater detail, the capitalists failed to achieve real power in Austria. Not only did they fail to bring into being liberal political institutions, but they also failed to inculcate the values of individual political and economic freedom in the Austrian people. As a result, real democratic revolution would have to await the coming to power of working-class parties. The Socialist Party of Austria would demand the abolition of aristocratic privilege and the creation of democratic political institutions. Nevertheless, the primary goal of the Socialists was economic equality, not individual freedom in the liberal sense of the word. Equality would be gained when the working class controlled the government; party organization, not individual political initiatives, was the key and democracy the means.

Thus, while the Socialist Party, in cooperation with the Austrian People's Party, has been very successful in achieving widespread economic equality and social well-being for the Austrian people, the full acceptance of individual civil rights and liberties as basic and sacred has not occurred. Nevertheless, a strong attachment to democracy as a procedure has been created, and with the passage of time these procedural safeguards should secure substantial individual protection.

LAGER SUBCULTURES

That national identity has not become linked to democratic values is very important, but also critical, and more divisive, is Austria's political fragmentation into three subcultures: the Christian Conservative, the Nationalist, and the Socialist. Many students of Austrian politics refer to them as *lagers* or camps in order to portray the sharpness of the divisions. Of particular importance to an understanding of Austria's present political system is the lager mentality or psychological differences which these subcultures interject into Austrian politics.

Historically, lagers grew out of the intense class conflict of the late nineteenth and early twentieth centuries, when industrialization began to restructure Austrian society. The original enemy of each of the lagers was the capitalist class and its liberal ideology. The Christian Conservatives attacked it because of their commitment to a traditional social order and, to a degree, their antisemitism; the Socialists attacked it because of the exploitation of the working class and because of their desire to bring about a socialist revolution; and the Nationalists attacked it because they perceived the capitalists to be predominately Jews who were oppressing the *Volk* and who would be willing to betray the fatherland in order to make a profit.

Under such a heavy and unified attack, liberalism died a quick death, but lager politics continued as the three blocs contended with each other. Both the Socialists and the Nationalists condemned the Christian Conservatives because of the excessive role the Catholic church played in national politics. On the other hand, the Christian Conservatives and the Nationalists denounced the Socialists as unpatriotic, un-German, as a cancer in the body politic. The Socialists countered by accusing the leaders of the other two lagers of being representatives of the capitalist class, which dominated and exploited the working class. Feelings ran deep and each lager proceeded to organize itself into independent subcultures, isolating its members from contact with members of the other lagers. The extreme right even organized paramilitary organizations comparable to the *Sturmabteilungen* (SA) in Germany. Violence escalated, climaxing in a short civil war in 1934. The Socialists were defeated, a dictatorship was established, and the Christian Conservative and Nationalist lagers moved increasingly to the right, eventually falling into the hands of the Nazis.

Following World War II, the lagers did not disappear. The Nationalists, however, were badly compromised by their collaboration with the Nazis. The Christian Conservative lager emerged embarrassed but still powerful. The Catholic church officially withdrew from formal politics, but still remained the bastion of Christian Conservative strength. However, the Socialists revived from the war years with increased vigor, undefiled because of their strong opposition to the Nazi cause.

From the point of view of political culture, this lager mentality is of great importance. It means that Austria's political processes cannot depend upon the broad social and political consensus enjoyed by other democratic systems. It further means that if stable democracy is to be achieved, political mechanisms must mediate subcultural cleavages, since these hostilities are not mediated by an extensive network of crosscutting cleavages or diluted by decentralized jurisdictions of political decision-making. Such mediating efforts are, however, facilitated by the deeply rooted values of cooperation and compromise. As a result of the lack of stress on individualism, the older and more permanent values of corporatism still exercise substantial influence. In effect, society as a whole and its various elements ought to function in an orderly and just fashion. All can benefit only when the many groups in society are integrated and perform their duties cooperatively. No one class or group within society ought to make such demands that it keeps other groups from fulfilling their functions. When conflicts occur, reasonable compromises based upon a live-and-let-live formula should be used to keep those conflicts from damaging the common good.

In summary, then, one finds many paradoxes in the political culture of Austria. A firm national identity linked to democratic institutions is taking root, yet the values of active local participation remain weak and the values of corporatism and equality supercede the values of individual civil rights and liberties. The country is ethnically and religiously rather homogenous, but horizontally its structure is split by gaping class cleavages. The values of cooperation and compromise continue to be widely held, while at the same time lager mentalities are filled with distrust and suspicion. To a degree, all political cultures have contradictions and some authors have even argued that balanced inconsistencies actually lead to political stability. However, in the case of Austria there are few inconsistent values which can independently span subcultural differences; it is rather in the area of political processes that these deep cleavages are compensated for and functional democratic government is achieved.

Internal Cleavages, Political Competition, and Citizen Participation

Switzerland

To this point, the underlying values, attitudes, and beliefs of the Swiss and Austrians have been analyzed. However, a full understanding of their politics requires that these values, beliefs, and attitudes be superimposed upon the institutions through which they are expressed. Let us begin with Switzerland's New Confederation.

The most immediate structural change in Swiss society occurred as a result of industrialization. It is important to stress that Switzerland was always one of Europe's most industrialized countries and that the full transformation of Switzerland from a principally agricultural to a highly advanced industrial economy proceeded smoothly at an average rate of decline in agricultural employment of 0.4 percent per year. The smooth and even pattern of industrialization combined with decentralized economic development around multiple core areas of growth softened the disruptive effects of industrialization upon Swiss institutions. This allowed ample time for adaptation and for localizing the focus of that adaptation.

The social impact of the industrial revolution was nevertheless substantial, for industrial development stimulated major demographic movement, which, combined with the new institutional guarantee of freedom of settlement discussed earlier, created tensions by upsetting preestablished lingual, religious, and rural-urban balances. Furthermore, industrialization created new economic conflicts as a growing working class demanded a large share of industrial profits and threatened farmers resisted the rationalization of the agricultural sector. In fact, Swiss experience is very much in harmony with current theory which argues that within most Western democracies the major political cleavages, that is the active conflict-generating divisions, are an outgrowth of the industrial revolution. Thus, the fundamental issues which animate Swiss political life, as well as the underlying political organizations such as pressure groups and political parties, are largely a response to the conditions created by the tremendous transformation occasioned by modernity.

Table 5.1, which describes shifts in the structure of the Swiss labor force, reveals the pace of transformation and the present structure of the work force. The fact that the industrial work force was already relatively large near the turn of the century is a sign of the early pace of industrialization. The fact that the service sector emerged thereafter as the most dynamic area of labor

TABLE 5.1

Swiss Working Population by Sector, 1798–1970 (In Percentages)*

Economic Sector	1798	1820	1850	1880	1900
Agriculture	65.8	62.3	57.4	42.4	32.1
Industry	26.3	28.8	32.5	41.8	48.0
Service	7.9	8.9	10.1	15.8	19.8
	1920	1941	1950	1960	1970
Agriculture	27.1	23.2	18.1	13.2	7.6
Industry	48.8	48.5	51.1	48.5	48.4
Service	24.1	28.4	30.8	38.2	44.1

*Column totals may not equal 100 percent due to rounding error.

Sources: F. Sneschaurek, "Wandlungen der schweizerischen Industriestruktur seit 1800," as reported in Jean-François Berger, *Problèmes de l'histoire économique de la Suisse* (Bern: Editions Francke, 1968); and Switzerland, Bureau fédéral de statistique, *Annuaire statistique 1972*.

market growth and presently employs almost as many people as the industrial sector is a sign of the advanced stage of economic development in Switzerland. Today, Switzerland has an economy based on high technology, with widespread prosperity and consumer-oriented production.

The transformation is further underlined by the process of urbanization. Whereas before 1847 there were few cities in Switzerland with more than 10,000 people, today the vast majority of Swiss live in urban areas and the pace of urbanization has proceeded in almost perfect inverse correlation to the decline of the agricultural sector. Thus as the agricultural sector became increasingly rationalized, the local inhabitants moved to the city to find industrial employment.

The major interest groups and political parties presently active in Swiss politics emerged from the conflict generated by this almost total restructuring of Swiss social and economic life. During the first fifty years under the New Confederation, interest groups and politics in general revolved around two major parties and a strong minor party. The Radical Democrats, who supported the movement toward the drafting of the new constitution, were in the majority, although the Liberal Democratic Party, which stood somewhat to the right of the Radicals, enjoyed a large constituency in the early years of the New Confederation. It subsequently lost ground to the Radicals and other splinter parties. The Conservative and Christian Social Party, now known as the Christian Democratic People's Party, was the second major party and represented the interests of the Catholic cantons. In a sense, the party structure reflected the issues of the *Sonderbundskrieg*. As already noted, these issues transcended religious disagreements over the separation of church and state. They helped create the basis for a modern capitalist economy by legally destroying the last vestiges of the feudal, guild, and commercial economies which existed at that time. The Radical Democrats represented the interests of the new middle class and the industrialists, while the Conservative and Christian Social Party sought to resist the intrusion of this new economy into the traditional mountain agriculture of central Switzerland.

However, this rigid two-party majoritarian system was ill-adapted to Switzerland. For one thing, it forced the interests of labor and the interests of the Protestant farmers to be reconciled in the Radical Party, which was at the same time promoting the interests of the commercial elite and industrial class. After World War I, these internal tensions came to a head. The General Strike of 1918 was called by leaders of labor and one of their principal demands was the institutionalization of proportional representation, a system of election which allocates seats in the legislature on the basis of the percentage of the national vote each party receives, rather than apportioning the legislature on the basis of the outcomes of hundreds of local voting district contests. The first year that this new system was used there was a major shift in the party structure. The Radical Democrats lost almost half their seats in the National Council and the Social Democrats emerged as the second strongest party in the council.

The shift to the proportional system was much more in keeping with Swiss tradition, for the Confederation had always been a coalition of cantons which resolved common problems through friendly accommodation rather than majority rule. Furthermore, it satisfied the Swiss preference for democracy, one in which every group's interests were considered, and the final process of policy formulation usually emerged as collaboration and consensus rather than the triumph of one group or party over another.

This goes a long way toward explaining why Switzerland has been spared the destabilizing and often violent confrontation between the demands of labor and interests of business. The system of proportional representation allowed labor to enter into the policy-making process and eventually to become the dominant party in the National Council. At the same time, the spirit of collaboration and Switzerland's cultural norms, stressing the necessity of cooperation in this small country with its precarious economy, tempered the more radical demands of labor and in general promoted mutual compromise. Thus, in 1937 the principal industries and labor unions signed an agreement called Peace in Labor, in which an institutionalization of procedures for contract negotiations was agreed upon. This agreement bore upon all subjects of mutual interest, including work hours and conditions as well as salary, vacation, and social benefits. Since that time, Switzerland has had virtually no strikes and the Swiss laborer has come to enjoy one of the highest standards of living in the world.

This Peace in Labor agreement would not have been possible had the Social Democratic Party not given up its ideological moorings, choosing to improve the conditions of the laborer pragmatically rather than through revolution. The Communist Party, which has until very recently held fast to the inevitability of violent revolution, has never enjoyed influence in Swiss politics, failing to garner more than a few percentage points of the vote. Of course the reasons for this go beyond those presented here and will be more comprehensively considered later.

The proportional system of representation made possible the emergence of two other parties reflecting the conflicts created by the industrial revolution. As already noted, the modernization of the Swiss economy inevitably led to the rationalization of Swiss agriculture. Thus, farmers banded together with interest groups representing small merchants and craftsmen to create a party called the Farmer, Artisan, and Citizen's Party. This party demanded governmental action to reduce the effects of economic rationalization upon farmers, craftsmen, and small businessmen. Fortunately for Swiss farmers, such demands could be defended on the grounds of national security, since Switzerland's foreign policy of perpetual neutrality necessitated a certain degree of autarchy and therefore required that the Swiss government pass legislation protecting the Swiss agricultural market against excessive foreign competition. This may also account in part for the smooth moderate rate of decline in agricultural employment over the last hundred years.

Nevertheless, the efforts of interest groups and parties such as the Farmer, Artisan, and Citizen's Party, now called the Swiss People's Party, to protect the incomes of their members against the increasing impact of economic rationalization necessarily created higher prices. In response, there emerged the Independent Party, which demanded lower prices for consumers by increasing the efficiency of product distribution and eliminating the protectionist privileges of less efficient sectors of the economy. In general, the Independent Party has supported all policies which promote the interests of the consumer in the marketplace. The founder, Gottlieb Duttweiler, was the first to introduce the mass marketing of groceries and other household products. He was so successful that he extended his efforts into other consumer sectors, and today the cooperative enterprises he started extend into such diverse businesses as banking, restaurants, and education.

Obviously, in order to maintain their strength, both the Radical Democratic Party and the Conservative and Christian Social Party have also adapted their platforms to the changing substance of Swiss politics and to the challenge of competing parties. The Radicals have come to support necessary social welfare policies as well as measures designed to secure economic equilibrium, but remain the staunch defenders of the capitalist nature of the Swiss economy.

Due to the increased secularization of Swiss culture, religious issues have declined in importance and the effects of the separation of church and state have become a fait accompli. Thus, the Conservative and Christian Social Party, now called the Christian Democratic People's Party or CVP, has shifted its emphasis to secondary issues such as defending the federal structure of government against the increasing centralizing pressures of the modern Swiss economy and conserving Switzerland's traditional norms and culture. In addition, however, Christian trade unions represent the second largest labor group in Switzerland and the left wing of this party supports labor policies in harmony with the social teachings of the Catholic church. Finally, because the CVP is almost entirely made up of Catholics, its influence is very strong in the politics of Catholic and mixed cantons and obviously in the Council of States, which, like the American Senate, accords representation on a geographic basis (with the canton being the basic unit of geographic representation).

The moderation and stability which typify Switzerland's contemporary political life have been buttressed by nearly 700 years of cantonal cooperation. Thus, prior to the founding of the New Confederation, an overarching sense of community, an identity in which the values of cultural diversity, local autonomy, religious coexistence, cantonal cooperation, consensual politics, democracy, equilitarianism, hard work, and individual responsibility had long since achieved legitimacy. In particular, the New Confederation inherited the deeply rooted popular conviction that the peace and prosperity which the Swiss had so long enjoyed depended upon a mutual give-and-take from all members of the community, and that compromise and practical action would in the long run bear the best fruit.

The radical politics which led to the *Sonderbundskrieg* and a federal constitution may appear to contradict these values. However, the liberal reforms and guarantees were very much compatible with Swiss tradition. Even the new federal institutions were designed to only slightly modify the degree of local autonomy that had heretofore existed. While in specific cantons the conflict between the Catholics and radicals continued after the end of the *Sonderbundskrieg*, the civil war did not create long-term religious hatred and the liberal reforms were soon accepted by the Catholic cantons.

Second, Switzerland's cultural and social fragmentation has been along crosscutting lines. The argument is as follows: when the cleavages which divide a society run parallel, they tend to reinforce each other and make intergroup cooperation more difficult; however, when they cut across each other, they tend to attenuate conflict and reduce the emotional content of any single cleavage. Thus, in Switzerland, the French-speaking population is divided by religion. The Calvinist Protestants of Geneva and Lausanne and the extremely orthodox Catholics of Fribourg and the Valais have opposed each other for centuries. Furthermore, the French-speaking population is divided economically, some living in cities and practicing a variety of nonagricultural professions, and others living in the countryside and practicing agricultural professions. Within the latter category, there is substantial occupational diversity. The French-speaking Swiss are divided in terms of their incomes; some earning large, others moderate, and some small incomes. The same crisscrossing patterns of cleavage exist in education. The same diversity can be found among the Swiss-Germans and to a degree among Swiss-Italians. In short, while, for example, a Swiss-French may have language and to a degree culture in common with other French-speaking Swiss, he might be separated from many of them by religion, education, and class. In fact, he might have more in common with Swiss-Italians and Swiss-Germans who share with him the same religion, education, and class. Thus, while in truth Switzerland is a country of great cultural diversity, the lines of division do not run deep and are weakened by the multiple crosscutting patterns which tie Switzerland's heterogeneous population into a whole.

These cross-pressures are clearly discernible at the interest group level of Swiss politics. Thus, agricultural pressure groups, whether French-, German-, or Italian-speaking, whether from Protestant or Catholic areas, cooperate politically to secure the interests of Swiss farmers. The same is true for the two major labor union groupings, Catholic and socialist, for business and professional groupings, and for cultural and religious organizations.

Swiss political parties also cut across the nation's cleavage structure Socialists and Radical Democrats are drawn from all areas, religions, languages, and cultural groups. The Christian People's Party is largely Catholic but cuts across occupational, cultural, linguistic, and regional cleavages. The same is true of the Independent and Swiss People's parties.

In summary, since the Swiss cannot invest their full interests and emotions in any single group and since social, economic, and cultural composition differs from organization to organization, the net effect is a limit to the degree of attachment and exclusivity any single interest can obtain. The inevitable political consequence is moderation and compromise.

The moderating influence of Switzerland's crosscutting cleavage structure is complemented and strengthened by a number of accompanying conditions. First, as has already been noted, the industrial revolution proceeded at a very smooth and even rate in Switzerland, allowing adjustment time for the hundreds of thousands of persons who left the countryside for the city and gave up farming for industrial or service employment. Many adjustments were of course necessary, but the important point is that the in-migrating populations had time to adapt to their new environment and to the new norms and lifestyles found in urban settings. In essence, the growing cities had sufficient time to accommodate the demands of the new population and assimilate them into their social and political fabric.

The importance of the smooth and even rate of social mobilization can in particular be seen in the area of ethnic relations. As a result of the rationalization of the agricultural sector, tens of thousands of Swiss-Germans from cantons such as Bern, Aargau, and Thurgau migrated to cantons other than that of their family origin, oftentimes to the French or Italian areas of Switzerland. Had the rate of mobilization been too rapid, it would have generated conflict, as the Swiss-Germans would have flooded the minority French- and Italian-speaking cantons with wave after wave of newcomers. The local residents would have interpreted the population shifts as an invasion and would have resisted the inevitable cultural dissolution that such numbers of Swiss-Germans would have signaled. In fact, however, the stream of immigrants proceeded at a constant rate, a rate which allowed each wave to be assimilated into the local culture. As implied by the territorial principle, the immigrant moving into an area where another language is the historical language is obligated to learn the local tongue. This has in fact taken place. If one opens the telephone book of Lausanne, Neuchâtel, or Geneva, all French-speaking areas, one will find a large percentage of Swiss-German names. However, the vast majority have been raised in the French culture and consider French their mother language. They have been assimilated to pose no threat to the ethnic integrity of the canton.

In a sense, then, the mobilization of the Swiss economy has bound the country together into a closer-knit society because a large number of French- and Italian-speaking Swiss have German-speaking relatives. Thus, they are bound together not only by crosscutting interests and values, but by blood as well.

The same factor has played an important role in diluting the geographic separation of the Protestants and Catholics. As migrants from the poor Catholic mountain cantons moved to the cities looking for work, they broke down the Protestant homogeneity of many of these urban cantons. Thus, cities like Geneva and Zurich, once the centers of Protestant fanaticism, now have very important Catholic populations. To a lesser degree, there has been a migration of Protestants into predominately Catholic cantons. Since the rate of mobility was smooth and even, segregation has been diluted and contact and intermarriage have increased without undue reaction and the result has been better mutual understanding between the religious groups.

The smooth and constant rate of economic modernization also cushioned the impact of the economic disruption which modernization inevitably imposes. Switzerland has never had large slums inhabited by proletarian workers. In many cases there was a transition period when farmers would work during the winter months at home or in local factories making watches, and in the summer spend the majority of their time farming. Or they would work part-time in local factories and the rest of the time on the farm; or some members of the family would work in the factory while the others worked on the farm. Furthermore, only recently have gigantic industrial firms emerged. Most Swiss production still takes place in small and middle-sized concerns where direct human contact between management and labor has been maintained and where owners of enterprises feel a deeper sense of responsibility for the well-being of their workers.

A slow, even mobilization of the Swiss economy led to greater integration, more intense division of labor, and more cross-pressures creating new interests and natural allies. The decentralized nature of economic modernization also reduced political conflict and the miseries of the industrial transition by furnishing local core areas where migrants could find work. It eased ethnic conflict by furnishing in all ethnic regions dynamic areas of core growth, and by reducing the need, in particular among the French-speaking Swiss, to migrate to Swiss-German centers. As a result, the Swiss-French population felt less vulnerability vis-à-vis the dominant Swiss-German cantons.

The success of Switzerland's economy has also facilitated political stability. With Sweden, Switzerland enjoys the highest per capita income of all Western industrial countries. According to almost any of the major indices of standard of living, Switzerland ranks first. Swiss workers enjoy far-reaching social benefits, low taxes, and stability of employment.

Historically, the upward mobility created by economic modernization was enjoyed by all classes of Swiss. Switzerland ranks as the European country where the upward mobility of all classes has been the broadest and where family position has been least likely to guarantee an automatically successful future to the children of an achieving parent.

Thus, from an economic perspective, one encounters the strange paradox of Europe's most capitalist economy having passed through the industrial revolution with the broadest conditions of upward mobility and social equality. This was possible because there was no deeply rooted aristocracy to displace. As a result, the class antagonisms characteristic of many other European countries are almost absent in Switzerland.

Industrialization sharpened Switzerland's division of labor, and intensified interdependence. The highly integrated agricultural, industrial, and financial structures of the Swiss economy function as a complex whole and therefore create a far stronger sense of common interest than the more loosely jointed and parochial preindustrial Swiss economy.

The last major category of moderating factors involves Switzerland's political institutions. As has been stressed, the historical practice of delimiting conflict through federalism, that is, granting to communal and cantonal jurisdictions the autonomy to resolve problems in keeping with the opinions of the local inhabitants, allowed the Swiss Confederation to grow from a small alliance to a strong political community. Of course, this requires tolerance for heterogeneity because the various cantons and communes are likely to resolve important questions in different and sometimes contradictory fashions. It also requires that conflict be largely geographically or spatially defined. This has often been the case with Switzerland's lingual, ethnic, religious, and economic populations.

Therefore, except for guaranteeing civil liberties, the national government has avoided the problem of having to formulate a comprehensive, nationwide cultural and lingual policy by allowing local cantons and communes to define their own policies. The same is true of religion. Beyond subsidizing Swiss churches and guaranteeing religious freedom, the Confederation has left the definition of religious policy to the cantons. The same has also been generally true of economic policy. Only recently, as a result of the need to create conditions of economic equilibrium in a highly advanced and complex national and world economic system, has the Swiss government begun to manage the economy and assume responsibility for conditions of economic growth, employment, and monetary stability.

Moreover, as has already been shown, the system of proportional representation in the National Council, combined with the cantonal representation in the Council of States, maximized the representation of all interests, geographically defined or otherwise. Thanks to proportional representation and the initiative and referendum, Switzerland has been forced to deal with its problems at one level of government or another. As has been shown, it could not leave problems to fester because the very structure of the system makes it almost impossible to ignore them. To forestall initiatives, the government as well as private organizations have had to anticipate what might be the reactions of the populace in general and of its divergent minorities.

Finally, Switzerland's foreign policy of neutrality has allowed the national government to avoid making decisions on foreign policy questions which might divide the population. Although the policy of perpetual neutrality had not been entirely formulated by the time of the Thirty Years' War, it was consciously used by the Old Confederation to keep religious questions from destroying the alliance. In modern times, in the midst of the fevered nationalism of the late nineteenth and early twentieth centuries and especially during World War I, neutrality protected the Swiss ethnic populations from the divisive passions of European nationalism and thereby sustained the integrity of the New Confederation.

Neutrality also means that Switzerland has only had to invest that amount of money in defense which was necessary to defend its mountaineous terrain. The money required for an offensive capability was either left in the private economy or invested in public areas to resolve domestic problems, a feature of Swiss life highly envied by most of this Alpine nation's Western European neighbors.

Austria

At first view, Austria might appear to be similar to other small Western European democracies, being approximately the size of Maine and having a population of only nine million. Yet while Austria has certainly passed through the industrial transition, statistics on sector transition point to the very special nature of the transformation of the Austrian economy. As late as 1961, 16.4 percent of the active population still worked in the agricultural sector. Since Austria is not particularly suited for an agriculturally oriented economy, this rather high figure appears to reflect a historical resistance to agricultural rationalization.

What is true of agriculture is also true of Austrian industrial development: rationalization of production was resisted and efforts were made to accommodate the new industrial system to the traditional corporate economy. In short, as has already been noted, Austria never fully accepted the liberal ideology. Competition has never acquired the legitimacy in Austria which it has enjoyed in England and the United States; to the contrary, it has traditionally been perceived as illegitimate and antisocial. As a result, the government nationalized important parts of the economy even before World War I. It gained increasing control over banking institutions, and by the end of World War II there was sufficient political support for the nationalization of most important banks and numerous industrial enterprises and for the purchase of stock—in most cases controlling interests—in many others. In fact, Austria may have the largest public sector in Western Europe. Steiner attributes 63 percent of corporate capital to the public sector, 14 percent of the gross national product to public or semipublic enterprises, and 6 percent of the working population to nationalized enterprises.[1]

In addition to outright nationalization, the government has historically supported protectionist legislation designed to preserve merchants and small *commerçants* from more efficient systems of product distribution, to preserve small farmers from land consolidation, and even to encourage or at least not punish firms for cartelization and market sharing. Almost any activity on the market requires some type of authorization, license, or certificate, and "fair trade" restrictions abound. All this reflects the desire to limit competition and to maintain the corporate and almost guild-like character of the traditional economy.

The pervasive role that the central government plays in Austria's economic life could also be portrayed, if space allowed, in an examination of the administrative functions of the national government. In a sense, it is but the continuation of a trend toward centralization and paternalistic bureaucratic rule which binds together Austria's vertical social structure. The economy, social groups, interests and pressure groups, and political parties are in general organized to provide inputs into the national political and bureaucratic superstructure. An analysis of Austria's political parties and their supportive lagers will further substantiate this fact.

The major political parties in Austria follow lager cleavages and furnish a clear example of the national and self-encapsulated nature of lager politics.

An examination of the Socialist Party of Austria, the SPO, will illustrate this point. The party was originally organized in the 1880s, and because it was excluded from participating in the political process, it turned its energies to building an independent socialist community capable of meeting the broad gamut of needs of its membership. It published newspapers, books, pamphlets, and other materials; it provided for political education; it organized trade unions and socialist clubs and associations for its members whatever their age, sex, or station, for the young, professional people, women, university students, sportsmen, etc. Even when after World War I the SPO gained the right of full political participation, its isolated, cohesive, and all-inclusive social organization remained intact. In the 1930s, as Austria embraced fascism and moved toward *Anschluss*, the SPO was forced to go underground. Many of its leaders were arrested and sent to concentration camps. After World War II, the party reemerged, supported by the same powerful vertical lager organization. In many ways, the party was much strengthened and its membership grew, as did its political power. As one of the government parties in the Grand Coalition, it benefitted from incumbency and in particular from the numerous patronage jobs which were filled in the nationalized sector and in the bureaucracy.

While the organizational isolation and complexity of the SPO has only slightly diminished, despite at least twenty years of postwar prosperity, the ideological intensity of its appeal has weakened substantially, particularly at the level of the masses. While more radical than the SPD (German Socialist Party), the SPO has become increasingly pragmatic in dealing with the substantive political, social, and economic problems facing Austria. Marxism continues to exercise influence among intellectuals, but the party has remained anticommunist, criticizing the policies of the Soviet Union and refusing all alliances with Austria's Communist Party. In fact, it is because of the power of the SPO, with its comprehensive organization and union dominance, that the communists remain so weak.

The Austrian People's Party, or the OVP, represents Austria's second major lager. It is a descendant of the prewar Christian Social Party, which itself was a merger of the highly antisemitic and nationalist Christian Social Party and the Catholic Conservatives. Although it represented broad interests running from Catholic workers to small farmers, the Christian Social Party gradually came to defend the position of large landowners and the business and commercial class. It was a core around which the governments of the First Republic were organized and in the 1930s reflected the influence of rabid nationalist and fascist elements in Austria. Eventually, it was to support the movement toward dictatorship.

After World War II the party reemerged as the Austrian People's Party, led by members of the Christian Social Party who had opposed facism. The party brandished new and appealing social doctrines designed to underline its shift away from the discredited programs of the Christian Social Party. In fact, however, the old business and agricultural interests soon came to control the party, moving it gradually back to the right. Recently, a new generation of leaders has come of age, but these political notables have devoted most of their attention to tactical questions rather than ideology. The OVP was the dominant element in the GrandCoalition until in 1966 it received enough seats in the National Assembly to organize a cabinet alone. In 1971, however, it suffered a defeat at the polls and moved into opposition.

Perhaps the most important political development for the OVP was the Catholic church's decision after the war to withdraw from partisan politics. This did not mean that the OVP would not remain the party of devout Catholics, but it did mean that many of the auxiliary organizations and facilities of the Catholic church would no longer be available. The party compensated by restructuring its organization around three internal federations: the Federation of Austrian Farmers, the Federation of Austrian Workers and Employees, and the Federation of Austrian Business. In addition to these, a broad gamut of specialized organizations for young people, for women, etc., continues to bind the Christian Conservative lager tightly to the party in a vertical organization similar to that of the SPO.

The Nationalist Party or *Freiheitliche Partei Oesterreich*, which is the successor to the prewar Nationalist Party, was heavily discredited because of its collaboration with the Nazis. While the secondary organizations of this lager still have influence, the popular appeal of the party has declined from almost 12 percent in 1945 to somewhat more than 5 percent in recent elections. The *Kommunistische Partei Oesterreich*, or the KPO, exercised considerable power in the initial postwar government due to the support of the Soviet occupation forces, but it was clearly rejected by the Austrians when in the first election the party only received about 5 percent of the vote. The party has since undergone destalinization and has become increasingly independent of the Soviet Union. Apparently it entertained hopes of combining with the SPO in the mid-1960s in order to create a majority coalition in the National Assembly, but all initiatives were rejected by the SPO. The electoral appeal of the KPO has dropped to less than 2 percent and it controls no seats in the National Assembly.

Governmental Institutions and the Policy-Making Process

Switzerland

Having completed our examination of the sociocultural makeup of both Switzerland and Austria, we can now turn our attention to their respective governmental institutions. It is quite clear that many of Switzerland's institu-

TABLE 5.2

Party Representation in Switzerland's National Council

Party	1975		1979	
	% Vote	Seats	% Vote	Seats
Social Democratic Party (SPS)	24.9	55	24.9	51
Radical Democratic Party (FDP)	22.2	47	24.0	51
Christian Democratic People's Party (CVP)	21.1	46	21.1	44
Swiss People's Party (SVP)	9.9	21	11.5	23
Independent Party (LdU)	6.2	11	4.2	8
Swiss Liberal Party (LPS)*	2.4	6	2.8	8
Republican Movement (Rep.)	3.0	4	0.6	1
Party of Labor (Communist)(PdA)	2.4	4	2.1	3
Evangelical People's Party (EVP)	2.0	3	2.3	3
National Action Against the Foreign Infiltration of People and Homeland (NA)	2.5	2	1.4	2
Progressive Organizations of Switzerland/Autonomous Socialist Party (POCH/PSA)	1.3	1	2.1	3
Others	2.1	0	3.0	3

*The Swiss Liberal Party was formed in 1977 from the Liberal Democratic Union of Switzerland

tions can trace their origins to the inception of the Confederation. At the cantonal and communal levels, many old-time political structures have survived and at the federal level, despite the revolutionary origins of the new constitutions, the principles of federalism and direct democracy definitely reflect Swiss tradition. In fact, the federal political structures were designed with great care to harmonize with Swiss tradition. The Swiss took the United States for a model rather than Great Britain, perhaps because the United States also originated as a confederation and then moved on to a more tightly knit federation.

Three structures form the heart of the federal political structures: the National Council, the Council of States, and the Federal Council. The National Council and Council of States correspond to the American House of Representatives and Senate. The Federal council is a collective executive made up of seven councilors.

THE NATIONAL COUNCIL

The National Council is the most important legislative body. Its two hundred members are elected directly by the people through a system of proportional representation. Cantons with a population over 36,000 form the primary electoral district to which a number of legislative seats are assigned according to the size of the population. Thus, the large cantons such as Zurich and Bern dominate, with the cantons of Vaud, Aargau, and St. Gallen exercising substantial influence.

The National Council is reconstituted every four years. Although the list system is generally used, when the number of seats each canton is allocated does not correspond with the breakdown of the vote, alternative procedures are invoked to determine the winner. In principle, any fifteen citizens can submit a list, but in practice the major parties propose the lists from which members of the council are elected.

As already noted, the system is particularly well-adapted to the needs of Switzerland. Its advantage is that it directly reflects the diversity of the country in the National Council (see Table 5.2). Obviously, since no one party can win a majority, it is necessary for parties to form coalitions, to negotiate, to compromise, and to take into account the interests of a broader number of groups in order to get the ruling majority necessary for the passage of legislation. Furthermore, because parties are more numerous, they tend to represent the views of specific interest groups, and thus, interest articulation in the National Council is more clear-cut than in a majoritarian system such as the United States. Of course, because of the subsequent need to build legislative coalitions, national elections are not the most decisive level of political competition; rather, parliamentary negotiation and bargaining determines which political groups and sets of policies will succeed.

Several European countries have shifted away from the proportional system because it has generally resulted in stalemate. The French Third and Fourth republics, the Weimar Republic in Germany, and the present republic in Italy have faced or now face the difficulties of arriving at a political formula that all parliamentary factions can accept so that a stable majority coalition can effectively rule. In the absence of such a coalition, a succession of unsure governments rises and falls with the arbitrary changes of the political barometer.

It is equally evident, however, that in small European democracies, the system of proportional representation has often worked well and has furnished the basis for an efficient and dynamic government. Such is the case of Switzerland. The crucial element is that the political culture reflects bonds of consensus sufficiently strong and sufficiently intimate to mediate the diversities expressed in the proportionally elected legislature. As already noted, the long tradition of coalition rather than majoritarian practices, the belief that both militarily and economically cooperation and conciliation of all Swiss were absolutely necessary, the dislike of radical rhetoric and violent politics, and the preference for practical, workable solutions over ideological programs have all tempered partisanship in Switzerland and have promoted compromise among the factions in the Swiss National Council. It is clear that such favorable conditions for proportional representation tend to exist in small countries, where social life is more intimate and less likely to be mediated by intervening social structures. One final note—Switzerland's decentralized federal political system has no doubt contributed to the effectiveness of proportional representation, for many of the issues which would otherwise be most divisive are resolved at the cantonal and communal levels according to the wishes of local populations. If one single solution, for example, to the problem of ethnic relations had to be imposed by the national government upon all local jurisdictions, the possibilities for conflict would be unending. It is easy to imagine how this could be duplicated in the area of religion and in the conflicts between large cities and the countryside.

THE COUNCIL OF STATES

The Swiss Council of States represents the interests of the cantons, and each canton enjoys the prerogative of determining the method and period of election to this legislative chamber. Each of Switzerland's federated cantons is entitled to two seats in the council, and specially designated districts, known as "half cantons," are each eligible for one seat.

Along with the National Council, the Council of States fulfills an important policy-making function and must approve all legislative and fiscal measures before they can be implemented by federal authorities. Moreover, these two legislative chambers, which together comprise the Federal Assembly, oversee the activities of the civil service and the military and select the members of the Federal Council and the Federal Supreme Court.

THE FEDERAL COUNCIL

Of all of Switzerland's federal institutions, the Federal Council is the most unique and the most Swiss, and such executive councils are also commonplace in the cantons and most communes. The Federal Council functions in accordance with the collegial principle, that is, a collective executive made up of seven councilors who are collectively responsible for all executive decisions. Its members are elected by the Federal Assembly, and once elected, they cannot be brought down by a vote of no confidence. They serve four-year terms and in fact are generally reelected until they choose to retire. A member of the council is also asked, on an annual basis, to serve as the President of the Swiss Confederation. Federal councilors are selected from all of the major ethnic communities, from diverse cantons, and from both principal faiths. Since the Great Depression, the political composition of the council has remained relatively stable, with the Social Democratic, Radical Democratic, and Christian People's parties having two councilors and the Swiss People's Party having one. Thus, the Federal Council reflects the diversity of Switzerland. Nevertheless, it is unified by its members' experience and professions. A strong majority of its members have had experience in cantonal or communal government and come from the legal profession.

Despite the fact that the federal councilors come from diverse backgrounds, they have historically shown a great degree of solidarity. They work together intimately over a long period of time to deal with the problems of the Confederation. They seldom disagree in public, and generally the councilor who is in charge of a particular ministry will have the decisive influence on any policy which concerns his ministry, although he will always take into account the opinions of the other councilors. Decisions taken by the council are collective decisions and can only be revised by a new collective decision. The cohesion of the Federal Council reflects the essential traits of Swiss politics: cooperation and compromise and the tendency of the Swiss to govern by committee.

The fact that this body functions as a unit and not according to the individual whims of its members is particularly important given the council's great power. When one considers that the Federal Assembly is out of session for most of the year and that the task of ruling falls almost completely into the hands of the Federal Council, it is not surprising that it is looked upon as the dominant institution of Swiss politics.

Despite its apparent efficiency, the Federal Council currently runs the grave risk of degenerating into a mere administrative body. The emphasis upon cooperation often promotes bureaucratic rather than political solutions to problems. In many ways, the Federal Council has become depoliticized and in doing so has failed to be creative. Its solutions tend to be patchwork compromises and lack overall planning. This critique may be unfair; it may not reflect the constraints which the multiple division of authority imposes upon the council, yet it remains a constant danger which the council must eventually be prepared to confront.

THE REFERENDUM AND INITIATIVE

In America, the court system has been the most effective avenue for constitutional reform, but in Switzerland the Supreme Court does not have the same power to interpret and amend the constitution. The amendment process in Switzerland is much more direct and requires only a majority of popular votes and a majority of the cantons. Thus, referenda and initiatives have become a much more important political structure than in America.

Referenda are most important at the cantonal and communal levels. At the national level, referenda are compulsory only if the Federal Council wants to amend the constitution and may be used on an optional basis when it wishes to gain the assent of the people on various pieces of federal legislation or on international treaties.

Initiatives represent a much more potent political instrument, for with fifty thousand signatures any political group can propose an amendment to the constitution. Some initiatives are simply recommendations that the federal government take action on certain problems, but others propose written texts which become binding upon passage.

The initiative is the heart of Swiss democracy and has a rich tradition in the history of Swiss constitutionalism. After its adoption at the federal level between 1892 and 1930, initiatives have been proposed in great numbers, and while they have not often been accepted, they have had a marked influence upon Swiss politics. The Federal Council and the Federal Assembly, fearful that a clear-cut policy proposal might generate an initiative, tend to refrain from long-term planning. When unpopular measures are necessary to meet economic crises, the fear that an initiative might be generated leads the federal government to season its legislation with benefits for all groups which might resort to the initiative. Furthermore, as economic and social policies have become increasingly technical and difficult to understand, the ability of the average citizen to make enlightened choices declines and the tendency of interest groups to simplify these issues in terms of immediate individual gains increases.

The most damning crituque of the initiative is the degree to which it weakens Swiss political structures. The initiative weakens the Federal Council, the legislative bodies, and the parties, and strengthens pressure groups because most pressure groups are capable of gathering fifty thousand signatures without the help of a party, and therefore their dependence upon party organization and the legislative process as a means of achieving policy change declines. Finally, the initiative allows interest groups to circumvent normal political procedures and safeguards created to secure well-designed and just legislation. Despite all of the criticisms of the initiative, it has been used with discretion, and controversial initiatives linked to the abrogation of civil rights have in almost every case been rejected.

On the positive side, the initiative has kept the political system supple. It has furnished the people a tool with which they can keep institutions and elites attentive to the major concerns of the common people and it has helped forestall bureaucratic sclerosis. While it can be used by powerful interest groups, it can also be used by small interest groups to keep the powerful and wealthy from dominating the political process. In a sense, the initiative makes it very difficult for the federal government to repress conflicts and ignore issues which are important to even a small population. Therefore, at all levels of Swiss government, not only is substantial participation elicited but the initiative allows the voters to communicate with the government on substantive issues. Finally, one must consider the broad legitimacy and strengths which Swiss institutions enjoy because they are close to the people and must deal with their real, felt problems.

THE COURT SYSTEM

The Swiss judicial system is one of the most decentralized in the Western world, with the conduct of judicial proceedings and the organization of the courts left in the hands of cantonal authorities. Prominent features of cantonal legal systems can often be traced back to local traditions, and some of the cantons even permit lay people to serve as judges in certain instances.

However, a great deal of uniformity does exist among the cantons in terms of important procedural and substantive judicial matters. A federal code of civil law was enacted in 1912, and a federal code of penal law was put into effect during World War II. Uniformity is also enhanced by the provision which permits the Swiss Federal Court to be the tribunal of last resort in both civil and penal cases. Moreover, conflicts of jurisdiction in civil or public law between the Confederation and the Cantons, or between two or more cantons, are also settled by the Federal Court.

With the expansion of state activities over the past few decades, administrative law has also become increasingly important. Practically every canton has now established independent administrative courts which have a mandate to protect Swiss citizens against unfair encroachment into their lives by state authorities. At the federal level, the Federal Court and, under certain circumstances, the Federal Council have jurisdiction over administrative law matters. Once again, the Federal Court has the final say in the ultimate disposition of cases involving the public administration.

Austria

Like Switzerland, Austria is a federal state, with the two major levels of jurisdiction being the federal government and the *Länder* governments (Länder are somewhat like states in the United States). Further down the line are district and city jurisdictions. However, the Länder governments do not exercise nearly as much authority as their cantonal counterparts. Although each of the nine states possesses its own provincial assembly and cabinet, the Austrian states can only legislate independently in limited and, with few exceptions, minor areas. Their most important responsibility is to elaborate, implement, and administer laws passed at the federal level.

THE PARLIAMENT

At the federal level, two legislative bodies compose the parliament: the National Assembly and the Federal Council. The government is a "weak-cabinet parliamentary system" in which a chancellor presides over a cabinet dependent upon the confidence of a legislative body which is elected by proportional representation for a fixed term. Thus, if the National Assembly withdraws its support from the cabinet by failing to pass a motion of confidence or by passing a motion of censure, the old cabinet falls and a new cabinet is formed, but no new parliamentary election is absolutely necessary in order to effectuate this change in cabinets.

The 183 members of the National Assembly are elected for four years by proportional representation, meaning that a political party is allocated the number of legislative seats which most closely corresponds to the percentage of the vote it receives in the general election.

The Federal Council is supposed to represent the various regions of Austria. Its 58 members are elected by the respective state legislatures, with not more than 12 coming from the largest state and no fewer than 3 from the smallest state. The exact ratio is worked out on the basis of the population distribution reported in the most recent census. However, the extremely powerful role that the highly centralized parties play in this selection process undermines the regional character of the body, since the major political parties in fact nominate candidates to the Federal Council. Once elected, these state councilors tend to reflect party interests rather than regional ones.

The limited powers of the Federal Council further limit its effectiveness in representing regional interests. The Federal Council can refuse to ratify laws passed by the National Assembly, but the National Assembly can override this refusal by simply repassing the law with a quorum of at least 50 percent of its members present and voting.

The two legislative bodies meet in joint session to form a third body called the Federal Assembly. The functions of this body are limited to the swearing in of the president of the republic, the passing of declarations of war, and a few other infrequent activities.

THE PRESIDENCY AND THE CABINET

The general public elects the president of the Austrian Republic for a six-year term. As in most parliamentary systems, the president's role is primarily to maintain continuity in periods of political change. He may appoint and dismiss the chancellor and on the request of the chancellor dismiss the members of the cabinet; he may also dissolve the National Assembly, but not more than once for the same reason. On the whole, the president has little real independent power, since no cabinet can survive without the confidence of the National Assembly. Therefore, the president has no choice but to appoint a chancellor acceptable to the ruling coalition or party. Even when exercising his constitutional power to declare a national emergency, it must be done with the recommendation of the cabinet and agreement of the Permanent Subcommittee, the National Assembly's watchdog committee during times when the legislature is in recess.

The important executive functions are, of course, exercised by the cabinet with the confidence of the National Assembly. The various ministers who make up the cabinet are chosen on the basis of bargaining among the members of the majority party in the National Assembly, or where this is lacking, among the coalition parties which form the ruling majority. The cabinet administers the affairs of the country with the aid of state secretaries, who are often chosen from different parties than the party of the minister to form a sort of check. The members of the cabinet are responsible both collectively and individually to the National Assembly. The chancellor directs the activities of the cabinet and assumes the primary role of formulating and executing public policy.

THE CHAMBER SYSTEM

Finally, the Austrian Constitution calls for the formation of chambers representing the corporations of the economy, the most important of which are the Chamber of Commerce, the Chamber of Labor, and the Chamber of Agriculture. These chambers are not simply pressure groups but have legal functions which they are assigned. Steiner points out:

> Federal law regulates their relations to their members—who are members by virtue of law—including their power to tax their members, which is exercised through federal agencies. The chambers have the right to present advisory opinions on government bills and important ordinances affecting the interests of their members, and to be represented on many government bodies, especially those dealing with the economy.[2]

Recruitment to these chambers differs with the body, but they are highly political, with the People's Party dominating the Chambers of Commerce and Agriculture and the Socialist Party dominating the Chamber of Labor. This unusual constitutionally sanctioned institution would appear to be a continuation of the corporatist structure of Austrian economic life which was commented upon earlier.

THE ADMINISTRATIVE COURT

Like other democracies, Austria has a court system designed to adjudicate criminal and civil breaches of law. The system begins with local district courts and rises in tier-like fashion to the Supreme Court. Of particular interest are the Administrative Court and the Constitutional Court, for they exercise the higher level judicial functions of a political nature.

The Administrative Court is appointed by the federal president on the recommendation of the cabinet. The cabinet may choose the president and vice-president of the court independently, but when other seats become available, the court itself meets and recommends three names for each vacancy. The cabinet must choose from these three. The influence of the court in selecting its own members tends to perpetuate a court which reflects the historical conservatism of Austria's judiciary and its law schools.

The Administrative Court reviews the application of public law by public agencies and enjoys full jurisdiction over administrative decisions and policies when there is a question of their legality, except when complaints involve questions of constitutionality. The Constitutional Court reviews all cases involving judgments of constitutionality, including conflicts over jurisdiction between the various levels of government. It also exercises final judgment on election conflicts and presides over trials of impeachment.

Its members are selected according to a complex process in which the cabinet recommends the president, vice-president, six additional members, and three substitutes for appointment by the Federal president. The remaining six judges and substitutes are selected from recommendations made by the National Assembly and Federal Council. In general, the process is quite political and the selection of court members tends to reflect the proportional power of the various political parties. Thus, the Constitutional Court has historically been more liberal, or at least less conservative, than the Administrative Court.

POLICY-MAKING WITHIN A CONSOCIATIONAL FRAMEWORK

Clearly, it is not sufficient to review the formal structure of a country's political institutions to gain full understanding of how the politics of that country occur and how government is possible. For under the mantle of formal institutions, one almost always finds a more complex political game which flows into and animates formal institutions, but which operates according to different rules. An analysis of Austria's political institutions alone does not help one understand how the fragmented layers of Austrian society have been able to cooperate so regularly and achieve effective government and political stability. Nor can one understand why Austrian politics remain so ideologically charged given the general decline in the salience of nationalist, religious, and economic issues during the postwar period.

Arend Lijphart, a Dutch political scientist, argues that like the Netherlands, Austria is a consociational democracy, a democratic system specifically designed to reduce conflict and promote compromise in highly fragmented societies. In a consociational democracy, the gaping cleavages separating the various segments of society, in the case of Austria the lagers, are purposely segregated by vigorous vertical organization. The actual game of politics and decision-making is played at the elite level; it is here, out of public view, that the segments of a fragmented society are bound together. For this cartel of elites to function effectively, they must be able to cooperate and compromise with each other without losing the allegiance and support of their own subcultures. Furthermore, all must accept the rule of proportionality. Majority rule could lead to violent confrontation, where more powerful subcultures might seek to impose unacceptable policies upon minority subcultures. Furthermore, the elites representing the various political subcultures of the country must recognize that there are certain fundamental interests that each constituent subculture cannot compromise. As Lijphart notes, it requires

> ... the pragmatic acceptance of the ideological differences as basic real-
> ities which cannot and should not be changed. The fundamental convic-
> tion of other blocs must be tolerated, if not respected. Disagreements
> must not be allowed to turn into either mutual contempt or proselytiz-
> ing zeal.[3]

Thus, since each of the constituent elites realizes that their fundamental interests will be respected, its representatives feel free to negotiate, bargain, and
accommodate each other on less essential questions. These bargains seldom
result in winner-take-all, yes and no decisions. Rather, the rule of proportionality and the relative importance of each group's cooperation for the issue
at stake determines the degree of influence each group will have on the final
outcome.

In order to be able to make compromises and hammer out public policy,
elites in a consociational democracy must enjoy a substantial degree of autonomy from their own subcultures. Such autonomy may be the result of long-
standing customs of elite deference, carried over from predemocratic political
institutions. Autonomy can be encouraged by surrounding the rule-making
process with secrecy and only making decisions public after all parties have
agreed upon a total package. Of course, autonomy can also be promoted by
limiting the opportunities that the masses have to cast their votes, as happens
in most weak-cabinet parliamentary governmental systems.

In addition to elite autonomy, consociational democracy requires an elite
consensus upon the value of cooperation. The leadership must agree that the
avoidance of subculture flare-ups is in the interest of all. It must accept consociational institutions as legitimate and be willing to protect and improve
them.

Finally, the probability of the success of consociational democracy is increased when the political load on decision-making institutions is low. A neutral foreign policy, geographically defined cleavages, and federalism can often
help in this regard. Also, a relative balance of power among the competing
subcultures lends stability.

The consociational model describes the postwar evolution of Austrian politics rather well. After World War II, it appeared equally clear to Socialists and
Christian Conservatives that some form of cooperation would have to be
achieved if Austria were to be united, self-governing, and economically viable. Because of the vertical and encapsulating structure of the lagers and because the political culture stressed deference to lager leadership, the political
elites were able to manage interlager conflict without intervention from the
rank-and-file membership.

The formula for mediating conflicts was and continues to be by proportionality and not by majority rule. The Grand Coalition in which the SPO and
the OVP ruled collectively until 1966 reflects this modified form of political
competition. The portfolios of the cabinet were distributed with scrupulous

TABLE 5.3

Party Representation in Austria's
National Assembly

Party	1975		1979	
	% Vote	Seats	% Vote	Seats
Socialist Party (SPO)	50.4	93	51.0	95
People's Party (OVP)	43.0	80	41.9	77
Freedom Party (FPO)	5.4	10	6.1	11
Communist Party (KPO)	1.2	0	1.0	0

observance of each party's electoral status; even small changes in the percentage of popular vote brought shifts in the relative power over cabinet policy. The same is true of the selection of members for the Constitutional and Administrative courts and of workers for the numerous patronage jobs available in the bureaucracy and the nationalized sector of the economy.

Since elections were generally held every four years and between elections there were few opportunities for mass participation in the political process, the elites were free to form public policy as they wished. Furthermore, the relative balance of power between the SPO and the OVP, as well as the general policy of neutrality, helped to maintain stability and equilibrium.

Even today, although the Socialist Party has long been able to rule without direct help from the Austrian People's Party, the proportional system of party participation in government is still applied. In a sense, the Socialists have resisted the temptation of majority rule. How long this will be the case depends largely upon whether the Socialist electorate continues to increase in numbers and how well the OVP is able to maintain its own solidarity (see Table 5.3).

In Austria, consociational processes require popular acquiescence in between elections, but mass mobilization during elections. During legislative campaigns, one is astonished that the two major parties competing for office could ever have cooperated so reasonably between elections. The People's Party warns of the socialist proclivity for collectivist solutions, whereas the Socialist Party drags out the "bloody shirt" by rehashing the Christian Conservative lager's "betrayal" of the First Republic as well as its partial collaboration with the Nazis. The propaganda machines of both parties flood the country with polemic rhetoric, each warning the people that the slightest change in the electoral balance in favor of the opposing party could bring disaster.

While in most Western democracies political campaigns are directed toward gaining the support of the undecided, generally middle-of-the-road voter, these campaigns are obviously designed to secure the strength and cohesion of the lagers and to keep traditional support from ebbing. To no one's surprise, some of these elections have been so caustic that it has taken months to recreate a working relationship between the parties in the legislature and in the cabinet. But with time, hard feelings soften among the elites and the masses return to their general political apathy.

In a sense, then, the cost of political stability in such a system is the artificial prolongation of political hostilities. Several studies have shown that at the level of the masses, the deep lager cleavages no longer elicit the same emotional response and are not of great daily concern to the average citizen. Even the top-level elites within each lager become accustomed to working with opposing elites, but apparently the more ideologically minded middle-level elites within each party, who link the top and rank and file, increase the ideological competition during elections, for it is at this time that they have greatest influence over political processes.

Policy Problems and Prospects

Switzerland

How is it possible that a country as divided and diverse as Switzerland has achieved such political harmony and stability? An explanation might be that offered by the Marxists, who argue that Switzerland has only the surface characteristics of a democracy. The Marxists insist that there is substantial political repression and the real political games actually are played by powerful corporate elites who manage the politics of the country behind the scenes.

This might be an acceptable explanation if it did not contradict squarely the facts of Swiss political life. In particular, few countries have institutions which offer such easy access to their citizens. Not only does proportional representation make it possible for any tendency of import to be represented in the National Council, but as previously noted, the initiative allows any group which can collect fifty thousand signatures the opportunity to offer amendments to the constitution and change any aspect of the Swiss government or statute law it wishes. Furthermore, at the cantonal and communal level, the local government is required to submit on a regular basis important legislation to public scrutiny in the form of a referendum.

No, the explanation for Switzerland's impressive stability is more complex than that offered by the Marxists. In effect, it can be said that the stability of modern Swiss social and political institutions depends upon a number of fortuitous circumstances. First, a seven-hundred-year heritage of common political action and political institutions furnishes a sense of continuity, legitimacy, and community which cements the common identity of the Swiss. Second, the crosscutting pattern of politically relevant cleavages has reduced the emotional impact and organizational exclusivity of Swiss cultural, social, and political divisions. Furthermore, the moderate and steady pattern of economic development not only minimized the social costs of modernization, but has bound the Swiss closer together by helping to create an interdependent system of labor, thereby helping to mitigate ethnic and religious differences. Finally,

Swiss institutions, founded upon the principles of full representation of all interests, consensual procedures of conflict resolution, and federalism sensitive to the need for local diversity in policy formulation, complement the cultural and structural elements of Swiss politics and promote political stability. These factors and perpetual neutrality have allowed Swiss political institutions to significantly reduce the emotional tenor and ideological character of Swiss politics.

Yet, conflict can be good; it can warn of problems and lead to solutions. But that conflict which exceeds the capabilities of existing political processes can threaten the stability of political institutions and of society itself. Over the last 125 years, Switzerland has known very little of this type of conflict.

However, the status of the Jura region was one issue area which came close to undermining Swiss political stability. The North Jura is a Catholic, French-speaking district in the predominately Protestant, German-speaking canton of Bern. Most of the North Jura became a part of Switzerland in 1815 through a decision of the Congress of Vienna and not as a result of its own choice. It was attached to the canton of Bern, which is one of the most centralist cantons of the Confederation. Jealous of its powers, the cantonal government of Bern has traditionally allowed little autonomy to local districts and communes. During the period leading up to the *Sonderbundskrieg*, Bern was one of the most radical cantons and in the latter part of the nineteenth century, the cantonal government continually harassed the Catholic clergy in the Jura and even sought to regulate ritual and the selection of priests. Furthermore, Bern was later very active in the pan-German movement. Prior to World War I, the cantonal policies favored German over French and even sought to annex certain French-speaking areas into the German-speaking part of Bern, in full contradition to the territorial principle. This was done because heavy Swiss-German (largely Bernese) migration into the Jura, stimulated by the pressures of economic modernization, had increased the number of German-speaking inhabitants to the point that many Swiss-Germans were demanding German-speaking schools. Furthermore, there is evidence that at the same time, the Jura was taxed more heavily than the rest of the canton and received fewer benefits derived from taxation. When one combines all of these conditions with the fact that the Jura is one of the poorer areas in Switzerland, one can understand the long-term Jurassian dissatisfaction with its political relations with the canton of Bern. Finally, within the Bernese Cantonal Assembly, the representatives from the Jura were a minority vis-à-vis the Protestant, German-speaking Bernese, and no party really seemed to represent the interests of the North Jura. The South Jura was also French-speaking, but it was Protestant and generally better off economically; thus it generally opposed the demands of the North Jura and supported the cantonal government at Bern.

Given these conditions, which seem so foreign to the general Swiss experience, it should not be surprising that the Jura has been in periodic revolt since the turn of the century. After the end of World War II, there was a growing separatist movement led by a capable elite. It used all sorts of techniques to gain the attention and support of the Jurassian people and to push for the creation of a separate canton of Jura. Members of the movement invaded the Cantonal Assembly, vocally disrupting the procedures. They created internationally embarrassing events, and some extremists even dynamited military facilities. The *Jura-Libre* movement eventually splintered into several wings, with the extreme left advocating violent methods of guerilla warfare, while the majority continued to harass the regime in Bern by conventional means, bordering on illegality. Partially as a result of this political activity, a referendum was eventually ratified by the inhabitants of the North Jura in which they voted to become a separate canton. In a nationwide referendum held in September 1978, the Swiss electorate voted overwhelmingly to amend the constitution and permit the Jura to become a separate canton. On January 1, 1979, the Jura officially became Switzerland's twenty-third federated canton, the first new canton since the Swiss Confederation was formed in 1848.

This example of political conflict, which for many years prior to the referendum polarized cantonal political relations, underlines two points made thus far. First, in the absence of crosscutting-cleavages and substantial local autonomy, the heterogeneity found in Switzerland can indeed yield major political conflict and even violence. Second, even this conflict can be limited, when it is of a geographic nature, by the decentralization of authority; in other words, by invoking the traditional political practice which has served to consolidate the Confederation over a seven-century time span.

The 6.3 million inhabitants of this small nation nestled in the Alps live in one of the most diversified societies in the world. Linguistically, three different languages are spoken by large segments of the population. Religiously, 48 percent of the people are Protestant and 49 percent are Catholic. Culturally, cantonal and communal roots run deep and regional loyalties are immensely resilient.

This Swiss societal mosaic has thus necessitated a great deal of give-and-take at the national level, as well as the creation of one of the most decentralized governmental systems in the world. In effect, the cantonal and communal authorities continue to exercise significant policy-making power, whereas the policy-making latitude of the national government located in Bern is extremely limited and is in fact the weakest of all central governments in Western advanced industrial societies.

Nevertheless, prospects for the future seem to be brighter for Switzerland than for many of its European neighbors. Because of their strong dependency on importing and exporting, the Swiss will certainly remain apprehensive about world economic uncertainties, but their economy continues to be robust and the Swiss are used to tightening the belt when conditions dictate.

Moreover, Switzerland continues to provide some of the best examples of direct democracy in action, and the Swiss governmental system remains eminently qualified to cope with possible problems on the horizon. For one thing, the four political parties which have dominated the Swiss governmental and political scene since 1959 have done a noteworthy job in articulating and satisfying the demands of Switzerland's diverse interest groups. Furthermore, the use of frequent referenda and initiatives has served the Swiss well and has helped to defuse some potentially explosive political situations, such as the North Jura affair. Initiatives, of course, have suffered a high failure rate. For example, several xenophobic-linked proposals calling for a drastic reduction in the number of foreigners working in Switzerland were decisively turned down by the Swiss electorate. The same fate greeted the three nationwide proposals voted on by the Swiss in 1977. These rejected proposals dealt with the implementation of a forty-hour work week, the legalization of abortions undertaken within the first twelve weeks of pregnancy, and the reform of the system of taxation on higher incomes.

However, the great publicity generated during and after referendum and initiative campaigns helps to educate the public and may eventually make issues once rejected by the voters more palatable in the future. For example, although far too late in the eyes of many outside observers, Swiss women were finally given the right to vote as a result of a 1971 nationwide referendum. The recognition of the claims of the North Jura residents was also slow to develop, but in the 1978 referendum, 82 percent of the Swiss voters favored the creation of the new Jura canton and not one cantonal majority anywhere in Switzerland opposed the proposal.

The Jura is not the only instance of institution-threatening conflict in recent Swiss political history. In the last several years violent youth rebellions known as the "Kravallen" have occurred in Zurich and to a lesser extent in Bern. While the immediate issue was the failure of the city of Zurich to fund a youth center although at the same time it was willing to fund the construction of an expensive opera hall, it is clear that the "kravallen" have a deeper significance. The very existence of a relatively large floating population of rootless and alienated young people in such a wealthy country where unemployment is almost unknown is a concern. It may well be that Switzerland may have more difficulty dealing with the effects of post-industrial affluence than it has had with its historical problems of ethnic diversity, class conflict, resource poverty and armed neutrality. The erosion of the traditional values of community, accommodation, cooperation and self-sacrifice and the appearance of an increasingly numerous group of aimless young people who find little meaning in traditional cultural forms could be a sign of trouble on the horizon. On the other hand, there are those who argue that it is a momentary period of adjustment, and in the same way that the Swiss have succeeded in the past at disarming such problems, they will respond to the problems of a troubled youth.

Thus, short of outright war or global economic depression, the Swiss political system seems to be well equipped to cope with and adapt to the challenges and vicissitudes of the 1980s. In essence, the Swiss have demonstrated that political stability is possible in an ethnically diverse society within the confines of noncoercive democratic institutions.

Austria

Austria too has achieved political stability within a formally democratic framework. Its government has ruled effectively since the end of World War II, not only in maintaining political order and balance, but in securing real prosperity for a high percentage of its citizens. This is no small achievement when one considers that prior to 1945 Austrian political culture, social and group structures, and historical institutions were antagonistic to democracy. The institutions of the First Republic had failed; the country was deeply divided by class, with little social trust to bind the self-contained segments of the society together; and the legacy of World War II was one of almost complete economic breakdown.

In some ways, however, World War II and its composite effects were beneficial to the development of democratic institutions in Austria. First, the authoritarian right had been once and for all discredited because of the atrocities and excesses of the Nazis. Second, the external pressures of the Cold War, which made stable government and real neutrality in foreign policy an absolute necessity, created common interests and constraints for all Austrian parties. Not only did it minimize the amount spent for defense, but Austria's neutrality made possible the development of a new identity—a new symbolic role—for Austria in the world. Very much in the same way that neutrality has allowed Switzerland and Sweden to affirm a positive and morally altruistic foreign policy, neutrality makes it possible for Austria to see itself as a meeting place for East and West, where peace talks can occur and world understanding and peace can be promoted. It is a foreign policy much more supportive to democracy than the hypernationalism of former years. Finally, the Marshall Plan furnished the substantive as well as the structural basis for economic recovery in Austria and Europe. Nevertheless, most of the credit for Austria's success must go to the pragmatic leaders of both major political parties who understood the existing limitations and avoided the temptation of opportunism.

On the other hand, historical circumstances and geographical location have at times thwarted Austrian initiatives in the international arena. Because of Austria's role in World War II, Allied occupation forces did not vacate the country until 1955, at which time the major Allied nations, particularly the United States and the Soviet Union, agreed that Austria would become an officially neutral nation, similar to Switzerland. The Russians have continued to keep a vigilant eye on Austria, mainly because it shares borders with several Eastern European nations. When Austrian officials made overtures in the 1960s to bring their nation into the European Community (EC), the Russians protested vehemently. The Kremlin claimed that Austrian neutrality would be irreparably compromised by membership in a Western-oriented organization and that such an action could not be condoned by the Soviet Union. Consequently, largely as a result of the Russian protests, Austria has resigned itself to being a member (along with Switzerland) of the European Free Trade Association (EFTA) and has been granted an associate trading status vis-à-vis the European Community.

The product of Austria's democratic experience is different than that of Switzerland. In fact, in many ways it is the opposite. Austria has a highly centralized, elitist system in which two or, more recently, one party has tended to dominate the government. The social and economic policies have certainly reflected socialist programs of collective action, with less attention paid to the claims of individualism. In Austrian democracy, the clear priority has been equality rather than freedom as economic liberals would understand the word. While politics in Switzerland tends to degenerate into administration, in Austria it flares into cyclical electoral campaigns of invective rhetoric designed to animate party loyalties and deepen class divisions.

At the same time, it should be remembered that despite proximity and similar size, Switzerland and Austria have extremely different political cultures, social structures, and institutional pasts. It is therefore not to be expected that democratic institutions which have been successful in Switzerland would be appropriate for Austria; in fact, such institutions might have exacerbated conflict among competing lagers, making a politically stable and balanced democracy impossible. In short, Austria's consociational democracy would appear to be fully appropriate to the present needs and expectations of the Austrian people, while furnishing sufficient flexibility for future evolution and change.

Finally, it should be noted that like the governments of Germany and Japan, the institutions of the Austrian Republic have yet to be fully tested. Unlike those of Switzerland, which have evolved over many centuries and have withstood religious war, industrialization, two world conflicts, and economic depression, the Austrian Republic has only known the relatively auspicious circumstances of post–World War II Europe. It is not clear whether Austria has acquired a national identity sufficiently strong and sufficiently separate from that of Germany to tide its government over in times of grave economic or political crisis. Furthermore, the consociational formula has shown itself an effective medium for the resolution of political conflict in the postwar period, but it is not impossible that under conditions of intense stress, such as a major economic recession, this medium could break down, precipitating a constitutional crisis similar to that of the early 1930s. On the other hand, it is also true that the longer democratic processes continue to deal flexibly and effectively with the conflicts and problems of Austria, the more institutionalized they become, the more legitimacy they acquire, and thus the more likely they are to meet the test in times of crisis. There is, of course, a third alternative. It may be that consociationalism is merely a form of political transition toward a one-party-dominant or a majoritarian system. The socialists have controlled a majority in the National Assembly for well over ten years. In addition, the socialist chancellor Bruno Kreisky has been in office so long that he is considered as almost a national hero. Even difficult economic times and scandal within the Austrian Socialist Party have failed to weaken his appeal.

In conclusion, then, in the same way that Switzerland is an example of the effectiveness of democratic government in resolving the problems of a multiethnic society, Austria is an example of how these same processes can succeed in a country which suffers from deep class divisions and lacks an immediate political heritage favorable to democracy. Such an example would then contradict the long-standing belief that democracy is a luxury only to be afforded by those few societies that are wealthy and have slowly evolved structures fostering democratic participation.

Notes

1. Kurt Steiner, *Politics of Austria* (Boston: Little, Brown, 1972), p. 85.

2. Ibid.

3. Arend Lijphart, *The Politics of Accommodation: Pluralism and Democracy in the Netherlands* (Berkeley and Los Angeles: University of California Press, 1968), pp. 139–140.

Selected Bibliography

Bohn, David. "Consociational Democracy and the Case of Switzerland." *Journal of Politics* 42, no. 1 (February 1980): 165–180.

Bohn, David. "Consociationalism and Accommodation in Switzerland." *Journal of Politics* 43, no. 4 (November 1981): 1234–1241.

Bohn, David. "Neutrality—Switzerland's Policy Dilemma: Options in the New Europe," *Orbis* 21 (Summer 1977): 335–352.

Bradfield, B. *The Making of Switzerland: From Ice Age to Common Market.* Zurich: Schweizer Spiegel Verlag, 1964.

Daalder, Hans. "On Building Consociational Nations: The Cases of the Netherlands and Switzerland," *International Social Science Journal* 23, no. 3 (1971): 355–370.

De Salis, J.-R. *Switzerland and Europe.* Translated by A. and E. Henderson. University: University of Alabama Press, 1971.

Gruner, Erich. *Die Parteien in der Schweiz.* Bern: Francke-Verlag, 1969.

Hughes, Christopher. *The Parliament of Switzerland.* London: Cassel, 1962.

Hughes, Christopher. *Switzerland.* London: Ernest Benn, 1975.

Katzenstein, Peter J. "The Last Old Nation: Austrian National Consciousness Since 1945," *Comparative Politics* 9 (January 1977): 147–171.

Lijphart, Arend. "Consociational Democracy," *Comparative Political Studies* 1 (April 1968): 3–33.

McRae, Kenneth D. *Switzerland: Example of Cultural Coexistence.* Toronto: Canadian Institute of International Affairs, 1968.

Powell, G. Bingham, Jr. *Social Fragmentation and Political Hostility: An Austrian Case Study.* Stanford: Stanford University Press, 1970.

Steiner, Jurg. *Amicable Agreement Versus Majority Rule: Conflict Resolution in Switzerland.* Chapel Hill: University of North Carolina, 1974.

Steiner, Jurg, and Obler, Jeffrey. "Does the Consociational Theory Really Hold for Switzerland?" In *Ethnic Conflict in the Western World,* edited by Milton J. Esman. Ithaca: Cornell University Press, 1975.

Steiner, Kurt. *Politics in Austria.* Boston: Little, Brown, 1972.

Steifbold, Rodney P. "Segmented Pluralism and Consociational Democracy in Austria: Problems of Political Stability and Change." In *Politics in Europe,* edited by Martin O. Heisler. New York: David McKay, 1974.

Waldheim, Kurt, *The Austrian Example.* Translated by Ewald Osers. New York: Macmillan, 1973.

Wenner, Manfred W.; Wenner, Lettie M.; and Flango, V. Eugene. "Austrian and Swiss Judges: A Comparative Study," *Comparative Politics* 10 (July 1978): 499–517.

6.

Scandinavia: The Experiment in Social Democracy

James L. Waite

The Historical Setting

An Overview

Scandinavia is the northern cap of Europe. The term Scandinavia has reference to a group of people that share the same language family. For purposes of this discussion, *Scandinavia* will refer to Denmark, Norway, and Sweden. It is true that many Finns speak Swedish, but the principal language is Finnish, which is *not* a Scandinavian language. Finland is a democratic republic. It has a written constitution, a president, a prime minister and cabinet, and a parliament. The country has a multi-party system and elections based on proportional representation. The more comprehensive label, *Nordic* countries, denotes five countries: Sweden, Denmark, Norway, plus Finland and Iceland. Iceland, to many, is not considered part of Scandinavia because of its distance from the mainland. It is a democratic republic, which elects a president, while actual power lies with a prime minister who directs the government with his cabinet. The country has a parliamentary form of government electing a sixty-member parliament.

Scandinavia has come to be regarded as a region of advanced industrial democracies. Collectively, Scandinavia encompasses over eighteen million people who share a common cultural heritage. Except for Denmark, the only member of the region connected to the central European land mass, Scandinavia has remained relatively aloof from the continent. At the same time, however, it has developed a history of unity which dates back to the days of Viking conquest.

As early as 1397, all of the Scandinavian countries were combined under the so-called Kalmar Union. This union lasted until 1523, when Sweden finally succeeded in effecting a permanent break. Nevertheless, Denmark and Norway remained together until 1814, at which time Denmark was forced at the Congress of Vienna to turn Norway over to Sweden. In 1905, this union also split, thus creating the three independent states as we know them today. Ever since, their political stability and economic prosperity have made them interesting subjects for comparative analysis. As Harry Eckstein points out:

> The Scandinavian countries are among the sadly few that have dealt remarkably well with certain vexing practical problems. Social welfare, land use, industrial relations, conservation, the promotion of the arts and aesthetics of life, and controlled economic growth come readily to mind: we can profit from studying their policies. . . . This is no plea for imitation, which rarely works, but for considering instructive experience when it is available.[1]

With these observations in mind, let us begin our comparison of the Scandinavian nations by examining the historical development of Sweden.

Sweden

Swedish history may be conveniently studied by dividing it into seven periods:

1. The Viking Epoch: 800–1050
2. The Middle Ages: 1050–1520
3. The Vasa Period: 1521–1611
4. The Age of Greatness: 1611–1718
5. The Era of Liberty: 1718–1772
6. The Period of Gustavian Absolutism: 1772–1809
7. The Emergence of Modern Sweden: 1809–1921[2]

Settlements began to appear in Sweden approximately 10,000 years ago, after the great ice sheet receded. By the year 1500 B.C., a considerable Bronze Age culture had emerged. Trade was carried on with the European continent and as time progressed the Swedes began to work with iron ore. By the seventh and eighth centuries A.D., Sweden had undertaken various far-reaching trading tours. In the ninth century, however, these tours took on a warlike character, as Vikings ravaged many of the Christian countries of Europe.

During the Middle Ages, Christianity spread throughout Sweden. Indeed, by 1164, Sweden was considered important enough to merit an archbishop. Also during this period, Sweden began to forge a new nation and suffer the agonies of nationalism. It began to separate itself from the other Scandinavian countries and, by increasing commercial ties with Germany, Sweden was able to strengthen its national cause. By 1430, the development of Swedish nationalism was well underway but was not completed for almost another century.

The Vasa Period is named for the impact on Sweden of its first king and first genuine national hero, Gustav Eriksson Vasa. Gustav Vasa's accomplishments in many ways parallel those of Henry VIII of England. In his fight for an independent Sweden in the early sixteenth century, he led a revolt against the Danes and crushed an attempt to patch up the Kalmar Union. He was elected king by the Riksdag (parliament) of Strangnas in 1523. By centralizing the government and nationalizing the administration, he laid the foundation for modern Sweden. Vasa cut the ties of the Swedish church with Rome, confiscated church property, and supported the Reformation. When he was succeeded by his sons, Sweden was on the verge of becoming a great power.

The Age of Greatness is regarded as a time when Sweden enjoyed its one grand fling as a major power. Though possessing scarcely more than a million inhabitants, victorious wars were waged against Denmark, Russia, and Poland. Sweden's contributions during the Thirty Years' War under Gustavus Adolphus enabled it to emerge from the Treaty of Westphalia in 1648 as one of the dominant political as well as religious powers of Europe. After the southernmost provinces were conquered in 1658 (they had belonged to Denmark), Swedish power embraced present-day Sweden, Finland, Ingermanland (in which Leningrad is now located), Estonia, Latvia, and important coastal towns in northern Germany. To a certain extent, the Baltic Sea could have been regarded as a private Swedish inland sea. Later, under Karl X and Karl XI, the empire continued to grow.

The Era of Liberty was characterized by a transfer of power from an absolutist monarch to the Riksdag. However, the preeminence of the Riksdag was only temporary, and by 1772 the power of the parliament had begun to slip noticeably. Weakened by internal dissensions, the Riksdag finally succumbed to Gustav III's demand for the restoration of royal supremacy.

The era that followed is known as the Period of Gustavian Absolutism. Gustav III was an energetic and at times reform-minded monarch who completely dominated the Riksdag. He instituted several changes which were beneficial, but he was scarcely loved by the nobility, which feared his strong power base. The king was finally assassinated in 1792 and the throne was held for a short time by Gustav IV Adolph. However, after Sweden's loss of Finland to Russia, the new ruler was deposed in 1809.

The final era of Swedish history we will discuss was the most dynamic in terms of the development of democracy. During this period, the line of monarchial succession was changed when Marshal Bernadotte assumed the throne in 1810. A Swedish constitution was promulgated and the parliament was transformed into a bicameral structure and picked up some legislative muscle. Moreover, the structure of government was changed with the introduction of Montesquieu's separation of powers doctrine and the notion of checks and balances.

Between 1907 and 1921, the most dramatic events occurred, with the expansion of the electorate and the rise of modern political parties. During

World War II, Sweden declared itself neutral and, except for certain concessions made under pressure from the Nazis, remained outside the world conflict. This position of international neutrality, which has served Sweden so well
during the twentieth century, continues to be a guiding principle for contemporary Swedish policymakers.

Norway

Norwegian history is connected at many points with that of the other Scandinavian countries. Between the years 800 and 1000, the territorial forays of
the Norwegian Vikings increased. Small agrarian communities began to appear and soon they were organized into larger administrative and military
regions. By 875, small Viking settlements were established in the Hebrides,
the Isle of Man, the Shetlands, the Orkneys, England, Ireland, and Normandy.
In Norway, the realm was unified under the leadership of King Harald Hår-
fagre (Fairhair). At Harald's death, the kingdom was split among twenty of
Harald's sons, with Erik Bloodaxe serving as overking. The temporary unity
collapsed as dissension occurred among the heirs. In addition to these domestic struggles, both Sweden and Denmark were trying to acquire Norwegian
territory.

In 995, Olaf I, a great-grandson of Harald I, became king. Prior to assum-
ing control over Norway, Olaf had lived in England and had been converted
to Christianity. When he became king he tried to force Christianity on Norway and was partially successful. It was also during this period that Greenland
and America were both discovered by Viking expeditions.

Several years after King Olaf's ascension to the throne, he quarreled with
Sven I, king of Denmark. In a naval battle at Svöld, he was defeated by combined Swedish and Danish forces. Olaf was killed in the battle and Norway
was divided by the coalition. After a short period of disorder, the country was
reunited by Olaf II, who drove out the foreigners and made himself king of
Norway in 1016. Olaf II continued the religious work of his predecessor, using
the sword against all who refused to be baptized. Because of the power of
Olaf, he aroused the enmity of the nobles, who, together with Canute II, king
of England and Denmark, drove Olaf into exile in Russia in 1028.

On the death of Canute in 1035, Olaf's son, Magnus I, was called from
Russia by partisans of his father to become king and unite Norway and Denmark under his rule. For the next three centuries a succession of native kings
ruled Norway. Although internal confusion and wars between rival claimants
to the throne disrupted the country intermittently, Norway began to emerge
as a united nation, enjoying comparative prosperity brought on by its great
trading fleets. The Norwegians had become predominately Christian and a
powerful clergy was one of the strongest influences in the kingdom. However,
the lineage of Norwegian nobility deteriorated during the next three hundred

years. By the year 1300, the old families had gradually descended to the economic status of well-to-do peasants, and for the most part the Norwegian people became a nation of peasants. Commercial activity declined greatly because of the increasing power of the Hanseatic League of northern German cities.

The relative tranquility enjoyed by Norway was abruptly shattered with the death of Haakon VI in 1380, at which time Norway was united with Denmark through the ascension to the throne of Haakon's ten-year-old son Olaf, who had already been proclaimed king of Denmark in 1376 upon the death of Denmark's King Valdemar. The dynastic union was actually realized through the design of Margaret, wife of the deceased Haakon VI of Norway and daughter of King Valdemar of Denmark. When the young King Olaf died in 1387, Queen Margaret was granted a "kingly" status and she succeeded in her plan to forge the Kingdom of Sweden, Norway, and Denmark into a single administrative unit, an action which was to be commemorated historically as the Kalmar Union of 1397. Margaret then proceeded to designate her adopted son, Erik of Pomerania, as her successor to this united Scandinavian court.

However, Norwegian prosperity and culture declined steadily after the union was consummated and the black death which swept over the country added to Norway's demise by wiping out as much as one-half of the population. In effect, policy that was made under the auspices of the Kalmar Union was generally in the interest of Denmark and to a lesser extent Sweden. Eventually Sweden was able to pull out of the union in 1523, but Norway remained subject to the dominance of Danish officials for another three centuries.

The Napoleonic wars which occurred at the beginning of the nineteenth century finally helped bring an end to the Danish-Norwegian union. Denmark, an ally of France, was compelled by the victorious European powers to sign the Treaty of Kiel, which ceded Norway to Sweden. Although quite pleased to be rid of Danish hegemony, the Norwegians were livid at being placed under Swedish tutelage and refused to recognize the provisions of the treaty. They eventually decided to declare themselves an independent kingdom, drew up a liberal constitution, and offered the crown to the Danish crown prince, Christian Frederik. War with Sweden three months later caused King Christian Frederik to resign and the Norwegian parliament (Storting) to agree to the union with Sweden.

By the Act of Union of 1815, Norway was allowed to retain its newly conceived constitution and was given its own navy, army, customs, and legislature. In essence, the country was permitted full liberty and independence within its own boundaries. During the tenure of the union, the Norwegians solidified their nationalism by resisting the closer relations with Sweden which had been provided for by the Act of Union. This period saw much political development in the country. In 1837, municipal self-government was inaugurated; in 1884, parliamentary government was introduced; the jury system was established in 1887; and in 1898, universal male suffrage was granted.

In 1905, Norway was proclaimed an independent kingdom and in a plebiscite in August, the Norwegian people voted overwhelmingly for separation from Sweden. The Swedish Riksdag ratified the separation in October. A month later, Princer Carl of Denmark accepted the Norwegian crown as Haakon VII.

The Norwegian government, dominated by ministers with liberal political backgrounds, became one of the most advanced in Europe in matters of social legislation, education, and political liberties. In 1907, Norwegian women became the first in Europe to be given the voting franchise, unemployment insurance benefits, and old-age pensions. Finally, liberal laws concerning divorce and illegitimacy made Norway famous for its advanced social policies.

During World War I, the governments of Sweden, Norway, and Denmark agreed to maintain the neutrality of the Scandinavian countries. This policy continued up to World War II, despite Norwegian sympathy for Finland during the 1939 winter war with Russia. On April 9, 1940, the Norwegian government was toppled and a Nazi-sponsored government was established under the leadership of Josef Terboven, the German commissioner for Norway. Haakon and his cabinet, after an unsuccessful attempt at resistance, withdrew to Great Britain to establish a government-in-exile. Upon the surrender of the German forces on May 8, 1945, Haakon returned to Norway. The death penalty was restored and leading German sympathizers were tried and either imprisoned or executed. The government-in-exile eventually resigned after temporary order was established. The Labor Party came to power in October 1945, and was faced with the tremendous task of rehabilitation.

Denmark

The first inhabitants of Denmark appear to date back as far as 50,000 B.C. However, really noticeable communities were not established until 10,000 to 3,000 B.C. In about 3,000 B.C., significant changes began to take place in the way of life. Farming became wide-spread and land cultivation became common. In approximately 2,000 B.C., a new people, probably nomadic horse-riders, pushed westward through Europe. These "Indo-Europeans," as they were called, changed the population significantly. Since the time of this migration, the people living in the country we now know as Denmark have spoken the Indo-European dialect and have tended to be blond-haired and blue-eyed.

The Viking period in Danish history lasted scarcely more than two hundred years, from 800 to 1050 A.D. During this period, Viking warriors swarmed out of Denmark and attacked England and other portions of the European continent. Denmark had profited during the Viking period through the acquisition of wealth and slaves; however, the constant drain of thousands of its men left the homeland relatively defenseless while the fleets were away. King Harald Bluetooth, who lived during the tenth century, was cognizant of the possibility of invasion from the south and took steps to consolidate several of the Danish kingdoms into one domain. Harald was also converted to Christianity and was largely responsible for its introduction into Denmark. Gradually, the influence of the church began to be felt throughout the country, with bishoprics being created, monasteries being founded, and local parishes being established.

Late in the twelfth and in the early part of the thirteenth centuries, the Danes expanded to the east. They conquered the greater part of the northern and southern coastal areas of the Baltic Sea, and the expanded realm was nearly twice the size of modern Denmark. During this period of expansion, the Danish nobility and upper clergy prospered, whereas the large masses of once free peasantry were relegated to virtual serfdom.

In 1380, Denmark acquired Iceland and the Faeroe Islands. By 1387, Denmark gained control of Norway and a decade later the Union of Kalmar was formed with Denmark as the dominant power within the union. Once the union was consolidated, the Danish national capital was eventually moved from Roskilde to Copenhagen.

The Reformation spread northward to Denmark and the Protestant cause was championed by Christian III. In fact, Danish support of Protestantism precipitated the nation's entry into the Thirty Years' War. Moreover, Denmark fought a series of wars with its regional rival, Sweden. The war efforts of 1611–1613, 1643–1645, and 1657–1660 generally went badly for the Danes and they were forced to forfeit some of their Baltic islands as well as their territory along the Scandinavian peninsula. The consequences of these territorial losses and the severe economic problems suffered during the wars helped to curtail some of the power and privileges of the nobility. In 1660, the monarchy, which had until then been largely dependent for its political power on the nobility, was made hereditary and in subsequent years became a dominant force.

In the eighteenth century, Denmark began to colonize Greenland. Danish trade in the Far East was also expanded and trading companies were established in the West Indies. Toward the end of the century, a series of economic and social reforms were introduced, bringing about a weakening of the monarchy and the abolition of feudalism. However, in the ensuing years, Danish power continued to decline. Because of Danish activities during the Napoleonic wars, the big powers at the Congress of Vienna decided to take Norway away from Denmark and to give it to Sweden. Denmark lost even more territory in 1864, when Schleswig-Holstein came under Prussian control.

A growing demand for constitutional government in Denmark finally led to the proclamation of the *grundlov* (charter) of 1849. The charter declared Denmark a constitutional monarchy, guaranteed civil liberties, and provided for a bicameral legislature which was to share policy-making responsibilities with the crown. In 1866, the Danish constitution was revised, and under a stable system of parliamentary government, commerce and industry began to prosper once again.

Along with the other Scandinavian countries, Denmark remained neutral during World War I. In 1917, Denmark sold its Virgin Island possessions to the United States, and on the domestic front several constitutional reforms were enacted, including the introduction of universal suffrage. A year later, Denmark recognized the autonomy of Iceland but continued to exercise control over Icelandic foreign policy. Denmark also remained the nominal head of the Icelandic government.

In May 1939, Denmark signed a ten-year nonagression pact with Hitler, but Germany invaded the nation one year later. While the Germans were occupying Denmark, the British took control of Iceland and the Americans established a temporary protectorate over Greenland. At the end of the war, Denmark was freed from the German oppression, Iceland retained its independence, which it had declared in 1944, and Greenland was once again returned to Danish jurisdiction.

Political Culture and Socialization

The Scandinavian countries possess political cultures which encourage a high degree of citizen participation. Moreover, in spite of past hostilities, Norway, Sweden and Denmark now have strong regional linkages. The widespread support for Scandinavian regionalism is tied to three main factors.

First, language has served to unite the Scandinavian countries. Though local dialects abound, no major language problems exist. Danish, Norwegian, and Swedish are closely related tongues. A citizen of one country can travel within either of the other two countries with some expectation of linguistic communication. Danish is the most unique of the three languages and is facetiously referred to by some Scandinavians as a "disease of the throat." Nevertheless, these minor differences have not been a barrier to regional cooperation.

Second, religion has also been a unifying force. Nearly all Scandinavians belong, at least formally, to the Lutheran church. Some Danish writers, in particular, distinguish between a "state church" and a "national church." They say that a national church merits the support of the state because a vast majority of the citizens are members. In fact, the Danish constitution uses the term *national church* (*folkekirke*) rather than *state church* (*statskirke*) in its religious references. In all of the Scandinavian countries, freedom of religion is a fact of life, enabling all members of dissenting churches to worship in accordance with their own faiths. However, just over a century ago, a person could suffer a fine or imprisonment for belonging to so-called free churches.

In Sweden, the "conventional edict" of 1726 even made it a crime for people to gather in private homes for worship or Bible-reading, and this provision was not repealed until 1858.

Finally, geography has played an important role in Scandinavian cultural development. Except for the trading lanes established during the Viking era, Scandinavia has been virtually cut off from the traditional intercourse of European society. For example, the major land wars of Europe have generally passed by Denmark and the Scandinavian peninsula. Consequently, this regional isolation has caused the Scandinavian countries to turn inward (this is less true of Denmark than of Norway and Sweden) and cultivate their own regional subcultures, distinct from the rest of Europe.

Sweden

THE FAMILY

In preindustrial Sweden, the family was the basic unit of social organization. The family was traditionally headed by an authoritarian father, and children were taught to be submissive to the demands of adults. Obedience took precedence over independence and children learned that the best way of doing things was the way they had been done in the past. Resistance was seldom seen, yet this pretense of compliance created insurmountable barriers between children and parents.

With the advent of industrialization and modernization, increased social mobility eroded traditional family patterns of authority. With women joining the labor market, patriarchal dominance declined, opening more avenues for women's independence and necessitating men's participation in child-rearing and household duties. The result is a family structure that has become "democratized"—equating the position of the sexes and placing parental emphasis on self-sufficiency among the children. This self-sufficiency has been forced, to a certain extent, by economic constraints. Families need two incomes to support their standard of living; this produces smaller families and a transfer of authority from the home to the school. It is the contention of some Swedish sociologists that this shift from authoritarianism to democratization of the family is more pronounced among the urban middle class than in the working-class families.

THE SCHOOLS

Because the Swedish schools have become such an important socializing agent, Swedish education has been a profound impact on the contemporary political system. Basic education is compulsory and extends for ten years beginning at age seven. The primary education is taken at *grundskolan* (elementary school) and secondary education is taken at *högskolan*, which is an integrated secondary school. In this school, there are twenty-two programs of two to four years' duration; also a variety of special vocational courses of differing lengths of time are offered.

After the third year in the theoretical programs, the student may enter a university—all of which have open admissions policies. There are six state universities, several state-owned professional schools, university-level institutes, and one semiprivate business school. Sweden has had a great commitment to education, particularly adult education. Evening and special courses are available to every adult citizen who wishes to continue his education. Table 6.1 illustrates the number of citizens involved in the Swedish educational process. The high standard of education and its widespread impact has led to a virtual elimination of illiteracy and has contributed to a national cohesion spanning the political, industrial, and cultural spectrum.

POLITICAL PARTIES AND INTEREST GROUPS

For the most part, political parties in Sweden are ideological in their design. Each party has established sections and subsections organized for the purpose of developing positions and support on key issues among the public. Seminars on foreign, economic, and domestic policy issues are often held by the various parties' subsections for student affairs. The purpose is to foster grass-roots interest and support for the issues.

The above process is also followed by the various interest organizations in the country. Labor and business both have their representative factions, which, in a very organized manner, spread their various points of view through the information and public affairs outlets in the country. One most curious organization is the National Organization of People and Defense (*Centralförbundet Folk och Försvar*). This interest group is an association of national organizations interested in defense, with its basic role being to inform the public about defense and to strengthen the defense will of the people. Even though this is a voluntary central organization, nearly three-fourths of its budget comes from the national government. As is evident, both interest groups and political parties play an important role in the political socialization process.

MASS MEDIA

Mass media play a direct role in the socialization process. All television and radio programs in Sweden are broadcast by *Sveriges* Radio, a private company operating under a state concession that makes it a virtual monopoly. Its share capital is apportioned among industry, the press, and the national social movements. The Board of Governors consists of eleven members, six appointed by the government (including the chairman) and five representing the shareholders. It is recognized by many observers that *Sveriges* Radio has begun to take a more active part in social and cultural issues and its programs

TABLE 6.1

The Swedish Educational System, 1975–1976

Academic Level	Students	Teachers*	Schools*
Primary:			
Grades 1–6	713,000	43,000⎫	
Secondary:		⎪	5,000
Grades 7–9	314,000⎫	⎬	
Integrated Upper	⎪	54,000⎭	
Secondary Schools	220,000⎭		800
Higher:			
Teacher Training	13,700	1,100	30
Universities and			
Specialized Colleges	108,000	NA	40
People's Colleges†	12,000	1,700	115
Municipal Adult Education	151,000	2,300	NA
Study Circles	2,468,000*	NA	NA

*Statistics for 1974–1975 academic year
†Courses of more than 30 weeks

Source: National Central Bureau of Statistics, Stockholm.

bear evidence of its increased commitment to urgent problems in Swedish society.

Specified limitations on freedom of speech in broadcasting are defined by the Enabling Agreement and the Broadcasting Liability Act. The latter law designates a person called the chief program editor as legally liable for the contents of any one program. Broadcast libel is defined with reference to the provisions of the Freedom of the Press Act.

Under the Freedom of the Press Act, no form of censorship may be applied to Swedish newspapers, magazines, books, or brochures. Swedes, incidentally, rank among the world's leading newspaper readers. In the first half of 1972, there were 151 dailies with a combined circulation of 4.5 million, which comes to about 560 copies per 1,000 inhabitants. With few exceptions, the newspapers of Stockholm, Göteborg, and Malmö appear seven days a week. The major newspaper ownerships also reflect ideological differences. Table 6.2 shows the ideological alignments of the leading Swedish dailies and their circulation figures for 1972.

Norway

THE FAMILY

The Norwegian family is similar to the Swedish family, but because Norway is less urbanized, modernization has had a lesser effect on the Norwegian family than on other Scandinavian families. The family holds to its traditional values and in a recent poll, 87 percent of the national population still favored

Table 6.2

The Political Allegiances of Sweden's Major Newspapers, 1972

Newspaper	Political Alignment	Daily Circulation
Expressen	Liberal	586,000
Aftonbladet	Social Democratic	470,000
Dagens Nyheter	Independent	441,000
Göteborgsposten	Liberal	298,000
Svenska Dagbladet	Conservative	152,000

marriage as the ideal form of social relation. In essence, the family is a fairly tight-knit social group that instills its values in the Norwegian child. The values as they apply to government are generally moderate and democratic. In terms of parental behavior, it is "moderately democratic" in that restrictions on children are used sparingly and relationships between parent and child are based on reason and persuasion. This possibly has produced the notable ease, freedom, and relaxed independence exhibited by Norwegian youngsters as they grow up.

THE SCHOOLS

Traditionally, the Norwegian schools have been regimented and authoritarian, though this is more true of the upper grades than of the elementary level. Social distance is maintained between teacher and student. In recent times, however, authoritarianism in the school system has declined somewhat.

Although certain sectors of the educational system lag behind their other Scandinavian counterparts, the system as a whole has been modernized and made accessible to many more people. For example, while only a quarter of those Norwegians over seventy years of age in 1970 had had any secondary education, 90 percent of the young adults had gone beyond the primary school level.

Education is compulsory for all children between seven and sixteen years. Elementary education lasts from seven to nine years. Generally, secondary education takes place at comprehensive schools (*ungdomsskole*). The pupil may then progress to an upper grammar school (*gymnas*), where a certain degree of specialization takes place. After the age of seventeen, a student wishing to further his education may enroll in one of the folk high schools for a six- to eight-month course. In addition to these schools, there are four universities, six colleges of university standing, and six regional colleges.

Two recent developments in Norwegian education are important. The first has been an increasing number of female students at the secondary level. The second, an effort by the state to bring education to the adult members of society— "distant education," as it has come to be called—has been widely

Table 6.3

The Political Allegiances of Norway's Major Newspapers, 1970

Newspaper	Political Alignment	Daily Circulation
Aftenposten	Conservative	201,000
Dagbladet	Liberal	111,000
Verdens Gang	Nonpartisan	96,000
Bergens Tidende	Liberal	82,000
Arbeidebladet	Labor	75,000
Adresseavisen	Conservative	74,000

accepted and concentrates on subjects taught on the secondary and vocational levels.

POLITICAL PARTIES AND INTEREST GROUPS

As is the case with Sweden, Norwegian parties and interest groups play an active role in cultivating attitudes on political issues. The activities of these institutions are most apparent among student organizations which discuss and debate the political issues relevant to contemporary politics. The organizations funnel information pertaining to their political persuasion to the students who are thus socialized and in turn help to socialize others along these ideological lines.

MASS MEDIA

It was not until the principle of freedom of the press was established in the Constitution of 1814 that the Norwegian press became an important factor in the formation of public opinion. The first daily paper was issued in 1819 (*Morgenbladet*), and Norway's largest newspaper today, *Aftenposten*, the only paper with two daily editions, was started in 1860. In 1970, the circulation of the Norwegian press was 1,810,000 and newspaper circulation has generally been going upward. Practically all of these newspapers are politically engaged. However, the political affiliation, circulation, and electoral support of the political parties seldom correspond. Thus the Labor Party, with 37 percent of the seats in the recent Storting election, has only 24.3 percent of the daily newspaper circulation. Table 6.3 lists the leading newspapers and their political allegiances.

All Norwegian radio and television transmitters are operated by the Norwegian Broadcasting Corporation (*Norsk Rikeskringkasting*, NRK), which has the monopoly to transmit in Norway. It is an independent entity whose director general is responsible for his decisions to a five-member board, all of whom are appointed by the king on the advice of the cabinet. With this centralized and monopolistic control over television and radio, there would seem to be a far greater risk of bias and news management than in a competitive media system. However, abuses have thus far been very infrequent.

Denmark

THE FAMILY

The Danish family is more liberal and democratized than either the Swedish or Norwegian family. It is possible that this is due to the fact that Denmark is more urbanized and that the nuclear family has become more decentralized because of the forces of urbanization. As a result, Danish children and adults are more independent than in many cultures.

The independence of the members of the family is evidenced by the rights of married women. A woman is deemed to be independent by Danish law with regard to sickness (provided she is a member of an unemployment fund). She is also entitled to a separate and distinct old-age pension. On marrying, a woman normally assumes her husband's surname, but if application is made before the wedding takes place, the wife may retain her maiden name. Similarly, the children can carry the mother's name on application to the government. Also, if the husband applies for state permission before the wedding, he can assume the wife's surname.

THE SCHOOLS

The educational system of Denmark must be viewed from the perspective of a couple of distinguishing historical developments: the commencement of compulsory public education for children in 1814, attributable essentially to an attitude of political liberalism and a mood of Danish nationalism; and the launching of the folk school movement in the 1840s, earmarking the emphasis on adult education in Denmark, a movement which extended shortly thereafter to Norway and Sweden and thus identifies a common Scandinavian characteristic of progressive education. Currently, Danish children are required to complete at least nine years of compulsory education. After the seventh year of classes, approximately 35 percent of the students decide to pursue vocational classes and 65 percent opt for advanced academic studies.

The Danish educational system is presently experiencing a profound transformation. From the basic primary school to the institutions of higher learning, the structure is changing. More pupil-centered instruction is replacing the previous emphasis on examinations. The system is also moving from the "selective principle" to the new "elective principle." The elective principle will, by means of counseling activities, help the students plan a program of instruction geared to their individual talents and aptitudes. There has also been a concerted effort to increase parent involvement in educational decisions. In 1970, the Educational Supervision Act was promulgated, giving parents "co-responsibility" for school activities and educational priorities.

The Danish state has a continuing commitment to adult education. More than 425,000 students are enrolled in general, spare-time educational courses, and vocational guidance is available to those seeking training in trade and technical skills. Denmark also has five universities and thirty-two other institutions of higher education. The country has an increasing commitment to education, and the institutions it has established are a major agent for inculcating political values and concepts.

POLITICAL PARTIES AND INTEREST GROUPS

Danish political parties and interest groups are virtually identical to those in the other Scandinavian countries with regard to their role in socializing new members into the political system. They actively state their policy positions and serve the public as information outlets on important issues.

MASS MEDIA

The Danish press has always been regarded as reflective of various interests. Of the fifty-five daily papers, one, *Statsidende*, contains only official announcements and another contains only building-trade news. The largest of the Danish dailies is the conservative *Berlingske Tidende*, which has a weekday circulation of 146,000 papers. It is closely rivaled by the *Radical Politiken's* circulation of 124,000. The only direct competition to these two papers is the Social-Democratic *Abtualt*, formerly *Social-Demokraten*, with a 52,000 circulation. It is still a party organ but freer and more popular in style. Other smaller papers bring the total Copenhagen circulation to 385,000 daily. It has fallen since 1950 from 492,000; however, the midday tabloids have risen from 200,000 to 477,000. The largest of the non-Copenhagen newspapers that is national in outlook and circulation is the independent conservative *Fyllands-Posten* (81,000), published at Aarhus.

Newspapers have been published in Danish since 1666; however, it was not until the freedom of the press was won in 1849 that newspapers achieved widespread circulation. Concurrently, with social-political development, there arose four groups of newspapers, each group associated with a definite party and definite social groups.

During the occupation, 1940 to 1945, the press was strictly controlled and in the last two years was subject to total German censorship and compulsory publication of articles. Except for this period, however, there has been freedom of the press, a freedom guaranteed in the constitution. Legal responsibility for signed articles rests with the author, and the legal limits of fair comment in speech and writing are broad. The government exercises no control over the press nor does it seek to control systematically the flow of news from the administration.

The electronic media are handled by Radio Denmark. It is a public and independent institution with the sole right of presenting radio and television programs under the Broadcasting Act of June 11, 1959. The day-to-day control of radio is exercised by the director general. He is assisted by various other directors responsible for personnel, finance, etc. Program directors are responsible to the director general for their respective programs. A program committee meets weekly to discuss programming, and it is through this committee that program control is exerted. The widespread access to radio and television in Denmark permits the electronic media to have a potentially profound impact on Danish political and social life.

Internal Cleavages, Political Competition, and Citizen Participation

Scandinavia as an area can be easily classified as stable, competitive, participant, and decentralized. Each country has an active electorate, with a large number of people participating in interest group activities and political party functions. But, despite the high degree of political fractionalization within Scandinavia, the region is still one of the most politically stable in the industrialized world.

Sweden

Interest organizations in Sweden are a vital part of the overall political system. Representatives of the different organizations sit in the parliament, serve on commissions of inquiry, and belong to administrative agencies. The organizations are invited to submit comments on all sorts of proposals forwarded inside the administration or parliament. Their views are recorded in the official publications of the political machinery. The interest organizations are varied; they include trade unions, salaried employees, employers, consumer and producer cooperatives, small landowners, industry, business, trade, women's groups, tenants, and landlords.

The principal Swedish trade union confederations are as follows:

1. The Swedish Trade Union Confederation (LO, Landsorganisationen) was founded in 1896 and consists of 25 national blue-collar unions. The organization has approximately 2 million members that are organized into 1800 regional organizations, with over 10,000 workplace organizations or local branches.
2. The Swedish Central Organization of Salaried Employees (TCO, Tjänstemännens Centralorganisation) was founded in 1944 and consists of 24 national white-collar unions with about 1 million members. These unions are organized into over 20,000 local branch organizations.
3. The Swedish Confederation of Professional Associations (SACO/SR, Centralorganisationen SACO/SR) was founded

in 1947 and consists of 27 national professional associations
with over 200,000 members, mainly white-collar employees
with university level degrees.

4. The Central Organization of Swedish Workers (SAC,
   Sveriges Arbetares Centralorganisation) was founded in 1910
   and is a syndicated trade union organization. It consists of
   nearly 260 "co-organizations" with a membership of 18,000
   members.

The counterpart to the labor organizations is the employer organizations.
The major ones include:

1. The Swedish Employers' Confederation (SAF, Svenska
   arbetsgivareföreningen) founded in 1902 and consists of
   more than 40 national employer associations, from different
   economic sectors. It has a membership of over 35,000 firms
   employing 1.3 million people.
2. The Swedish Association of Local Authorities (Svenska
   Kommunförbundet) is an employer organization of the
   country's 277 municipal governments. The scope of this
   sector includes about 475,000 employees.
3. The Federation of Swedish County Councils
   (Landstingsförbundet) is the employer organization of the
   country's 23 county councils, the scope of which includes
   320,000 employees.
4. The National Swedish Agency for Government Employers
   (Statens arbetsgivarverk) represents the state in negotiations
   with the national civil service, which has over 540,000
   employees. Until January 1, 1979, the organization was
   known as the National Swedish Collective Bargaining Office
   (SAV, Statens Avtalsverk).
5. The Collective Bargaining Board for State-owned
   Enterprises (SFO, Statsföretagens förhandlingsorganisation)
   represents businesses that are owned by the national
   government. The scope of this organization covers 170
   companies with about 75,000 employees.

These unique social structures help to focus labor policy and resolution of
conflicts between management and labor at national central points of arbitration. The issues and debates become national rather than local. This point
extends also to the solution, with rare exceptions.

At the top level, in the government chancery, leading personalities from
management and labor, industry and trade, etc., are invited to serve on certain advisory committees. Thus they sit on consultative bodies for matters re-

TABLE 6.4

Party Representation in Sweden's National Parliament

Party	1976		1979	
	% Vote	Seats	% Vote	Seats
Social Democratic Labor Party	42.9	152	43.2	154
Center Party	24.1	86	18.1	64
Conservative Party	15.6	55	20.3	73
Liberal Party	11.0	39	10.6	38
Left Party—Communists	4.7	17	5.6	20
Christian Democratic Party	1.4	0	0	0
Communist Party of Sweden	0.3	0	0	0

Source: *Nordisk Kontackt* no. 3, 1982.

lating to such issues as employment policies and building questions. Not only are the interest groups involved in public discussion, but they play a responsible part in the actual administration at all levels.

There are five political parties which are represented in the parliament and two additional parties which are not. Table 6.4 shows the parties, their seats held in the parliament, and their percentage of the national vote. Listed below are the general policy stances of the major Swedish political parties:

1. The Social Democratic Labor Party (*Socialdemokratiska Arbetarepartiet*) is closely allied with the worker's trade union movement (*Landsorganisationen*, LO), which has a number of representatives in the parliament as Social Democrats. This relationship dates back to the 1880s. The party's program is one of socialist economic reform and support of the United Nations.
2. The Liberal Party (*Folkpartiet*), as a nationwide organization, was constituted in 1902. It has backed the traditional philosophy reflecting liberal values, such as universal suffrage and women's rights.
3. The Center Party (*Centerpartiet*) was constructed in 1922 through the coalition of two smaller parties formed in 1913 and 1915, respectively. Its program emphasizes social development, with concentration on governmental decentralization.
4. The Conservative Party (*Moderata Samlingspartiet*) was founded in 1904 but derived its conservative tendencies during the latter part of the nineteenth century. The chief points in its program are social and economic progress along traditional Swedish lines and a liberal, market-oriented economy.

5. The last of the five parties seated in the parliament is the Left Party—Communists (*Vänsterpartiet Kommunisterna*). This party was formed in 1917 as the Left Social Democratic Party of Sweden and affiliated with the Communist International in 1919. At the party congress in March 1921, it was renamed the Communist Party and in 1967 the name was changed to the Left Party (*Communisto*). The policy of the party is based on the principles of Marxism.

6. Two remaining minor parties, the Christian Democratic Party (*Kristen Demokratisk Samling*, KDS), formed in 1964 to promote Christian values in political life, and the Communist Party of Sweden (*Sveriges Kommunister Partiet*), a small Maoist party, have never been seated in the parliament.

From 1932 until 1976, the Social Democrats were in office continuously—except for an interregnum of one hundred days in 1936. Between 1933 and 1936 they had a working agreement with the Center Party. Coalition governments of Social Democrats and the Center were in power from 1936 to 1939 and from 1951 to 1957. During the Second World War, 1939–1945, all parties except the Communists were in coalition. During the years 1945 to 1951, and 1957 to 1976, the Social Democrats were in office alone. In 1976, in a dramatic upset, a coalition of the opposition parties (Liberal, Conservative, Center) turned the Social Democrats out of office. However, this tri-party coalition was short-lived. In 1978, it was replaced by a Liberal Party government. The opposition parties have never been able to achieve the necessary concensus to retain power and build on a common base. As the 1979 election returns indicated there appears to be a Social Democratic resurgence and there is every indication that this will continue to build in 1982.

Since 1966, state subsidies have been paid to every political party which has any significant support from the voters in the general elections. These subsidies are paid in the form of "party subsidies" and "secretariat subsidies." As of 1974, a party has been eligible for party subsidies if it has received at least one seat in the parliament or 2.6 percent of the votes throughout the whole country for either of the previous two elections.

To qualify for secretariat subsidies, a party is required either to have won a seat in parliament in the next to the last election or to have received at least 4 percent of the votes in the whole country at that election. The size of the subsidies is related to party strength. Secretariat subsidies are also larger for opposition parties than for parties represented in the cabinet. A party with seats in the parliament receives party subsidies amounting to Skr 85,000 per year per seat. No conditions are attached to the subsidies, nor is there any public audit of the party's expenditures.

Norway

Norwegian interest organizations are varied and cover the wide spectrum of political life. They include mining interests, fishing and maritime concerns, labor, agriculture, and newly acquired petroleum interests. Many of the interest groups have a regional outlook and maintain close links with their counterparts in the other Scandinavian countries. For example, labor has had much the same history and development in Norway as in Sweden. The Norwegian LO (*Landsorganisationen*) was formed as a major central union in 1899, shortly after it was established in Sweden.

Norway has a multiparty system and many of the interest group organizations work closely with particular political parties. For example, the referendum on Norwegian membership in the Common Market in September 1972 became a catalyst for the formation of new parties. At that time, several interest groups attempted to form their own distinctive political movements. The fractionalizing of the parties continued until, in the 1973 general election, a total of thirteen parties took part in the election, including an amalgamation of three parties from the left wing of the Labor Party. Recently, endeavors have been made to combine these groups into a single party called the Socialist Electoral League. Eight of the Norwegian parties were represented in the Storting (parliament) following the general election. Table 6.5 shows the various major parties along with their percentage of total votes and number of seats acquired in the Storting. The trend of these figures shows a dramatic shift to the right in the 1981 Norwegian elections. The Labor party, which has enjoyed a comfortable edge until recently, dropped from 76 seats in 1977 to 66 in 1981. Concurrently, the Conservative party jumped from 41 seats in 1977 to 53 seats in 1981. This apparent shift to the right with its corresponding Conservative party cabinet underscores the heterogeneity of the Scandinavian governments. Much can be written of a common culture, but unique independent politics is thriving among the northern countries.

Interestingly, there were no political parties in Norway when the Constitution of 1814 was adopted. Gradually, ideological differences were crystallized in the Conservative (*Høyre*) and Liberal (*Venstre*) parties, both of which were established as political organizations in 1884. This simple party alignment endured until the turn of the century, when the Norwegian Labor Party (*Arbeiderparti*) entered the political stage, electing its first representative to the Storting in 1903. Subsequent years saw the formation of several other parties. The Center Party (*Senterpartiet*) was founded in 1920 to promote the interests of farmers. It now aims at attracting voters from other sectors. The Christian People's Party (*Kristelig Folkeparti*) was formed in 1938 to promote Christianity as a basis of political life, and the Socialist Electoral League is a radical offshoot of the Labor Party. The policy stances of the various Norwegian parties follow:

TABLE 6.5

Party Representation in Norway's National Parliament

Party	1977		1981	
	% Vote	Seats	% Vote	Seats
Labor Party	42.4	76	37.2	66
Conservative Party	24.7	41	31.7	53
Christian People's Party	12.1	22	9.3	15
Center Party	8.6	12	6.7	11
Socialist People's Party	4.1	2	4.9	4
Communist Party	0.4	0	0.3	0
Liberal Party	3.2	2	4.0	2
Progressive Party	1.9	0	4.5	4
New People's Party	1.7	0	0	0
Others	0.9	0	1.4	0

Source: *Nordisk Kontackt* no. 3, 1982.

1. The Liberal Party (*Venstre*) has backed programs of liberal reform, for example, universal suffrage, social reforms on taxation, health insurance, and old-age pensions.
2. The Conservative Party (*Høyre*) has advocated lower taxes, favored business, and is against the Norwegian government controlling the economy. It was very much in favor of Norway joining the Common Market.
3. The Norwegian Labor Party (*Arbeiderparti*) has had a close relationship with the trade union movement. From the start, the Labor Party was a reform party, but as socialist and later communist tendencies gained ground, serious internal conflicts arose. In 1921, the moderate social democratic wing broke away and formed a new party, and in 1923 the main party came into conflict with the Communist International. The result was the formation of the Norwegian Communist Party (*Norske Kommunistiske Parti*). For four years, the country had three different labor parties, until 1926, when the Social Democrats rejoined the Labor Party. The party has undergone significant changes in its outlook on several questions of principle: first it was a democratic reform party, then a revolutionary party, and finally a more moderate socialist movement. This moderation led to a left-wing opposition in the party which in 1961 helped to create the Socialist People's Party.
4. The Socialist People's Party (*Socialistisk Folkeparti*) advocates a neutralist, anti-NATO foreign and defense

policy and a policy closer to the original social democratic
line on domestic questions. It provides a noncommunist
alternative for the neutralist elements in the electorate.

5. The Center Party (*Senterpartiet*) was previously called the
   Farmer's Party. Since 1945 the party had steadily increased
   its number of votes and has now become the fourth largest
   party. Its political importance was enhanced when Per
   Borten of the Center Party was chosen in 1965 to head a
   nonsocialist coalition government which remained in office
   until 1971. The party was one of the main leaders in the
   defeat of the promarketeers in the referendum on EEC
   membership in 1972. In principle, the party is opposed to
   socialism, but favors extensive economic and social planning.

6. The Christian People's Party (*Kristelig Folkeparti*) has
   shown special interest in educational and cultural matters,
   which it seeks to influence in a Christian direction, and is a
   strong supporter of NATO.

7. The New People's Party (*Det Nye Folkpartiet*) was the
   direct outcome of the bitter controversy within the Liberal
   Party on whether Norway should join the Common Market.
   After the people rejected membership through the
   referendum in 1972, the Liberal Party was unable to heal
   the rift between supporters and opponents. In November
   1972, the pro-membership wing left to form a separate
   party. This was later to become the New People's Party. Like
   the Liberals the new party regards itself as a social liberal
   party at the center of Norwegian politics.

8. The Norwegian Communist Party (*Norske Kommunistiske
   Parti*) has been in steady decline since World War II. In the
   1969 election the party obtained 1 percent of the total votes
   cast.

9. The remaining parties are relatively new and have thus far
   had a minimal impact on Norwegian politics. They are (1)
   Anders Lange's Parti—regarded as a protest party against
   growing state control and the increasing burden of taxes and
   duties—which appears to draw support not only from right-
   wing conservatives but also from other parties, including
   Labor; (2) Democratic Socialists—AIK (*Demokratiske
   Sosialester*)—founded by Labor Party left-wingers who
   would not compromise on their opposition to Common
   Market membership (AIK stands for Worker's Information
   Committee against the Common Market); (3) Red Electoral
   Alliance (*Rød Valgallianse*), which represents former
   Socialist People's Party supporters who aim at the

introduction of socialism by revolutionary means and is
sometimes referred to as "Maoist "; and (4) the Progressive
Party—a minor party which lost its four seats in the most
recent parliamentary election.

When the Norwegian constitution was adopted in 1814, only a limited
number (approximately 7 percent) of citizens were given the right to vote:
higher civil servants, members of the urban middle class, and farmers. According to the provisions now in force, all Norwegian citizens, both men and
women, are entitled to vote if they have reached, or will reach, the age of
twenty before the end of the year in which the general election is held. Thus,
out of a total population of some 4.1 million people, approximately 2.8 million
have the right to vote.

Norway's electoral system is based on proportional representation. The essential feature is that each party has a percentage of the seats in the parliament corresponding to its share of the votes. However, the system favors the
bigger parties so that large and moderately large parties obtain a numerically
higher representation in the Storting than would accurately correspond in
mathematical terms to their electoral support. This is done to avoid the com-
plication of a parliament highly fractionalized by a multitude of small parties.
In addition, the election system is based on geographical representation, since
the country is divided into a number of separate counties, each of which sends
a set number of representatives to the Storting. This arrangement also limits
the proportionality between the parties' share of the votes and their respective
percentage of the seats in the parliament.

The Storting is elected for four years and cannot be dissolved. A motion was
proposed in May 1973 to make dissolution possible, but it failed to achieve the
necessary two-thirds majority required to amend the constitution.

Denmark

Denmark, like the other Scandinavian countries, is a land of organizations.
The interest groups which are most actively seeking to influence public policy
come from agriculture, business, industry, and labor. Politically, the interest
groups are involved at five levels of the political process. They include (1)
direct and indirect ties and influence with party organizations; (2) economic
assistance to parties; (3) promoting of representatives in the parliament
(Folketing); (4) lobbying; and (5) activity in administration of government
policy.

Danish politics demonstrate that no interest group can guarantee a program, and the major parties realize that if they are to be successful they must
appeal to a broad spectrum of interest groups. In the multi-party framework
that exists, a coalition must be formed of several interests and parties in order
to secure adoption of a particular program. This enhances the role of bargain-

TABLE 6.6

Party Representation in Denmark's National Parliament

Party	1979		1981	
	% Vote	Seats	% Vote	Seats
Social Democratic Party	38.3	68	32.9	59
Progress Party	11.0	20	8.9	16
Liberal Party	12.5	22	11.3	20
Conservative Party	12.5	22	14.4	26
Center Democrats	3.2	6	8.3	15
Socialist People's Party	5.9	11	11.3	21
Communist Party	1.9	0	1.1	0
Radical Liberal Party	5.4	10	5.1	9
Christian People's Party	2.6	5	2.3	4
Justice (Single-Tax) Party	2.6	5	1.4	0
Left Wing Socialist Party	3.7	6	2.6	5
Others	0.4	0	0.4	0

Source: *Nordisk Kontackt* no. 3, 1982.

ing and causes the parties and interest groups to attempt to strike a balance and compromise on a program beneficial to those most concerned.

The Danes are inundated with appeals from a broad spectrum of political parties. The single problem that affects each of the major parties is finding allies strong enough to enable the alliance to gain and hold office as the governing coalition. The chance of turning a plurality in the electorate into a legislative majority is the complicated system of proportional representation followed by the Danes. The major political parties, their allocation of seats in the parliament, and their percentage of the nationwide vote are shown in Table 6.6. Listed below are the general policy stances of the major Danish parties:

1. The Social Democratic Party (*Socialdemokratiet*) was founded in 1871 and has been the largest party in Denmark since 1924, when it formed its first government. As with the other Social Democratic movements of Scandinavia, the Danish Social Democrats have had a close association with labor. Today, its chief adherents are found among workers, some employers, and civil servants. The party has supported traditional liberal domestic programs and, following World War II, abandoned its perennial position in favor of international neutrality and opted for Danish membership in NATO.

2. The Liberal Party (*Venstreparti*) was formed in 1870 and its main support has traditionally come from farmers. In recent years, however, its votes have been distributed almost

equally between urban and rural dwellers. The main planks of the party platform are free trade, minimum government interference in economic affairs, and a general social security system.

3. The Conservative Party (*Konservative Folkeparti*) came into existence in 1916 and has continuously advocated free initiative and the maintenance of private property. The party does, however, defend the right of the state to act as an arbiter to make sure that a proper economic and social balance is preserved. Danish conservatives in general see themselves as representing the center, rejecting reactionary arguments and old-style liberalism on the one hand and all types of socialism on the other. The Conservatives have supported the country's membership in NATO, EFTA, and most recently the European Community.

4. The Radical Liberal Party (*Det Radikale Venstre*) was founded in 1905, and even though it is considered one of the four "old parties," it has fared little better than fifth in most of the post–World War II elections. The Radicals consider themselves a "social-liberal" party and, like so many of their competitors, perceive themselves to be near the center of the political spectrum and a little to the left of the other nonsocialist movements. The party favors international detente and cooperation within regional and world organizations, social reforms without socialism, workers' participation in industry and state intervention in industrial disputes, and state control of trusts and monopollies while at the same time retaining a viable private economic sector.

5. There exists a wide variety of parties other than the aforementioned "old parties." The largest of these is the Socialist People's Party (*Socialistisk Folkeparti*). It was formed in 1959, and has consistently pursued a program of socialist policies. The other "new" party movements include the following: (1) the Independent Party (*De Uafhaengige*), which was founded in 1953; (2) the Justice Party (*Danmarks Retsforband*), which was formed in 1920 and has extolled the virtues of free trade and a single tax system; (3) the Danish Communist Party (*Danmarks Kommunistiske Parti*), which dates from 1919 and has remained a small fringe party within the Danish political structure; (4) the Left-Wing Socialist Party (*Venstresocialisterne*), which was pieced together in 1967 as a result of a split in ranks among

the members of the Socialist People's Party; (5) the Center
Democrats (*Centrum-Demokrater*), which came together in
1974 and has strongly supported Denmark's inclusion in the
European Community; (6) the Christian People's Party
(*Kristeligt Folkeparti*), which was established in 1970 with
the major goal of being an interdenominational grouping
strongly opposed to pornography and abortion; and (7) the
Progress Party (*Fremskirdtspartiet*), which was founded in
1972 and which supports the gradual abolition of the
income tax, the disbandment of a large sector of the civil
service, and dismantlement of the diplomatic service, and
the dismembering of a large part of Denmark's legislation.
As evidenced by the last parliamentary election and recent
public opinion polls, the future for the Center Democrats
and the Socialist People's party looks bright. This is true also
for the Conservative party, although recent polls show
support falling off. The remaining parties appear to be
declining in growth, with the exception of the Social
Democrats, who have maintained constant electoral support.
Unlike Norway, which has experienced a recent swing to the
right or Sweden, with its noticeable leftist momentum,
Denmark continues to waffle between the two positions.

Under the Constitution of June 5, 1953, the Danish parliament consists of
one chamber of 179 members. The country is divided for electoral purposes
into three zones: Greater Copenhagen, the Island, and Jutland. These are divided into seventeen electoral areas, which are divided into 103 constituencies
in all, so that there are, in each area, from 2 to 10 constituencies.

The division into electoral areas is based on the division between local governments, a county area being comprised of the primary, local government
areas. The three other large areas comprise the metropolitan municipalities of
Copenhagen and Frederiksberg. Local administration of elections is vested in
special election committees formed in each of the 103 constituencies from
delegates of the local government councils.

The right to vote at a parliamentary election is held by every Danish citizen of twenty-one and over who is permanently domiciled in Denmark. The
right to vote is also subject to enrollment in the annual electoral lists. Every
person entitled to vote is eligible for election, unless he has been punished for
any act which renders him unworthy to be a member of the parliament.

Any person may submit himself for election, provided that his candidature
is supported by at least twenty-five electors. The candidate must state which
party he supports or whether he is independent of parties. Under the electoral
law, 135 of the 179 members of the Folketing are elected to what are called

area seats and 40 to supplementary seats. The electoral concept is a form of proportional representation and the distribution of seats is according to a modified form of what is known as the Sainte Lagues method. In addition to the 175 members from metropolitan Denmark, 2 more are elected from the Faeroe Islands and 2 from Greenland.

Government Institutions and the Policy-Making Process

Sweden

THE CONSTITUTION

Until 1975 the Swedish constitution consisted of four separate documents: the Instrument of Government dating back to 1809; the Act of Succession (for the present royal family) to 1810; the Parliament Act to 1866; and the Freedom of the Press Act to 1949. However, in the spring of 1973 the parliament (Riksdag) passed the new Instrument of Government and new Parliament Act. The new constitution was confirmed and went into effect January 1, 1975.

THE MONARCHY

The Swedish king is a constitutional monarch and exerts no political power and takes no part in politics. The king represents the nation, and according to the constitution, is the head of state. The responsibility for the policy decisions rests with his Councillors of State (*Statsråd*), i.e., the cabinet ministers. Under the new constitution, the king is not required to sign government legislation and the Speaker of Parliament selects the new prime minister. Moreover, the Swedish parliament voted in 1978 to abrogate the Salic Law, which since its introduction in 1810 limited the succession to the throne to male heirs.

THE CABINET

Real political power rests with the cabinet and the party or parties it represents. Cabinet ministers may be heads of ministries or ministers without portfolio. The cabinet as a whole is responsible for all government decisions, although in practice a great number of routine matters are decided by individual ministers and only formally confirmed by the government. The principle of collective responsibility is reflected in all forms of governmental work.

THE PARLIAMENT

Since 1971, Sweden has had a unicameral parliament. The entire parliament is constituted by direct elections based on suffrage that comprises all Swedes who are eighteen years of age or older. Parliament has 350 members, who serve three-year terms. Eligibility is subject to Swedish citizenship and the attainment of voting age. All elections are by proportional representation. There is one exception to the rule of proportional representation: a quota rule intended to prevent very small parties from gaining representation in the parliament. A party must thus score at least 4 percent of the national popular vote to qualify for representation. In any one constituency, however, a party will gain a seat by obtaining 12 percent of the votes even if its national popular vote falls short of 4 percent.

The trades and professions of Swedish society are fairly well represented in the parliament. The unicameral parliament has a presidium consisting of the speaker and three deputy speakers. Every session of parliament appoints sixteen standing committees, of which one is on the constitution, one deals with budgeting and finance, and the remainder are specialized bodies, largely corresponding to the division of ministries. Ad hoc committees may be called during the session based on need. Committees may allow cabinet ministers to attend their meetings in order to provide information.

Although the right of cabinet ministers to speak is practically unlimited, it is not possible—by filibustering or otherwise—to avoid a decision on a matter which is before the house. Since the rules of procedure are clear and detailed, procedural debates are rare.

The parliament is in session during roughly seven months, the months of June through September being free. The government has the right to dissolve the parliament and to order extraordinary elections. Votes of confidence are not taken in the parliament as separate items and cannot be moved by members. If a cabinet wishes to make a bill or a legislative matter a "question of confidence," the rule is that it makes this known before the vote is taken.

The Ministries and Administrative Organizations

The ministries (departments) are small, each as a rule consisting of no more than one hundred persons (including clerical staff). The ministries have five major functions: (1) preparing the government's bills to the parliament on budget appropriations and laws; (2) issuing laws and regulations and general rules for the administrative agencies; (3) conducting international relations; (4) recommending higher appointments in the administration; and (5) hearing certain appeals from individuals, which are addressed to the government.

Except for these appeals, the ministries are, in most fields, not concerned with details of administration. The details of administration and the carrying out of government decisions are entrusted to a number of central administrative agencies. For example, under the heading of the Ministry of Health and Social Affairs fall the National Board of Health and Welfare, the National Social Insurance Board, and certain smaller agencies. Every such agency is headed by a director general, who is appointed by the government for a period of six years. Occasionally, these appointments are partisan. The board of an agency consists of the director general as chairman and a number of the senior officials serving directly under him. It also includes laymen representing organizations or sections of the population who have special interest in the matters dealt with by the agency. All members of the board are appointed by the board itself.

THE JUDICIAL SYSTEM

In Sweden the judiciary and the executive are separate. Judges are appointed by the government. A judge can be removed by an authority other than a court, but in such an event he may always call for a judicial trial of the decision. The *Domstalsverket* supervises the courts in administrative matters. This central authority has no control over the judicial process, in which the court is independent, even of the government.

Some state officers exercise control over the judiciary and the administrative authorities. The Chancellor of Justice and four ombudsmen supervise the courts and the general administration, including the armed forces.

There are three levels of courts in Sweden and a series of special courts and administrative courts. The basic courts include (1) Courts of the First Instance (*Tingsratt*)—these have jurisdiction in both civil and criminal cases; (2) Appellate Courts (*Hovratt*)—these courts have appellate jurisdiction in both civil and criminal cases, they are often called Courts of the Second Instance; and (3) the Supreme Court (*Hogsta Domstolen*)—this court has twenty-five members and works in divisions of five members. In some instances cases are decided by full session of the Supreme Court.

OMBUDSMAN

The post of ombudsman (*Justiombudsman*) was created to supervise the manner in which judges, government officials, and other civil servants observe the laws, and to prosecute those who act illegally, misuse their position or neglect their duties. The ombudsman is allowed access to all documents and information and has the right to be present at court hearings and other proceedings. Government ministers in Sweden are not subject to supervision by ombudsmen. Currently, there are four ombudsmen.

Norway

THE CONSTITUTION

The present constitution of Norway was drafted at the end of the Napoleonic War in Europe and proclaimed on May 17, 1814. In its original form, the constitution contained features derived from the U.S. Constitution and was also influenced by both France and the United Kingdom.

The constitution established a constitutional monarchy and a parliamentary form of government. The most important features of the constitution include due process of law, freedom of the press, free speech, and the illegality of ex post facto laws.

THE MONARCHY

The king of Norway reigns but does not govern. That power is exercised by the cabinet. The king can exercise the right of veto to suspend legislation, but this authority has not been used for years. The king is nominally the supreme commander of the country's armed forces and he is the head of the Church of Norway, to which he himself and at least half of his cabinet must belong. By law, the king can do no wrong. In addition, the throne is hereditary and is still limited to males.

THE CABINET

The cabinet, which is also known as the State Council (*Statsråd*), is regarded as the "government" of the nation and is composed of the prime minister and no fewer than seven Councillors of State. Councillors must be over thirty years of age.

Formally, the constitution empowers the king to appoint cabinet ministers. In practice, however, the leaders of the political party or parties which hold a majority in the parliament will tell the king who should be elected for cabinet positions.

All important matters of administration are decided by the King-in-Council, which is a euphemism for deliberations of the cabinet. The cabinet is also responsible for upholding the constitution and directs the government administration in collecting the taxes and duties imposed by the parliament; issuing regulations concerning commerce, customs, trade, industry, and the police; supervising education and the state church; declaring war in defense of the country; and making and denouncing treaties with other nations (treaties of major importance do not become binding until approved by the parliament).

THE PARLIAMENT

The Norwegian representative assembly is known as the Storting. The Storting must pass all legislation and also must approve cabinet appointments made by the king. By virtue of its power to control the government's purse strings, the Storting certainly plays a significant role in the governing of the nation.

The Storting may be described as a modified single-house legislature, with its 155 members elected for four-year terms. At the beginning of the first session following the election, the legislators select one-quarter of its members to serve in the *Lagting* (the second chamber), while the remaining three-quarters constitute the *Odelsting* (the first chamber). All legislative proposals which affect the citizen's rights and duties are considered separately by the two divisions of the Storting, while resolutions relating to constitutional amendments, treaties, and budgetary and financial matters are dealt with in joint plenary sessions. The *Lagting* also is empowered to join ranks with the Norwegian Supreme Court to form the High Court of the Realm to hear cases raised in the *Odelsting* against members of the government.

The main work of the Storting is done in standing committees and, unlike the U.S. Congress, the length of a representative's service in the parliament has little bearing on his appointment to or rank in a committee. The chairman of a standing committee is authorized to call meetings and may use his vote to break a deadlock. Yet aside from these powers, the chairman has little of the discretionary authority which until recently has belonged to the chairmen of U.S. congressional committees.

When a piece of legislation has been approved by the *Odelsting* and *Lagting* or the Storting in plenary session, it automatically becomes law. Constitutional amendments are also ratified by the Storting with a two-thirds vote of its membership. In compliance with a provision of the will of Alfred Nobel, the Storting has also been accorded the responsibility of selecting a special committee which awards the prestigious Nobel Peace Prize.

NATIONAL AND LOCAL ADMINISTRATION

Governmental authority in Norway is essentially centralized but the nation as a whole is divided into various administrative units and some discretionary power is exercised by local officials. As of the mid-1970s, the country was divided into 19 countries (*fylker*), 47 municipalities (*bykommuner*), and 397 rural districts (*landkommuner*).

Major decisions involving the administration of the country are settled by the cabinet in its role as King-in-Council. Each member of the cabinet controls and is responsible for the activities of a government ministry. Foreign Affairs, Educational and Ecclesiastical Affairs, Justice and Police, Social Affairs, and Local Government and Labor are among the most important ministries.

Local self-government was legally instituted in Norway in 1837, and local officials are elected for four-year terms in elections held midway between the national elections. Local authority is exercised by county governors, commissioners of police, and by other publicly elected county, municipal, and rural officials. Norwegian citizens pay taxes on income, capital, and other property to both the central and local governments.

On the whole, however, the central government establishes the major priorities for the nation, and as long as the cabinet enjoys majority support in the Storting, it is definitely the pivotal policymaking institution in the nation.

THE JUDICIAL SYSTEM

The Norwegian judicial system is organized into a hierarchy consisting of four main levels. Conciliation Councils (*Forliksrådadene*) lie at the bottom of the hierarchy. Each municipality contains a council of three elected members which acts as a mediator between the plaintiff and the defendent. If the council is unable to resolve their dispute, the case may be taken to the local court (*Herredsrettene og byrettene*) for formal consideration. Local courts comprise the second level in the judicial hierarchy. These courts of first instance are presided over by a single professional judge, though lay assessors may sit with the regular judge if either party to the dispute so requests. The third level in the Norwegian system is composed of courts of civil and criminal appeals (*Lagmannsretten*). The proceedings in these courts are conducted by a senior judge and two other professional associates. In criminal cases a ten-member jury decides the verdict, while the judges decide the sentence. Finally, located at the top of the hierarchy is the Supreme Court of Justice (*Høiesterett*). It is composed of a Chief Justice and seventeen permanent judges, though only five judges sit on any one case. Like those courts below it, the Supreme Court has the power to declare legislative acts unconstitutional. Moreover, it possesses the authority to review all aspects of any case which it hears on appeal from a lower court.

Denmark

THE CONSTITUTION

The Constitution of June 5, 1849, abolished the absolute monarchy in Denmark and established a system of parliamentary democracy. Most of the provisions of this original constitution remain in force, but significant revisions have been made in the document, the most recent in 1953. The framers of the Danish constitution were heavily influenced by the Norwegian and Belgian constitutions, and the original Danish document established a form of separation of powers based on the theories of Montesquieu. Legislative power was vested jointly in the parliament (Folketing) and the monarch, with executive authority exercised primarily by the monarch and judicial authority by an independent judiciary.

While the concept of separation of powers is theoretically preserved in the 1953 revisions, the system of parliamentary rule has essentially spelled an end to any real separation between the legislative and executive branches. In addition, the 1953 revisions provided for a unicameral legislature.

THE MONARCHY

The powers of the monarch in contemporary Denmark are basically symbolic and predominately ceremonial. Under the constitution, all important government measures are scrutinized by the Council of State, which is presided over by the monarch but which is dominated by the prime minister and his cabinet.

Under the Act of Succession of 1953, which is part of the constitution, access to the throne is based on heredity, with the descendants of King Christian X and Queen Alexandrine first in line. However, male heirs are still given preference over female heirs.

THE CABINET

The constitution stipulates that the monarch shall appoint and dismiss members of the cabinet, but the real impetus for appointments and dismissals is in the hands of the leaders of the dominant party or parties in the Folketing. Generally, the cabinet operates in much the same way in Denmark as it does in Norway and Sweden. The ministers are each responsible for a government department and collectively they render decisions on bills which will be submitted to the parliament. As is the case in most parliamentary systems, as long as the cabinet can count on disciplined majority support in the Folketing, policy decisions made by the prime minister and his associates will generally be sustained by the legislative body.

THE PARLIAMENT

The Folketing is a unicameral body with 179 members, elected for four-year terms (subject to early dissolution) through a proportional respresentation electoral system.

The vast majority of all bills are introduced in the Folketing by a cabinet minister after the cabinet has deliberated on the proposal and then agreed to pass it along to the legislature. Even though the constitution grants every member of parliament the right to introduce legislation, few do so because of their lack of specific knowledge and expertise necessary for formulating a detailed proposal. Consequently, the Folketing is highly dependent on the cabinet for specific policy recommendations, much like the dependency of the U.S. Congress on proposals submitted by the White House.

The Folketing does closely scrutinize bills but debates on the floor of the parliament are usually severely limited. In effect, time constraints are imposed and most of the parties generally select one spokesperson to represent the party in the debate.

In addition to its strictly legislative function, the parliament is also charged with the important task of overseeing the activities of the state administration.

With the consent of the Folketing leadership, members of the parliament may submit questions to cabinet ministers concerning their specific areas of jurisdiction. At times, these questions may provoke heated debate in the parliament and lead in the end to a request for a vote of no confidence against the government.

Along with abolishing the upper chamber, the *Landsting*, the Constitution of 1953 provided for the holding of a referendum in certain limited cases. Within three working days after the passage of a controversial bill by the Folketing, a parliamentary group consisting of at least one-third of the membership may petition the Speaker for a referendum to decide whether a majority of the Danish electorate supports the new law. The purpose of the referendum is to prevent the governing party or parties from ramming through a piece of legislation which might be opposed by the people in general. In addition, the threat of a referendum helps to encourage wider collaboration among the parliamentary parties in the passage of key legislation.

THE ADMINISTRATION

The ministers in the cabinet are responsible for overseeing the daily activities of the central administration, whereas a wide variety of administrative units exist at the regional and local levels. Recently, administrative consolidation into regional units has occurred in Denmark with the creation of the *Kommuner*. The *Kommuner* units now handle many of the administrative problems once assigned to the county and local governmental units. Denmark has also been segmented into fourteen counties (*amter*), each headed by a county administrator (*amtmand*). Formerly, these county administrators performed a wide variety of local activities including chairing the popularly elected county councils. However, with the introduction of the *Kommuner*, the duties of the county administrator have been sharply curtailed.

THE JUDICIAL SYSTEM

In Denmark, the judiciary is essentially independent of government control. Judges are appointed by the crown on the recommendation of the Minister of Justice, and cannot be dismissed from the bench except in rare cases of gross incompetence or criminal conduct.

The court system is stratified into three levels: lower, higher, and supreme. There is a lower court for each of the eighty-four judicial districts in the country and it assumes responsibility for hearing most of the minor cases. The two higher courts hear cases from Jutland and the island dependencies and also serve as appeals courts for cases emanating from the lower courts. At least three judges hear each case which comes before the higher courts.

The Supreme Court is the court of appeal for cases from the two higher courts. Usually, only one appeal is allowed for any case, but in special instances the Minister of Justice may give permission for a second appeal, to the Supreme Court, of a case which started at the lower court and was then appealed to the higher court. A quorum consisting of at least five judges hears cases before the Supreme Court.

THE OMBUDSMAN

The Constitution of 1953 established the office of ombudsman, fashioned after the Swedish prototype. The ombudsman is elected by the Folketing after each general election. It is his responsibility, on behalf of the Folketing, to keep watch on the activities of the administration and those of the local districts. Any citizen may lodge a complaint with the ombudsman, who may not alter a decision but may express his dissatisfaction and bring the case before the court.

The ombudsman submits annual reports to the Folketing and his ideas have prompted its members to sponsor legislation creating changes in the existing laws and procedures. Since the creation of the office in 1955, the number of complaints has averaged one thousand annually.

Policy Problems and Prospects

Sweden

The major problem faced by Sweden today is economic. The consequences that this brings extends into domestic and foreign policy. The election of the opposition parties coalition government in 1976 and its succession to the Conservative party leadership has marked a transition in Swedish domestic politics. It appears that this transition may be short-lived with the reemerging power of the Social Democrats. In addition to this political realignment, Sweden has experienced a spiraling inflation rate and increased taxation. Except for Israel, Sweden has the highest tax rate in the western world. This circumstance has caused many within the Swedish economic system to challenge the premise of the social welfare system. The inability of the Government to control the economic situation has bolstered the Social Democratic bid for power and enhanced the call for cutbacks in government programs. The worldwide energy crises have enflamed the issue of nuclear power and the "fallout" of the debate has been detrimental to the opposition parties. Sweden in the past has maintained its economic well-being only by drawing itself closer to Europe, by adhering to the Common Market's free trade agreement and strengthening ties with Great Britain, the United States, and the other Nordic countries. This integrated policy cuts both ways; not only has Sweden benefited by this close relationship but she has also suffered from the problems.

The western European dependence on the Middle East and the complexities of integrated economic policies are two major complications.

This increased integration has sharpened the focus on the dilemma that occurs with the professed policy of neutrality. The official position of the country is to remain nonaligned during peacetime in order to be neutral during times of war. In recent years it has become increasingly difficult for Swedish foreign policy decision-makers to maintain strict neutrality while domestic, economic, and international realities are forcing Sweden to become more dependent upon European and worldwide integration. Swedish political problems that are mostly economically based seem to stem from this dilemma.

In 1981 a Soviet submarine went aground on a beach within Swedish territorial waters. The incident occurred within the vicinity of a sensitive Swedish naval base. Some analysts have come to feel that the presence of the submarine in the area was due to the degenerating credibility of Swedish armed neutrality. With the high cost of military armaments and the reduced armament procurement policy of the Swedish government, some NATO analysts are becoming concerned over the vulnerability of the northern flank.

The success of any government that comes to power in Sweden will hinge on how they cope with the problems of energy, growth, employment, inflation, and reconfirming a credible neutral posture in international affairs. The question remains: Will the decision-makers be able to adjust their policy to allow latitude for economic growth and development without weakening or seeming to contradict Swedish foreign policy?

Norway

The key issue in Norway's future can be summarized in one word: *oil.* National oil policy, its development and implementation will influence both internal and external Norwegian political affairs.

As early as 1963, Norway began a comprehensive policy of oil resource development. During that year, Norway proclaimed sovereignty over her segment of the continental shelf after concluding bilateral treaties with the United Kingdom, Denmark, and Sweden defining her area on the shelf. The Norwegian section of the shelf was found to be rich in oil reserves.

Until 1969 oil exploration in the Norwegian sector was very limited, but in that year Phillips Petroleum struck large oil and gas deposits in the Ekofisk field. Later, deposits were located in both the Frigg field and the Statfjord field, which straddles the boundary line with the United Kingdom.

Several problems confront Norway. The first is to maintain control over the exploration and production of the petroleum products pumped from her sector. Norway would like the petroleum from her sector landed in Norway; however, the depth of the Norwegian trench has precluded the building of pipelines. As a result, oil from the Ekofisk field is landed in England and gas is piped ashore to Scotland and the Federal Republic of Germany across the Danish zone.

The second problem for Norway is the increased need for Nordic cooperation on energy. It was not until 1973 that a committee of experts was assigned the task of evaluating the potential for Nordic cooperation. Norway is inclined to cooperate with her Nordic neighbors, particularly in exchange for Swedish industrial assistance.

Finally, the question of the Barents Sea area has produced Norwegian-Soviet tensions. The likelihood of finding oil deposits has developed the problem of establishing a dividing line for the two states' continental shelves. One question to be solved is: Does the island of Svalbard have its own shelf (which must be divided) or is it on the Norwegian shelf? Security questions related to the shelf have arisen, particularly regarding Soviet military navigation.

Norwegian petroleum developments may be summarized in three terms: *price, pace* and *profits*. The price structure for North Sea oil depends mainly on two factors, the expense of production and the Middle East situation affecting the price as a function of supply. The pace of the development of Norwegian oil has been modest. Environmental concerns have overridden economic concerns in Norway's full employment economy. Norway's current production is one-tenth of its potential and may be accelerated in the case of a future oil embargo by OPEC. In terms of profits, most are yet to be realized. In recent years Norway's trade has rung up a significant deficit. At the current rate of production, Norway does not plan to realize a surplus until the early 1980s. Expectations are running high regarding the potential effects of the profits. Meanwhile, the government has tried to stabilize these expectations by beginning, in 1975, a continuing income tax reduction program. In general, Norway's policy is to retain as much of the profits as possible for social programs while at the same time keeping the oil companies interested in exploration.

Norwegian oil has left its mark on Norway's political and social future. Norway's role both on a regional level and in Europe is bound to increase because of its new resource. This will bring increased interaction with its neighbors as they face common problems in the North Sea. In summary, Norwegian policy has been abruptly altered by its newly found resource and the implications touch every avenue of political and social life.

Denmark

Danish public policies and future prospects revolve around one central concept—European integration. European integration has become manifest in two major policies of the Danish state. These are membership in the Common Market and alliance with the NATO community.

The issue of the Common Market was raised in a referendum on October 2, 1972. The veto power of the people was absolute on the matter of Danish sovereignty versus joining an integrated Europe. In a record 90 percent turnout, membership in the Common Market was approved by a 63.3 to 36.7 percent margin. Survey data collected at the time of the election indicated that the vast majority of Danes support the membership decision on economic pragmatic grounds rather than ideological considerations.

In Danish society support for the European Community seems to go hand in hand with positive attitudes regarding "universalism" and Atlanticism. In a study conducted in 1970, a strongly negative assessment by the Danish people was recorded with respect to Nordism. In other words, response to regional integration (narrowly defined) was not as positive as to European integration. This leads one to expect a continued emphasis on policy favoring European integration.

The implications of this increased integration are not fully known. For example, to what extent will the crises in Poland affect attitudes about Danish defense? As the Polish crises have seemed to strengthen Danish NATO ties, the European anti-nuclear/pacifist movement seems to pull Denmark in another direction. Danish politics in the past has been caught in the middle of these forces, resulting in a mixed political profile.

Notes

1. Harry Eckstein, *Division and Cohesion in Democracy: A Study of Norway* (Princeton: Princeton University Press, 1966), pp. 5–6.

2. Joseph B. Board, Jr., *The Government and Politics of Sweden* (Boston: Houghton Mifflin, 1970), p. 21.

Selected Bibliography

Anderson, Ingvar. *Swedish History in Brief*. Stockholm: Swedish Institute, 1965.

Andren, Nils. *Modern Swedish Government*. Stockholm: Almquist and Wiksell, 1968.

Ausland, John C. "The Challenge of Oil to Norwegian Foreign Policy," *Cooperation and Conflict* 10, no. 2 (1975): 189–198.

Bjornsen, Mette Koefoed, and Hansen, Erik, eds. *Facts About Denmark*. Translated from the Danish by Erik Langkjaer. Copenhagen: Politikens Forlag, 1972.

Blitsten, Dorothy R. *The World of the Family*. New York: Random House, 1963.

Board, Joseph B., Jr. *The Government and Politics of Sweden*. Boston: Houghton Mifflin, 1970.

Derry, T. K. *A History of Modern Norway: 1814–1972*. New York: Oxford University Press, 1973.

Eckstein, Harry. *Division and Cohesion in Democracy: A Study of Norway*. Princeton: Princeton University Press, 1966.

Friis, Henning, ed. *Scandinavia: Between East and West*. Ithaca: Cornell University Press, 1950.

Hancock, M. Donald. *Sweden: The Politics of Postindustrial Change*. Hinsdale, Ill,: Dryden Press, 1972.

Kjersgaard, Erik. *A History of Denmark*. Copenhagen: Royal Danish Ministry of Foreign Affairs, 1974.

Miller, Kenneth E. *Government and Politics in Denmark*. Boston: Houghton Mifflin, 1968.

Nordic Democracy, Copenhagen: Det Danske Selskab, 1981.

Oakley, Stewart. *A Short History of Denmark*. New York: Praeger, 1972.

Oakley, Stewart. *The Story of Denmark*. New York: Praeger, 1972.

Oakley, Stewart. *The Story of Sweden*. London: Faber and Faber, 1966.

Orvik, Nils. "Nordic Cooperation and High Politics," *International Organization* 28 (Winter 1974): 61–68.

Petersen, Nikolaj. "Europeanism and Its Foreign Policy Attitude Correlates: A Political Belief System," *Cooperation and Conflict* 10, no. 3 (1975): 143–166.

Popperwell, Ronald G. *Norway*. New York: Praeger, 1973.

Royal Danish Ministry of Foreign Affairs. *Denmark: An Official Handbook*. Copenhagen: Press and Information Division, 1970.

Scott, Franklin D. *Scandinavia*. Cambridge, Mass.: Harvard University Press, 1975.

Scott, Franklin D. *Sweden: The Nation's History*. Minneapolis: University of Minnesota Press, 1977.

7.

The Regional Organizations of Western Europe

With few exceptions, the national governments in the Iberian, Benelux, Alpine, Adriatic and Scandinavian regions have played pivotal roles in the fostering of greater cooperation in Western Europe as a whole. Moreover, many of the citizens of these nations long for the day when petty national rivalries and jealousies will be cast aside in order for a new era of European solidarity and unity to be ushered in.

This chapter will chronicle the efforts made in post–World War II Western Europe to facilitate pan-European cooperation. In addition, the institutional characteristics and policy-making activities of the two most prominent regional organizations in Western Europe, the European Community and the North Atlantic Treaty Organization, will be examined. Special emphasis will also be placed on the contributions of the Benelux, Iberian, Scandinavian, Adriatic and Alpine governments to these regional organizations in particular and to the quest for European unity in general. (See Table 7.1 for the membership rosters of Western Europe's best-known regional organizations.)

The Quest for European Integration

Europe emerged from the Second World War a devastated continent with a demoralized populace. Over thirty-five million Europeans had perished in the cataclysmic conflicts and national economies were in a state of utter ruin. Some Americans were of the opinion that the Europeans were infected with a virulent strain of nationalism which periodically spawned an epidemic of warfare. As Stanley Hoffman has written, some among the new generation of American foreign policy-makers perceived Europe as "a prostrate victim of a self-inflicted war, a continent in need, not of redemption or probation, but of treatment, for the rehabilitation of the damned and the cure of the sick."[1] Indeed, three times in the span of seventy years, the Germans and the French

TABLE 7.1

Memberships in Western Europe's Regional Organizations

	C of E	EC	EFTA	NATO	OECD	WEU
Austria	X		X		X	
Belgium	X	X		X	X	X
Cyprus	X					
Denmark	X	X		X	X	
Finland			X		X	
France	X	X		X*	X	X
Greece	X	X		X*	X	
Iceland	X		X	X	X	
Ireland	X	X			X	
Italy	X	X		X	X	X
Luxembourg	X	X		X	X	X
Malta	X					
Netherlands	X	X		X	X	X
Norway	X		X	X	X	
Portugal	X		X	X	X	
Spain				X	X	
Sweden	X		X		X	
Switzerland	X		X		X	
Turkey	X			X	X	
United Kingdom	X	X		X	X	X
West Germany	X	X		X	X	X

*Both France and Greece have withdrawn from the military organization but remain members of the North Atlantic Alliance.

C of E — Council of Europe
EC — European Community
EFTA — European Free Trade Association
NATO — North Atlantic Treaty Organization
OECD — Organization for Economic Cooperation and Development
WEU — Western European Union

had squared off on the battlefield, and twice in the first four decades of the twentieth century, European nations had precipitated conflicts which eventually engulfed much of the world.

Thus, following the cessation of hostilities in 1945, Europeans faced some monumental decisions. Most aspired to the rapid recovery of the continent, somewhat reminiscent of the Phoenix rising majestically from the rubble. On the other hand, their optimism had to be tempered by the memories of past aberrations and by their recognition that ideological cleavages were once again tearing the Eastern and Western halves of the continent asunder. As Jean Monnet rather harshly remarked: "The countries of Europe faced a fateful decision. How could Europeans escape from the pattern of their history? How could nations suddenly learn to behave like civilized men?"[2]

Monnet became the principal architect and chief spokesman for a movement dedicated to the creation of a United States of Europe, hoping in the process to render the more destructive aspects of nationalism obsolete. Many critics considered the effort of Monnet and his compatriots to be in the same league with Don Quixote's quest. With little doubt, the magnitude of the task was awesome, and perhaps the following analogy will help to show the problems faced by the pro-European integration forces. A little more than two hundred years ago, thirteen colonies, located in a relatively small geographical area sheltering a population of a mere two million, cast off the colonial yoke and created an independent nation. This new nation, which benefitted substantially from having a population which largely shared a common heritage and a common language, struggled mightily to maintain its unity. In fact, the first constitution of the land, the Articles of Confederation, failed to unite the new states and served at times as a source of disintegration. Fortunately, a group of farsighted leaders eventually decided to scrap the first constitution altogether and to bring forth a new document which provided for stronger national authority while at the same time safeguarding certain fundamental powers belonging to the individual states. But even after this document was ratified and put into effect, growing pains and regional and ideological cleavages produced widespread disenchantment, eventually culminating in a civil war fought for the very purpose of determining whether the union would stand or fall. Consequently, even seventy years after the new constitution had been ratified by the states, the question of unification was still in doubt.

The situation in post–World War II Western Europe was infinitely more complex than that in 1776 America. Today, the western part of the European continent is composed of approximately twenty nations with a combined population of 350 million (the United States currently has a population of 230 million). At least thirteen major languages are spoken in this region, with other lesser languages and dialects abounding. Moreover, several of these nations once possessed vast world empires and their customs and traditions have influenced the life-styles of most of the other nations of the world.

In terms of geographical size, the Western European region is somewhat more than twice the size of the state of Alaska and would fit snugly into the quadrant running from Seattle in the northwest, to the Montana-North Dakota border in the northeast, to Houston in the southeast, and on to San Diego in the southwest. If one were to travel at a leisurely pace between San Francisco and Denver, two cities within the quadrant, he or she would have difficulty determining significant differences in the traditions and life-styles of the people who lived along the route. The distance between San Francisco and Denver is 2,117 kilometers, a little less than the distance travelled by a person covering the following itinerary: Copenhagen, Denmark, to Hamburg, West Germany, to Paris, France, to Basel, Switzerland, and finally to Milan, Italy. Along this route, however, the traveler would have crossed eight nations and would have mingled with people who spoke at least seven distinctive languages and who reflected many easily distinguishable traditions and lifestyles.

In this American-Western European comparison, one can readily see that the task which Monnet and his colleagues envisioned was prodigious. In essence, they contemplated ever-increasing cooperation and even economic and political integration in a region of 350 million people, twenty nations, and thirteen major languages, representing a mosaic of cultural backgrounds which often had roots tracing back not just for centuries, but indeed, for tens of centuries. Obviously, this ambitious venture would take many years to complete, and even today, a great deal remains to be accomplished. In fact, there is still no guarantee that the movement has as yet transcended the threshold which would ensure more than a modicum of pan-Western European cooperation.

The Integration Process

As a precondition for the receipt of Marshall Plan assistance to the war-torn continent, American officials insisted that the participating European nations first meet together and jointly determine which economic sectors would receive priority consideration. This American insistence on European cooperation was definitely linked to the view which Stanley Hoffmann ascribed to postwar architects of U.S. foreign policy. In effect, these leaders perceived Europe as "suffering from fragmentation which threatened to . . . reproduce the very discord and hatred that had already engendered two world wars."[3] As a result of this American demand, the Europeans joined together and formed in 1948 the Organization for European Economic Cooperation (OEEC) and the European Payments Union (EPU) to administer the Marshall Plan financial aid. In that same year, several European leaders also met in The Hague and endorsed the establishment of a European Parliament. In 1949, the Council of Europe was set up in Strasbourg and has served as a forum for the discussion of political, cultural, social, and economic issues pertinent to all of Western Europe.

The dire need for economic assistance and a concomitant fear of past nationalist excesses had undoubtedly helped to precipitate the formation of these intergovernmental organizations in the late 1940s. The growing fear of Soviet intentions and the advent of the Cold War also spurred on efforts to cooperate on a military basis. In a famous speech delivered at Fulton, Missouri in March 1946, Winston Churchill warned of an "iron curtain" which was rapidly descending over Europe. In 1947, the Soviet Union pressured its Eastern European allies into declining Marshall Plan aid, even though a handful of the nations had originally expressed a keen interest in the assistance program. During that same year, the French communists were kicked out of the Ramadier government for allegedly being too sympathetic toward Soviet policy priorities and too disruptive in the French domestic arena.

By the late 1940s, tensions had been accentuated noticeably in Europe, and in the aftermath of the Prague coup of 1948, which overthrew the democratic government of Czechoslovakia and replaced it with a pro-Soviet regime, several Western European nations finally decided to join together and form a military alliance. Within two weeks after the Prague takeover, the United Kingdom, France, and the Benelux nations created the Brussels Treaty Organization, which provided for mutual military assistance and protection. The Berlin blockade of June 1948, and a general distrust of Stalin's intentions toward Europe, eventually prompted an expansion of military cooperation in the West. In April 1949, the North Atlantic Treaty Organization (NATO) was created in Washington with ten Western European nations (the Brussels treaty signatories plus Denmark, Norway, Italy, Portugal, and Iceland) initially signing the document along with the United States and Canada. Greece and Turkey became members of the alliance in 1952, West Germany in 1955, and Spain in 1982.

The sense of security provided by the new Atlantic alliance undoubtedly created a more favorable climate for European integration efforts. In May 1950, French Foreign Minister Robert Schuman publicly endorsed Jean Monnet's bold plan to pool the coal and steel resources of France, West Germany, and other interested European countries. Naturally, the plan was intended to help cultivate more harmonious relations between France and West Germany, two nations which had often been bitter enemies during the previous decades. However, Monnet's concept also called for the creation of a High Authority, which would oversee activities in the coal and steel industries and which would render decisions binding on the member countries. This High Authority proposal represented a new phase in European integration efforts. The organizations which had previously been established in postwar Europe certainly fostered cooperation, but the member governments continued to retain the right to ignore any policies thought to be injurious to their own national interests. The High Authority, on the other hand, was to be vested with some supranational powers. In other words, the member governments first had to agree to transfer some of their sovereignty to the High Authority and agree to abide by High Authority decisions in the coal and steel sector, *even if* a member government vehemently opposed the decision. In essence, this new program, dealing only with coal- and steel-linked policies, was somewhat comparable to the American states agreeing in the ratification of the new constitution to transfer significant authority to the national government and to abide faithfully by the decisions rendered by national officials in certain well-delineated policy areas.

The Treaty of the European Coal and Steel Community (ECSC) was signed in April 1951, with France, Germany, Italy, Belgium, the Netherlands, and Luxembourg becoming charter members. Many Europeanists were keenly disappointed, however, that the British refused to join the new organization. In spite of Churchill's pleas in 1946 to build a kind of United States of Europe, many British officials continued to be suspicious of continental activities and adamantly refused to transfer sovereign authority to any European supranational organization. In addition, some of these British policy-makers worried about the ramifications which continental involvement might have on the United Kingdom's Commonwealth commitments. Consequently, the British disheartened the prointegrationist forces by deciding to remain aloof from the new ECSC organization.

Integration forces were to suffer another setback when the proposed European Defense Community (EDC) failed to materialize. Spurred on by the creation of the ECSC, French Prime Minister René Pleven recommended the formation of an integrated European army under a unified command structure. The Eisenhower administration enthusiastically supported this concept, and in May 1952, the six signatories to the ECSC pact also initialled the new EDC Treaty. With the ECSC and the EDC, some of the more optimistic prointegrationists thought that the establishment of the European Political Community (EPC), dedicated to the formation of a Western European political union, would be just around the corner. However, the EDC Treaty had to be ratified by each of the national parliaments before it could go into effect. In spite of a thinly-veiled warning from Secretary of State John Foster Dulles that the United States would have to make an "agonizing reappraisal" of its Western European commitment if the treaty were rejected, the French National Assembly voted it down in the summer of 1954. A coalition of Gaullists and communists, who objected to transferring French sovereign authority to any supranational organization, and a significant number of socialists, who were suspicious of rearming West Germany within the EDC framework, spearheaded the defeat of the treaty. As a hastily arranged compromise motion, the British government proposed the creation of a substitute organization, the Western European Union (WEU). The WEU was finally approved in 1954 and did provide a framework for integrating Germany into the European military structure as well as establishing an organization for intra-European military cooperation within NATO. On the other hand, the WEU was basically devoid of the supranational elements which were to be an integral part of the defunct European Defense Community.

At a 1955 meeting in Messina, Italy, ministers of the ECSC nations commissioned a panel under the direction of Belgian Foreign Minister Paul-Henri

Spaak to explore the feasibility of creating a general economic union and an organization which would coordinate the joint development of peaceful uses for atomic energy. Acting favorably upon the subsequent Spaak Committee recommendations, the ministers convened two years later in Rome and signed the treaties establishing the European Economic Community (EEC) and the European Atomic Energy Community (Euratom). Officials from France, Germany, Italy, Belgium, Luxembourg, and the Netherlands had thus agreed to expand the ECSC program and to attempt to gradually merge the national economies of the individual member states into one large economic community. The merger of the separate national markets into a single market was to be completed by 1970. Initially, a customs union was set up to foster the free movement of goods, people, and capital within the new community while at the same time establishing uniform tariffs on imports. The Six also agreed to establish common policies in the spheres of competition, agriculture, transport, and world trade.

This new European Community (EC), which brought together under one umbrella organization the ECSC, EEC, and Euratom, went into effect in 1958. One year later, the European Free Trade Assocation (EFTA) was created. EFTA was formed by the United Kingdom, Austria, Denmark, Norway, Portugal, Sweden, and Switzerland. Originally, these nations, which were all members of the OEEC, attempted to convince the six states in the European Community, fellow OEEC members, to form a free trade area covering industrial goods but not agricultural products nor seafood. The French rejected this proposal, claiming that it was not a practical plan. As a result of the French rebuff, the so-called Outer Seven agreed to form EFTA, an organization which would promote free trade within the member states but which would not contain provisions for common tariff policies nor for limited supranationalism, both of which were included in the treaty creating the European Community. Today, EFTA continues to function and is headquartered in Geneva. The United Kingdom and Denmark have both withdrawn from EFTA in order to join the European Community, but Finland joined EFTA as an associate member in 1961 and Iceland as a full member in 1970. EFTA currently represents the interests of forty million Europeans and each of the member states now has a special bilateral trade arrangement with the European Community. As for the OEEC, it was later expanded to include the United States and Canada and was formally transformed in 1961 into the Organization for Economic Cooperation and Development (OECD). Other advanced industrial nations in the West have also joined the OECD since its inception.

With the dismantling of much of its empire and the reluctant realization of the demise of its once-extensive world role, the United Kingdom finally began to recognize that its chief area of interest and concern had been narrowed to the European region. Consequently, the Conservative government under

Harold Macmillan applied for membership in the European Community in 1961 and began intensive negotiations for entry in 1962. Denmark, Ireland, and Norway also applied for membership during this same time period. President Charles de Gaulle abruptly ended this process by claiming that the United Kingdom was not sufficiently "European" in its orientation and values and was still too closely linked to the United States. Because of the stipulation that all six of the original member states would have to approve the expansion of the organization, de Gaulle's statement represented a de facto veto of membership for Great Britain and the other applicants. De Gaulle once again cut off renewed negotiations with the United Kingdom in 1967. However, once President Pompidou succeeded de Gaulle as leader of the Fifth Republic, talks were again resumed and the United Kingdom, Ireland, and Denmark formally joined the Community on January 1, 1973.

The aspirations expressed by prointegration forces for the gradual increase in supranationalism in the European Community were thwarted somewhat by General de Gaulle's personal repugnance toward any transfer of national sovereign authority. De Gaulle firmly believed in the concept of a European Confederation which would one day evolve into a Third Force rivaling the two superpowers in importance. Nevertheless, de Gaulle's vision of this confederation, which would eventually spread from the Atlantic to the Urals, was firmly anchored on the notion of national sovereignty, and not on supranationalism. In essence, cooperation on a Pan-European basis would be greatly encouraged, but ultimate decision-making authority would continue to reside in the nation-state, and no policy would be supported by a national leader which was perceived as being detrimental to his people. In the long run, General de Gaulle considered alliances to be inherently unstable and believed that nation-states would continue to be the common denominator in world affairs. Moreover, de Gaulle argued that an international system consisting of sovereign nation-states could indeed be stable, especially if the nations were able to develop a second-strike strategic capability and were thus able to deter any possible outside aggressor.

To say the least, the General did not share the opinions of those who considered increasing supranationalism the direction which Western Europe must take in order to guarantee order and stability in the latter part of the twentieth century. Reacting strongly to European Commission decisions on agricultural and budgetary policies, which he considered detrimental to French interests and which he claimed smacked of supranationalism, de Gaulle ordered a French boycott of European Community activities for a seven-month period in 1965 and 1966. The French returned only after the other Community members had tacitly agreed to shelve the majority voting provision in the Council of Ministers and to accept the right of any member government to veto proposals perceived by that government as injurious to its interests. In effect, de Gaulle had struck a serious blow against pro-supranationalism forces by guaranteeing that ultimate decision-making authority within the Community over important issues would remain within the purview of the individual nation-states.

In spite of this major setback, the Community continued to consolidate its policy-making apparatus. In 1967, a single Council of Ministers and single European Commission were created to oversee the activities of the ECSC, EEC, and Euratom. Moreover, the customs union was fully implemented in 1968, eighteen months earlier than had been stipulated in the original Rome Treaty. The Community, currently representing 270 million people and wielding tremendous economic and trade power, has currently assumed a "presence" which goes far beyond its limited geographical boundaries. For example, the Community signed the Yaoundé agreement in 1963, which extended associate status and special trade concessions to eighteen African nations. Twelve years later, the Lomé Convention was put into effect with the Community initiating agreements with forty-six African, Caribbean, and Pacific nations, agreements which extend special trade benefits to these developing areas. The Community also effectuated its own internal expansion from six nations to nine in 1973 and to ten in 1981 with the inclusion of Greece. It is also highly likely that Spain and Portugal will join the Community before 1985. In addition, the Community has signed free trade treaties with several members of EFTA and has negotiated various agreements with the United States, including the Kennedy Round pact to reduce tariffs on industrial goods. The Community has also opened discussions with the Eastern European economic organization, the Council for Mutual Economic Assistance (COMECON), and has exerted influence in the worldwide trade and tariff organization known as the General Agreement on Tariffs and Trade (GATT).

Within the military realm, Western Europe's defense structure is still integrally linked to NATO and its deterrence capability is inextricably tied to the American nuclear umbrella. Two of the members of NATO, France and Greece, have withdrawn from the military command but have remained members of the North Atlantic alliance. Some Europeans claim that the Western half of the continent cannot emerge as a true superpower unless it develops a strategic capability independent of the United States. Thus far, however, the Western European governments have shown little inclination to make the awesome economic sacrifices which would be necessary in order to develop credible conventional and strategic prowess.

The remainder of this chapter will examine in detail two of the most visible and powerful regional organizations in Western Europe, namely the European Community and NATO. With the exception of Austria, Finland, Sweden, and Switzerland, all of the nations covered in this book are either members of one or both of these regional bodies, or are now actively seeking membership in at least one of these organizations (see Table 7.2 for a general outline of the development of postwar cooperative efforts among the Western European nations).

The European Community

The Institutional Structure and the Policy-Making Process

A cherished goal of the founders of the European Community (EC) was the achievement of greater economic, social, and political cooperation among all of the nations of Western Europe and the harmonization of key policies among the member states of the Community itself. As mentioned previously, a major step toward increased coordination within the Community was taken in 1967, when the EEC, ECSC, and Euratom were all placed under the supervision of the Council of Ministers and the European Commission. Today, the council and the commission continue to serve as a dual executive for Community affairs, whereas certain limited legislative functions are fulfilled by the European Parliament and the judicial duties are entrusted to the Court of Justice.

EXECUTIVE AUTHORITY

The European Commission may be perceived as the European Community's "motor," taking the lead in initiating and cranking out policy recommendations in all areas covered by the Rome Treaty. The commission is a collegiate body composed of fourteen members, two each from France, Germany, Italy, and the United Kingdom, and one each from the other EC countries. Although members of the commission are selected by their national governments for four-year renewable terms, they are expected to act independently and to expound that which is for the good of the Community as a whole rather than in favor of their individual nation-state.

With the assistance of the 11,000-member European Community bureaucracy, the commission acts as the guardian of Community treaties and makes sure that the member governments and the companies and individuals doing business within the EC are complying with the numerous provisions contained in the treaties. Suspected violators of these treaties may be brought before the commission or the Court of Justice and sanctions imposed if found guilty.

The commission also plays an integral role in the EC's policy-making process. Each member of the commission is assigned a particular area of responsibility, such as agriculture or foreign affairs, and supervises the activities of pertinent administrative departments, which are called directorates general. In collaboration with the official bureaucracy, as well as selected interest groups, the commission formulates proposals which will then be submitted to the Council of Ministers for its stamp of approval. Once the council has

TABLE 7.2

The Development of Cooperative Ties in Western Europe

1945—World War II ends.

1946—Churchill warns of an "iron curtain" descending on Europe and of the need for a United States of Europe.

1948—The Marshall Plan is put into effect and the Organization for European Economic Cooperation (OEEC) is created to administer U.S. aid to Europe. Following the Prague coup, the Brussels Treaty Organization, a Western European defense alliance, is formed.

1949—The North Atlantic Treaty Organization (NATO) is created and the Council of Europe is established with headquarters in Strasbourg.

1951—The European Coal and Steel Community (ECSC) Treaty is signed.

1952—Greece and Turkey join NATO.

1954—The European Defense Community (EDC) is rejected by the French National Assembly. As a substitute organization, the Western European Union (WEU) is created later in the year.

1955—West Germany joins NATO.

1957—The European Economic Community (EEC) and Euratom treaties are signed in Rome.

1958—The Rome treaties go into force.

1959—The European Free Trade Association (EFTA) is founded in Stockholm.

1961—With the inclusion of the United States and Canada, the OEEC is transformed into the Organization for Economic Cooperation and Development (OECD).

1963—De Gaulle vetoes the British request to join the European Community.

1964—The first Yaoundé Convention agreement between the Community and eighteen African nations goes into effect.

1965—The French begin a seven-month boycott of Community activities, protesting supranational tendencies within the organization.

1966—France withdraws from the NATO military command and orders U.S. and other allied troops off French soil.

1967—A single Council of Ministers and Commission are created for the ECSC, EEC, and Euratom. De Gaulle again forestalls British entry into the Community.

1968—The Community customs union is completed eighteen months earlier than stipulated in the Rome Treaty. The first Kennedy Round tariff cuts go into effect.

1971—The second Yaoundé Convention is implemented.

1972—The Community signs free trade treaties with EFTA members Austria, Iceland, Portugal, Sweden, and Switzerland.

1973—Denmark, Great Britain, and Ireland formally join the Community.

1974—Greece withdraws from the NATO Defense Planning Group as a protest over U.S. treatment during the Cyprus affair.

1975—The Lomé Convention is signed between the Community and forty-six African, Caribbean, and Pacific nations. A British referendum reaffirms that nation's desire to remain in the Community.

1977—The Community-sponsored European University Institute opens in Florence.

1979—The European Monetary System (EMS) is instituted and direct elections to the European Parliament are held for the first time.

1981—Greece becomes the tenth member of the European Community.

1982—Spain becomes the sixteenth member of NATO.

reached a final decision, the commission is then in charge of making sure that the new policy guidelines are implemented and obeyed.

To a certain extent, the commission personifies the supranationalism which many European integrationists have always favored. For example, each commissioner is expected to have the interests of the entire Community at heart, even if his stance on an issue may run contrary to the desires of his home government. Furthermore, decisions rendered by the commission are based on a simple majority vote and no member state is entitled to veto a proposal before the commission. In effect, the commission is supposed to represent the European point of view, and the members of the bureaucracy which it supervises are expected to act as "Eurocrats" rather than as nationals of individual member states.

The Council of Ministers, on the other hand, exemplifies the "national" point of view in Community proceedings. The council is definitely the Community's predominant decision-making institution and issues (1) regulations, which are binding on the member states, (2) directives, which are binding in respect to ends but not in terms of means, and (3) recommendations and opinions, which are not enforceable. The council meets three or four times a month and is composed of one minister from each of the national governments. A permanent secretariat and the Committee of Permanent Representatives (COREPER), consisting of the ten ambassadors from the member states to the EC, are in charge of keeping the council abreast of Community affairs and they actually perform much of the groundwork for the formal council sessions.

For routine matters, decisions are rendered by the Council of Ministers on the basis of a weighted majority voting system. France, Italy, Germany, and the United Kingdom are each entitled to ten "weighted" votes, the Netherlands and Belgium to five each, Denmark, Ireland and Greece to three each, and Luxembourg to two, making a grand total of sixty-one. For a proposal to pass, forty-five favorable votes from at least six countries must be registered. As a result of this voting formula, two of the four large countries can join together to block any action. All council decisions are based on proposals submitted by the European Commission, and amendments to these proposals can only be made by a unanimous vote of the assembled ministers.

On issues of "vital concern" to the member states, unanimous agreement on commission proposals is required and one negative vote registered by any council member is sufficient to veto the measure. During the mid-1960s, some of the member governments attempted to extend the weighted majority system to these vital issues, but General de Gaulle adamantly refused, contending that France would never relinquish its sovereign authority over issues of paramount importance to the French people. De Gaulle then ordered a French boycott of Community affairs which lasted from July 1965 until January 1966. Because of the French president's strong stance on this issue, the entire framework of Community cooperation was threatened during the duration of the boycott.

Although the General has long since departed from the earthly scene, the specter of "veto" within the Council of Ministers still hangs over Community activities and remains a stumbling block in the way of greater European integration efforts. However, in 1982 the council refused to recognize a British veto of a proposal which would raise farm prices. Several members of the council claimed that farm price increases fell within the category of "continuing policies" and thus could only be resolved through the regular weighted majority voting system. The British have disputed this point of view and along with the Danes and Greeks have attempted to re-establish the principle that any member government can veto a proposal considered to be of significant importance to that government. The resolution of this key issue will go a long way toward determining the supranational character of the European Community.

LEGISLATIVE AUTHORITY

Even though the European Parliament has traditionally been regarded as a rather toothless organization, many observers feel that it will eventually play a pivotal role in future European integration endeavors. This perception is linked specifically to the first direct elections to the European Parliament which were held in June 1979. Prior to these elections, the 198 members of this assembly had been appointed by national legislatures. Now, however, the expanded membership of 434 is elected directly by the voters in each of the member states, with each nation determining its own method of election to the legislative body (see Table 7.3 for the distribution of seats by party group following the June 1979 elections). Prointegration groups assert that the active involvement of the national electorates will foster a sense of community in Western Europe and that the handful of eminent politicians and other dignitaries elected in 1979 symbolizes the growing commitment to a united Europe. Indeed, 110 million people cast ballots in the 1979 elections, approximately 61 percent of the eligible voters (8 percent higher than the turnout for the 1980 American presidential contest). Moreover, seating at the European Parliament is not on the basis of national origins, but rather on the basis of political affiliation. In other words, representatives from the socialist movements within the Community all sit together in the same location, as do the communists, liberals, christian democrats, and other political groups. Although the notion of "European" political movements is still premature, party groupings throughout the Community met together prior to the 1979 elections in an attempt to map out coordinated electoral strategies and common

TABLE 7.3

Results of the First Direct Elections to the European Parliament, 1979

Country*	Voter Turnout (%)	Communists	Socialists	Christian Democrats	Liberals	Conservatives	Progressive Democrats	Others	Total Seats
France	60.8	19	21	0	26	0	15	0	81
Germany	65.9	0	35	42	4	0	0	0	81
Italy	85.5	24	13	30	5	0	0	9	81
United Kingdom	32.1	0	18	0	0	60	0	3	81
Netherlands	58.1	0	9	10	4	0	0	2	25
Belgium	82.0	0	7	10	4	0	0	3	24
Denmark	47.1	1	3	0	3	3	1	5	16
Ireland	60.0	0	4	4	0	0	5	2	15
Luxembourg	85.6	0	1	3	2	0	0	0	6
Total	61.0	44	111	99	48	63	21	24	410

*Greece joined the EC in 1981 and was granted 24 seats in the European Parliament, upping the membership in this legislative body to 434. In the Greek elections held in October 1981, the communists won 4 seats, the socialists 10 seats, the liberals 8 seats, and other parties won 2 seats.

platforms. Integrationists anticipate that this interaction among the European parties will stimulate greater transnational linkages and thus mitigate some of the past national differences which have divided the political movements.

On the other side of the coin, the European Parliament basically remains a forum for the discussion of European issues, and is certainly hamstrung when it comes to the exercising of significant legislative responsibilities. Through its dozen committees and plenary sessions, the parliament oversees the activities of the commission and the council and may ask these executive institutions to justify their policy priorities. In the event of an extreme impasse between the parliament and the commission, the parliamentarians even have the power to censure and dismiss the commissioners by a two-thirds vote. The parliament also enjoys limited authority over the budget of the European Community, particularly in the area of institutional allocations. Nevertheless, the parliament only meets eleven times a year for week-long sessions and has absolutely no veto authority over decisions rendered by the Council of Ministers. Thus, as a legislative body, it remains a very weak-kneed organization.

Certainly, a strong dose of enthusiasm has been injected into the European Parliament by the 1979 direct elections, and the parliament's reputation as *the* debating forum of the Community has been enhanced. It should also be expected that the parliament's sphere of competence over Community affairs will grow, albeit in a very incremental fashion. However, the new optimism expressed by European integrationalists in regard to the parliament's expanding role in Community affairs must be tempered by the fact that some members of the EC still resist handing over supranational authority to the legislature. For example, in agreeing to hold direct elections to the parliament, the French National Assembly stipulated that any decision rendered by the European Parliament which did not coincide with France's interpretation of the Treaty of Rome would be viewed by French officials as null and void. Thus the decision taken by the members of the Community to hold direct elections to the parliament is indisputably a significant step in the direction of greater European cooperation, but the road ahead leading to European unity is wearingly long and marked with many potential chasms.

JUDICIAL AUTHORITY

The European Community's "constitution" is comprised of the ECSC, EEC, and Euratom treaties and other pertinent statutes, and the Community's "supreme court" is the European Court of Justice. The Court of Justice is composed of ten judicial experts, with each member nation choosing one representative who will serve a six-year term on the bench. The court accepts cases from member governments, from individuals and companies affected by Community law, and from the European Commission or the Council of Ministers. It is not a substitute for the high courts of each of the member states and it is confined to the interpretation and administration of Community law. However, as the years have passed since the creation of the Community, laws and methods of litigation within the EC have become more uniform and a fairly large body of "European" cases now provide precedents for many judicial decisions rendered at the national level.

Four advocates-general are also assigned to the court, and they have the major responsibility of evaluating the facts of each case coming before the court and of presenting their own recommendations based on the best interests of justice. Although the findings of these advocates-general are not binding, their conclusions often do have a dramatic impact on the final verdict issued by the court. For example, in one case, the European Commission had levied approximately ten million dollars in fines against sixteen sugar companies accused of monopolistic practices. The companies protested this commission action and appealed the decision to the Court of Justice. After reviewing the facts, the advocate-general assigned to the case contended that the commission's decision was too harsh and that national governments, more than the individual companies, were responsible for the exorbitant price of sugar within the Community. The court essentially agreed with the findings of the advocate-general and substantially reduced the fines assessed against the sugar companies.

Although major differences continue to exist among the judicial systems of the ten member states, particularly in terms of common law and civil law practices, the European Court of Justice has become a more influential body in recent years and without a doubt, a type of "European" system of justice is slowly but surely being created.

The Community's Problems and Prospects

The ten members of the European Community have made great progess in instituting a customs union which provides for free trade within the Community and a common external tariff for goods coming from countries not affiliated with the Community. With only a few exceptions, goods, services, and capital now enjoy freedom of movement throughout the ten nations.

On the other hand, important decision-making is still dominated by the Council of Ministers and real authority still resides in the ten capitals of the EC nations. Moreover, the organization has continued to experience major difficulties in harmonizing commercial and monetary politics, let alone political and defense priorities. The fragile nature of European unity is aptly illustrated by the events which transpired after the imposition of OPEC oil restrictions in 1973. At that time, the Arab members of OPEC designated France and Great Britain as friends and did not impose any limitations on oil deliveries to these countries. Six other Community members were subjected to a gradual decrease of 5 percent per month, whereas the Netherlands, labeled an ally of Israel, was embargoed altogether. Instead of closing ranks to confront this new challenge, the Community members failed to come to the assistance of the Dutch and went their own separate ways in coping with the energy crisis. In effect, when the chips were down, unity quickly dissipated and national concerns took clear priority over Community needs.

The member states learned bitter lessons from the OPEC incident and have now formulated common programs to help combat the serious economic problems precipitated by the swift rise in petroleum prices. The Community members have also attempted to harmonize their monetary affairs through the introduction of a European Monetary System (EMS) and other related programs. Although the United Kingdom postponed its entry into the EMS when it went into effect in early 1979, West Germany and France led the way in implementing this ambitious project. In essence, the EMS links the currencies of the member countries within an approximate 2.5 percent range and all of the national currencies "float" together vis-à-vis the value of the American dollar, Japanese yen, and other prominent world currencies. A reserve fund of more than 30 billion dollars has been established to help prop up national currencies which might experience particular difficulties in order to keep them within the 2.5 percent allowable range. Although the EMS is off to a shaky start, many believe that it represents a significant step toward the eventual introduction of one common monetary unit for the European Community.

Regional problems within the European Community also exacerbate efforts to bring about greater unity. Scotland, Wales, Northern Ireland, Greenland, Wallonia, Flanders, southern Italy, Brittany, Alsace-Lorraine, and Corsica are among the regions within the ten member states which have particular problems and consider that the Community has not been responsive enough to their specific needs. Many of these same regions also personify the significant economic disparities which continue to exist within the Community and which help to fuel animosity among the "have less" areas.

These regional disparities will undoubtedly increase when the European Community expands to include Portugal and Spain. In fact, the entire issue of enlargement presents many problems and challenges for the Community, even though the argument for expansion southward is certainly very pursuasive, both politically and morally. The Mediterranean region is certainly strategically vital to Europe, but perhaps even more importantly, the Treaty of Rome stipulates that all democratic governments in Europe should be welcomed into the Community fold. The two Southern European nations have asked for membership in the Community, and it is expected that their requests will be honored and that they will attain full membership during the 1980s.

Although receptive to the desires of Spain and Portugal, the ten member governments have approached enlargement with some trepidation. Some of the existing members will undoubtedly suffer a financial drain because money from the North will have to be funneled into the South in order to bolster the relatively weak and nondiversified Mediterranean economies. In particular, some significant changes will have to be made in the Community's Common Agricultural Policy (CAP) to prepare for the influx of farm products from the agrarian-dominated economies of the South. CAP already consumes almost three-quarters of the Community's budget and monopolizes a large part of the Community's annual agenda. French and Italian farmers, who will be most noticeably affected by the southward expansion, will certainly demand special concessions which will push up the CAP budget to even higher levels.

Greece, Spain, and Portugal suffer from high unemployment rates, and because of the free flow of labor provision within Community statutes, the heavily industrialized northern tier countries can expect added pressure from Southern European workers clamoring for jobs. It is possible, of course, that changes will be made in Community statutes to mitigate this movement of laborers, but such an action would be a step backward in the quest for European integration.

These three Mediterranean nations also have long authoritarian pasts and have only recently adopted democratic forms of government. Their democratic institutions are still somewhat fragile, their political systems remain highly radicalized, and their economies suffer from endemic unemployment and rampant inflation, conditions which signify that challenges from either the extreme left or right might suddenly and decisively curtail their noble experiments with democracy. Just by adding three new members with stable democratic systems, consensus-building within the Community would naturally be more difficult to achieve. But if one or more of these new members were to cast aside its democratic structures and resort to authoritarian practices, Community policy-making activities might grind to a sudden halt.

Furthermore, the Common Market provisions in the European Community treaties are largely based on capitalist principles, principles which are not heartily supported by many of the leftist parties in Southern Europe. Consequently, future leftist-dominated governments, such as the Papandreou regime in Greece, might demand major changes in Community policies which would threaten this capitalist base and polarize the Community decision-making process.

In spite of the myriad challenges which it will face, the European Community, which recently welcomed Greece into the fold, should extend the same opportunity to Spain and Portugal, as long as their governmental systems remain essentially democratic. Community membership will help these Southern European countries to solve their major political and economic problems and enhance their chances of maintaining viable parliamentary systems of government based on universal suffrage. Denial of membership, of course, would strengthen the cause of radical groups in the Mediterranean region and might eventually transform the southern flank of Europe into an adversary of the EC. With this ominous scenario in mind, expansion remains the best option now available to the Community, for both humanitarian and strategic reasons.

The integration of European political systems and the formulation of common and binding foreign and defense policies will not occur in the near future. Moreover, some prominent European nations are effectively excluded for the moment from seeking membership in the Community. Austria has openly sought membership, but international limitations stemming back to Austria's involvement in World War II preclude that country from joining the organization. Finland is also in the same predicament as Austria. Furthermore, Sweden and Switzerland have declined opportunities to join the Community because they feel that their traditional posture of international neutrality would be compromised by accepting Community membership.

Thus the Community faces formidable challenges in the future and Jean Monnet's vision of a United States of Europe is still largely unfulfilled. The integration of member state activities has often seemed to progress at a snail's pace and some commentators cynically assert that the Community has recently taken more steps backward than forward in the quest for European unity. Nevertheless, a comparison of the European scene today and at the end of World War II clearly illustrates that regional cooperation has increased dramatically. In fact, by the end of the present century, it is certainly conceivable that a European confederation could be forged among a dozen or more European countries. This confederation would assign specific supranational duties and authority to the institutions of the European Community, while at the same time permitting the individual member states to retain autonomy over important "domestic" affairs. Such a European political configuration falls short of what Monnet aspired to, but it would at least usher in an era of pan-European unity and cooperation unparalleled in the continent's long and turbulent history.

The North Atlantic Treaty Organization

An alliance is a formal agreement between the governments of two or more states which specifies the behavior of the parties to the agreement in the event that one or more of them becomes involved in a military conflict. Commitments in an alliance agreement may range from a detailed list of forces that will be furnished by each party under specified contingencies, to a guarantee of neutrality if any alliance members are attacked, to the requirement of consultation if hostilities should occur. Over time, states have changed the type of commitments that they were willing to enter into. The rapid expansion of force capability brought on in the late nineteenth century by improvements in weapons technology gave rise to long-term, highly specific alliance commitments. Statesmen were either unable or unwilling to bear alone the costs of developing the capability to ward off potential aggressors who now could wage war with unprecedented military might. Yet the defensive alliances that were created usually did not spawn much in the way of formal organizations. Indeed, when the foundations were laid for NATO in the late 1940s, in all probability none of the signatory parties envisioned the kind of organizational structure that would gradually be developed to implement their new commitments. However, following the communist attack on South Korea, the NATO allies began to assemble a decision-making apparatus that would be able to coordinate their actions if a similar attack occurred in Europe.

The Institutional Structure and the Policy-Making Process

Civil Organization

The highest authority of NATO is the North Atlantic Council. The council is a forum for political, military, and economic consultation between the sixteen member governments. It is chaired by the secretary-general of NATO, and it conducts its business on both the ambassadorial and ministerial levels. At least once a week, ambassadors from the allied nations meet in permanent session. In contrast, the Ministers of Foreign Affairs, Defense, or Finance come together in an attempt to coordinate their nations' policies on a less frequent basis.[4] All decisions are reached on the basis of "common consent" rather than by majority vote. In other words, the issues being considered are usually discussed informally and agreed upon prior to the official meeting. If a dissenting voice is raised, no decision will be taken.[5]

Those allies which participate in NATO's integrated defense system also take part in the Defense Planning Committee (DPC). Like the council, the DPC is chaired by the secretary-general and meets at the ambassadorial and ministerial levels.

Both the council and the DPC are assisted by a number of committees and working groups. The main committees of the council-DPC deal with political, military, and economic affairs, plus more specialized topics like national armaments, nuclear planning, civil defense, and so on. Each committee and working group is composed of representatives from all member countries.

Aside from chairing the North Atlantic Council and several committees, NATO's secretary-general also heads the International Staff of roughly one thousand people drawn from all member nations. The staff is organized into a number of administrative offices, as well as into the divisions of Political Affairs, Defense Planning and Policy, Defense Support, and Scientific Affairs. An assistant secretary is in charge of each division, while a deputy secretary assists the secretary-general in promoting allied consultation. By convention, the secretary-general has come from a European rather than a North American country.

The highest military authority of NATO is the Military Committee. It is made up of the chiefs-of-staff from all states who participate in the military functions of the alliance. Although the chiefs-of-staff meet infrequently during the year, they appoint permanent military representatives, who conduct the committee's affairs in their absence. The presidency of the committee rotates annually, while the chairmanship is an elected position which is held for a period of from two to three years.

The primary role played by the committee is that of advising the North Atlantic Council and the DPC on military issues. It is assisted in this role by the International Military Staff (IMS). In a nutshell, the IMS engages in military studies, some planning, and generally is responsible for ensuring that the policies of the committee are implemented. The IMS is headed by a director, who oversees both the IMS secretary and the six assistant directors, who are in charge of the organization's operational divisions.

One of the most notable military features of NATO is its integrated command system. Three commands currently exist: Allied Command Europe (ACE), Allied Command Atlantic (ACLANT), and Allied Command Channel (ACCHAN). Of these, ACE is by far the most important. It is under the Supreme Allied Commander (SACEUR), who is based at Supreme Headquarters Allied Powers Europe (SHAPE) in Belgium. The SACEUR exercises control over the ACE Mobile Force and, in the event of war, he would be responsible for all military operations conducted in his area. During peacetime, the SACEUR is expected to develop defense plans, coordinate logistical arrangements, and make recommendations to the Military Committee on issues that pertain to the defense of Europe. In these tasks, he is assisted by a number of military and scientific advisors.

Besides the formal civil and military organizations which we have mentioned, NATO also has ties to certain informal consultative bodies. One such body is the Eurogroup. Composed of all the European members of NATO except France, Spain, and Iceland, this organization has worked to coordinate and improve the Western European contribution to the alliance. Since its formation in 1968, the group has been particularly active in cooperative training and planning.

Another body which lies outside the so-called official NATO structure is the North Atlantic Assembly. Its origins can be traced back to 1955, when a conference was held in Paris by parliamentarians from various NATO countries. Until 1966, their follow-up meetings were known as the NATO Parliamentarians' Conference. But between 1966 and 1968, a number of changes occurred that altered the role of the assembly, the most important of which was the willingness of the North Atlantic Council to discuss and report back to the assembly their views on the proposals that the former had passed. In summary, then, NATO has developed a complex organizational structure which has ties to both informal and unofficial bodies. Yet, within this structure, there still remains a wide variety of views on the problems faced by the alliance.

NATO's Problems and Prospects

Following the Greek victory over Persia's Aegean ambitions in 478 B.C., Athens forged an alliance with other Ionian states in order to thwart future Persian aggression. However, the nascent Delian League eventually deteriorated into an Athenian empire. As Adda Bozeman has pointed out: "The Greeks did not succeed in finding a working relationship between the principles of equality and security as long as they professed to retain the political system of multiple independent states."[6] NATO presently is confronted with a similar dilemma. Composed of a heterogeneous group of sovereign states, the alliance faces a number of difficult problems today, many of which have long threatened to divide its members.

The problem which historically has received the most attention is burden-sharing. Ever since the alliance was first established, contributions to the collective defense effort have varied with member perceptions of the Soviet threat. Many NATO officials question the alliance's capability to halt a Soviet attack. Table 7.4 shows some of the data that led these officials to their conclusions. The most pessimistic of the group claim that a Soviet blitz could reach the Rhine in a matter of days. Given that even the most optimistic officials concede that the Warsaw Pact would hold an enormous advantage until NATO reinforcements could be brought into the fray, what impact will this have on NATO defense spending? Table 7.5 shows the burden of military expenditures on NATO's European members. Since the United States has contributed the largest share to NATO defense, it is not surprising that Washington has pushed to have the European members take up more of the financial burden.

A second problem for NATO is a lack of weapons standardization. In recent years, for example, NATO has used seven different main battle tanks, twenty-two different antitank weapons, and twenty-three different kinds of combat aircraft. If greater standardization could be achieved, the alliance's supply system would be simplified and, in turn, its military effectiveness increased.

TABLE 7.4

The Theater Balance Between NATO and the Warsaw Pact

| | North and Center Theaters | | Southern Theater | |
	NATO	Warsaw Pact	NATO	Warsaw Pact
Combat and Direct Support Troops Available	630,000	945,000	560,000	390,000
Main Battle Tanks in Operational Service	7,000	20,500	4,000	6,700
Tactical Aircraft in Operational Service	2,050	3,525	825	1,375

Source: *U.S. Defense Policy: Weapons, Strategy and Commitments* (Washington, D.C.: Congressional Quarterly, Inc., 1978), p. 25.

TABLE 7.5

The Military Burden, 1978

	Military Expenditures (billion $ constant)	Military Expenditures as % of GNP	Military Expenditures as % of Central Government Expenditures
Warsaw Pact	165.1	10.8	39.3
NATO	169.1	4.3	18.1
NATO, without North America	64.1	3.6	13.6
Europe, without NATO and Warsaw Pact	9.6	2.4	11.0

	Military Expenditures per Capita ($ constant)	Total Armed Forces (thousands)	Armed Forces per 1,000 Population
Warsaw Pact	447	6,162	16.7
NATO	298	4,926	8.7
NATO, without North America	198	2,746	8.5
Europe, without NATO and Warsaw Pact	104	821	9.0

Source: U.S. Arms Control and Disarmament Agency, *World Military Expenditures and Arms Transfers, 1969–1978* (Washington, D.C.: Government Printing Office, 1980), pp. 34–36, 76–78.

Nevertheless, many Europeans are skeptical of Washington's willingness to support standardization if it might result in foreign-made weapon components replacing those previously manufactured in the United States.

The third problem faced by the alliance pertains to the control of nuclear weapons. Owing to the possibility of massive retaliation against American cities, some Europeans have wondered whether U.S. assistance would actually be forthcoming to allies who faced a nuclear foe on the field of battle. At the same time, other Europeans have feared that America's allies might be unwillingly pulled into a confrontation between the superpowers because of the existence of U.S. weapons on their soil. Thus U.S. domination over both strategic hardware and strategic policy has clashed with the sentiments of national sovereignty held by many NATO members. Several approaches have been taken in an attempt to deal with this potential source of discord. During the Kennedy administration, for instance, the possibility of an allied Multilateral Force (MLF) was raised. In brief, this ill-fared proposal would have placed a seaborne nuclear force under miltilateral control. However, the British felt that a better idea would be to put all existing nuclear systems in Europe under an Atlantic Nuclear Force (ANF) composed of those allies which already had the bomb, while President de Gaulle saw any attempt at nuclear integration totally unimaginable. As a result of the stillbirth of these kinds of nuclear sharing formulas, the United States has continued to act as nuclear trustee for the alliance. That is, deployment and targeting of American weapons in Europe are based on mutual understandings reached under the auspices of NATO's Nuclear Defense Affairs Committee.

Finally, a fourth major problem facing the alliance concerns the fact that the political relations between members are at times far from the harmonious picture NATO presents to the general public. Some members, like Norway, have at best one foot in NATO. Norway's "base and ban" policy excludes foreign troops from being based on Norwegian soil and bans nuclear weapons. Another category of NATO states is exemplified by Portugal, which has committed no troops for alliance defense outside of its national boundaries. In still another category, states have sporadically been at odds with one another, as the Cyprus dispute between Greece and Turkey and the fishing dispute between Iceland and Britain have demonstrated. As these examples all show, despite the complex organizational structure which has developed since the late 1940s, one thing has remained the same: intra-alliance relations have continued to be extraordinarily delicate.

In conclusion, European unity has been a dream for many individuals ever since the dissolution of the Holy Roman Empire. While NATO has neither accomplished as much as its most vocal supporters have suggested, nor done as little as its greatest detractors have charged, nevertheless NATO has been a shield from behind which efforts toward European unification could be promoted.

Notes

1. Stanley Hoffmann, *Gulliver's Troubles* (New York: McGraw-Hill, 1968), pp. 96–97.

2. Jean Monnet, "Organizing for Peace," *European Community* (December 1967): 4.

3. Hoffmann, p. 97.

4. Although, in theory, the ministers should meet twice a year, since the mid-1950s they have not always done so.

5. William T.R. Fox and Annette Baker Fox, *NATO and the Range of American Choice* (New York: Columbia University Press, 1967), p. 26.

6. Adda B. Bozeman, *Politics and Culture in International History* (Princeton: Princeton University Press, 1960), p. 81.

Selected Bibliography

Beer, Francis A. *Integration and Disintegration in NATO*. Columbus: Ohio State University Press, 1969.

Cook, Chris, and Francis, Mary. *The First European Elections*. London: Macmillan, 1979.

Fedder, Edwin H. *NATO: The Dynamics of Alliance in the Postwar World*. New York: Dodd, Mead, 1973.

Feld, Werner J. *The European Community in World Affairs*. Port Washington, N.Y.: Alfred, 1976.

Fox, William T. R., and Fox, Annette Baker. *NATO and the Range of American Choice*. New York: Columbia University Press, 1967.

Galtung, Johan. *The European Community: A Superpower in the Making*. Oslo: Universitets Forlaget, 1973.

Harrison, Reginald J. *Europe in Question: Theories of Regional International Integration*. New York: New York University Press, 1974.

Henig, Stanley. *Power and Decision in Europe: The Political Institutions of the European Community*. London: Europotentials, 1980.

Kissinger, Henry A. *The Troubled Partnership*. New York: McGraw-Hill, 1965.

Lindberg, Leon N., and Scheingold, Stuart A. *Europe's Would-Be Polity*. Englewood Cliffs, N.J.: Prentice-Hall, 1970.

Myers, Kenneth, ed. *NATO: The Next 30 Years*. Boulder, Colo.: Westview, 1980.

Osgood, Robert E. *NATO: The Entangling Alliance*. Chicago: University of Chicago Press, 1962.

Palmer, Michael. *The European Parliament*. New York: Pergamon, 1981.

Pentland, Charles. *International Theory and European Integration*. New York: Free Press, 1973.

Serfaty, Simon. *Fading Partnership: America and Europe After 30 Years*. New York: Praeger, 1979

Stanley, Timothy. *NATO in Transition*. New York: Praeger, 1965.

Taylor, Philip. *When Europe Speaks With One Voice*. Westport, Conn.: Greenwood Press, 1979.

Tsoukalis, Loukas. *The European Community and Its Mediterranean Enlargement*. Boston: Allen and Unwin, 1981.

Usher, John Anthony. *European Community Law and National Law: The Irreversible Transfer?* London: Allen and Unwin, 1981.

Wallace, Helen; Wallace, William; and Webb, Carole, eds. *Policy-Making in the European Communities*. New York: John Wiley, 1977.

Warnecke, Steven J., ed. *The European Community in the 1970s*. New York: Praeger, 1972.

8.

A Comparative Overview of the Other Western Europe

The "other" Western Europe which has been highlighted in this book encompasses more than one-half of Western Europe's land mass and almost one-half of its population. In certain respects, most of the nations comprising the other Western Europe have much in common with the so-called Big Three—France, Germany, and the United Kingdom. Most importantly, the nations of Western Europe share the advantages and accompanying challenges associated with democratic parliamentary systems of government. Other similarities are borne out in the social, economic, and political indicators found in Tables 8.1 through 8.3. For example, public expenditures on education as a percentage of GNP, per capita GNP, infant mortality rates, and unemployment rates in the Big Three are quite similar to those in many of the nations of the other Western Europe. In fact, some of the "other" countries rank significantly above the Big Three in certain key categories. As illustrations, Switzerland and Sweden rank one and two in Europe in terms of per capita GNP and are among the top five nations in the world. Moreover, the less than one percent unemployment rate of Switzerland and Luxembourg are well below those of the Big Three and are the envy of almost all other countries around the globe.

On the other hand, the other Western Europe also illustrates the great diversity in the western part of the European continent. Some of the nations have long traditions of democratic rule, whereas Austria has had a viable democratic framework only in the post–World War II period, and Portugal, Spain, and Greece have only recently cast aside authoritarian regimes. Furthermore, some of the southern tier countries still evince characteristics commonly found in developing nations. In 1981, Portugal suffered from an inflation rate of 25.0 percent and Greece a rate of 22.5 percent, whereas Austria's rate was only 6.4 percent. Spain's unemployment rate was also a staggering 13.7 percent and Portugal's infant mortality rate was four times that of Sweden. In addition, a much smaller percentage of the people in the Mediter-

TABLE 8.1

Selected Social Indicators for the "Other" Western Europe

Nation	Public Expenditures on Education (% GNP)	Full-Time School Enrollment for Children Aged 15–19 (% of age group, 1975 through 1979 data)	Public Expenditures on Health (% GNP)	Infant Mortality Rate (deaths in first year per 1,000 live births)
Portugal	6.1	33.4	3.1	26.0
Spain	2.5	41.3	2.3	11.1
Greece	2.4	45.4	2.1	18.7
Italy	5.4	43.9	6.5	14.3
Belgium	7.7	61.3	1.1	11.2
Luxembourg	5.6	37.3	0.9	11.5
Netherlands	8.4	65.0	0.3	8.7
Austria	5.8	32.0	5.3	13.9
Switzerland	5.2	70.1	2.1	8.5
Denmark	6.8	57.4	4.8	8.8
Norway	7.7	65.0	0.6	8.8
Sweden	8.6	56.3	6.2	6.7
France	5.8	55.9	5.5	10.0
Germany	5.2	45.4	5.7	13.5
United Kingdom	6.0	46.2	4.8	11.8

Sources: U.S. Arms Control and Disarmament Agency, *World Military Expenditures and Arms Transfers, 1969–1978* (Washington, D.C.: Government Printing Office, 1980), and *OECD Observer* (March 1982).

TABLE 8.2

Selected Economic Indicators for the "Other" Western Europe

Nation	Per Capita GNP ($ U.S.—1981)	Unemployment Rate (1981)*	Inflation Rate (1981)	% Employed (1981) in: Agricultural Sector	Industrial Sector	Service Sector
Portugal	2,430	7.6	25.0	28.4	35.7	39.5
Spain	5,650	13.7	14.5	18.9	36.1	45.0
Greece	4,210	2.2	22.5	29.7	30.0	40.3
Italy	6,910	8.3	18.1	14.2	37.8	48.0
Belgium	11,820	10.9	8.1	3.0	34.8	62.2
Luxembourg	12,570	0.7	8.0	5.7	38.4	55.9
Netherlands	11,850	7.5	7.2	6.0	31.9	62.1
Austria	10,250	2.5	6.4	10.5	40.3	49.2
Switzerland	15,920	0.2	6.6	7.2	39.5	53.3
Denmark	12,950	8.3	12.2	8.1	28.6	63.3
Norway	14,020	2.0	11.9	8.5	29.7	61.8
Sweden	14,760	2.5	9.1	5.6	32.2	62.2
France	12,140	7.5	14.0	8.8	35.9	55.3
Germany	13,310	4.3	6.3	6.0	44.8	49.2
United Kingdom	9,340	11.2	12.0	2.6	38.0	59.4

* Unemployment rates for Greece, Luxembourg, and Portugal are for 1980.

Source: *OECD Observer* (March 1982).

TABLE 8.3

The Performance of the Major Political Movements in the "Other" Western Europe*

Nation	Voter Turnout (%)	No. of Parties in Parliament	Liberal	Christian Democratic	Socialist and/or Social Democratic	Communist	Others
Portugal (1979)	82.9	9	—	—	72.4	19.0	8.6
Spain (1977)	80.0	13	—	—	28.5	9.0	62.5
Greece (1981)	78.7	3	35.9	0.2	48.1	12.3	4.5
Italy (1979)	89.9	12	1.9	38.3	13.6	30.4	15.8
Belgium (1981)	87.6	12	21.5	26.4	25.1	2.3	24.7
Luxembourg (1979)	84.0	7	21.3	34.5	30.3	5.8	8.1
Netherlands (1982)	80.6	12	23.1	29.3	30.4	1.8	15.4
Austria (1979)	92.2	3	6.1	41.9	51.0	1.0	0
Switzerland (1979)	47.8	12	24.0	21.1	27.0	2.1	25.8
Denmark (1979)	85.6	10	17.9	2.6	47.9	2.3	29.3
Norway (1981)	79.3	7	3.9	9.4	42.1	0.3	44.3
Sweden (1979)	90.0	5	10.6	1.4	43.3	5.6	39.1
France (1981)	74.5	11	—	—	37.0	16.0	47.0
Germany (1980)	87.8	4	10.6	44.5	42.9	0.2	1.8
United Kingdom (1979)	76.0	8	13.8	—	36.9	0.1	43.9

* Based on the percentage of vote received in the most recent national parliamentary election

ranean countries are employed in the service sector than in Northern Europe. A high percentage of the work force in the service sector is generally considered a sign of a highly advanced industrial society. In addition to Iberia, other regions of Western Europe, such as southern Italy, western France, Greece, Wallonia, Scotland, Ireland, and Corsica, have also experienced severe economic privations.

The Western European mosaic is further illustrated by the fact that some of the societies are highly homogeneous, whereas a few are noted for their major subcultural cleavages. The Basque problem in Spain and the persistent turmoil in Northern Ireland rank as the most serious conflicts. Among the consociational democracies, Belgium, Switzerland, Austria, and the Netherlands, the Walloon-Flemish schism has been the most disruptive, but all of the parliamentary systems in these countries have retained their stability in spite of the major subcultural differences.

Politically, most of the nations of Western Europe have multiparty systems and governments are generally formed by so-called main-stream parties ranging from the liberals on the right to the social democrats on the left. However, some countries do have significant conservative movements and a few have viable Marxist-oriented socialist and communist parties. Nonetheless, even though a few communist movements have done fairly well electorally, especially in Italy, communist parties are at best fringe movements in many nations and the communists will continue to face tough sledding in their efforts to dominate any Western European cabinet.

The majority of the Western European countries have also adopted unitary systems of government, with governmental authority concentrated at the national level. West Germany, Switzerland, and Austria are among the few which have federal systems, dividing governmental authority among national and regional government units. In particular, the latter two countries have resorted to federal systems in order to more fully accommodate the demands of major subcultural groups. In the future, it is also possible that both the United Kingdom and Belgium will modify their unitary structures and permit some policy-making latitude to be transferred to regionally based groups.

As are the Big Three, most of the nations in the other Western Europe are committed to the objectives of the Atlantic alliance and several are active members of the North Atlantic Treaty Organization. Yet even in the defense sphere there are divergent priorities. Although generally supportive of Western causes, Sweden, Switzerland, and Austria remain officially neutral in the realm of international affairs and because of this neutrality, none of these nations is likely to become attached to the European Community or NATO in the foreseeable future.

Finally, in the area of European unity, several of the countries in the other Western Europe have been in the forefront of efforts to promote a broad spectrum of regional cooperation. For example, military and economic agreements among the three Benelux nations were important precursors to the eventual formation of NATO and the European Community. And in spite of the literal potpourri of languages and cultures, definite progress has been made in the effort to forge solid cooperative ties among the Western European nations. The European Community has expanded in the past decade from six to ten members, and it is likely that Spain and Portugal will join the club in the 1980s. Moreover, the European Community and the European Free Trade Association countries have also agreed to broaden their areas of cooperation. In recognition of the increasingly interdependent nature of European society, the Big Three and the other Western Europe have already made significant progress in the postwar era toward coordinating and harmonizing policies both in the inter-governmental and the transnational spheres.

Nevertheless, Western Europe remains a region of diversity and paradoxes, and formidable barriers still stand in the way of the achievement of European unity. For though intergovernmental and transnational ties have been strengthened dramatically, nationalism still reigns as the dominant force, and national interests continue to dictate the major policy priorities enunciated by the governmental leaders of Western Europe. In addition, ethnoregionalism has undoubtedly been on the upswing in an era of increasing regional cooperation. As an apt example, Belgium has been a pivotal force in the shaping of greater continental cooperation in the political, military, and economic sectors, but internally, the nation has experienced significant difficulties because of the persistent demands of its two linguistic communities for greater autonomy. Indeed, large segments of the Walloon, Flemish, Basque, Catalan, Scot, Welsh, and Breton ethnic groups, among others, passionately desire autonomy and would therefore prefer to see Western Europe fragmented into an even greater number of sovereign national units. Consequently, on a continent traditionally known for its great diversity, the quest for some form of confederation composed of the Big Three and the nations of the other Western Europe will continue to face stern challenges in the 1980s and beyond. Yet in view of Western Europe's troubled existence during the first four and one-half decades of the present century, it seems imperative that the search for greater solidarity and unity among the people of Europe relentlessly push forward.

INDEX

A

269

M

About the Authors

Earl H. Fry is Associate Professor of Political Science and Program Coordinator, Center for International and Area Studies, Brigham Young University.

Gregory A. Raymond is Associate Professor of Political Science, Boise State University.

David Bohn is Associate Professor of Political Science, Brigham Young University.

James L. Waite is Associate Professor of Political Science, Central Missouri State University.